Legal Notice

BOOKS FROM THE GET 800 COLLECTION

28 New SAT Math Lessons to Improve Your Score in One Month
    Beginner Course
    Intermediate Course
    Advanced Course
New SAT Math Problems arranged by Topic and Difficulty Level
320 SAT Math Problems arranged by Topic and Difficulty Level
SAT Verbal Prep Book for Reading and Writing Mastery
320 SAT Math Subject Test Problems
    Level 1 Test
    Level 2 Test
The 32 Most Effective SAT Math Strategies
SAT Prep Official Study Guide Math Companion
Vocabulary Builder
320 ACT Math Problems arranged by Topic and Difficulty Level
320 GRE Math Problems arranged by Topic and Difficulty Level
320 AP Calculus AB Problems
320 AP Calculus BC Problems
Physics Mastery for Advanced High School Students
SHSAT Verbal Prep Book to Improve Your Score in Two Months
555 Math IQ Questions for Middle School Students
555 Advanced Math Problems for Middle School Students
555 Geometry Problems for High School Students
Algebra Handbook for Gifted Middle School Students

CONNECT WITH DR. STEVE WARNER

www.facebook.com/SATPrepGet800

www.youtube.com/TheSATMathPrep

www.twitter.com/SATPrepGet800

www.linkedin.com/in/DrSteveWarner

www.pinterest.com/SATPrepGet800

plus.google.com/+SteveWarnerPhD

28 ACT Math
Lessons to Improve
Your Score in One Month

Advanced Course

For Students Currently Scoring Above 25
in ACT Math and Want to Score 36

Dr. Steve Warner

Table of Contents

ACTIONS TO COMPLETE BEFORE YOU READ THIS BOOK

1. Purchase a TI-84 or equivalent calculator

It is recommended that you use a TI-84 or comparable calculator for the ACT. Answer explanations in this book will always assume you are using such a calculator.

2. Take a practice ACT from the Real ACT Prep Guide to get your preliminary ACT math score

Your score should be at least a 25. If it is lower, you should use *320 ACT Math Problems* until your score on practice tests increases to 25 or higher.

3. Claim your FREE bonus

Visit the following webpage and enter your email address to receive solutions to all the supplemental problems in this book.

www.satprepget800.com/28LesAdv

4. Like' my Facebook page

This page is updated regularly with ACT prep advice, tips, tricks, strategies, and practice problems.

www.facebook.com/ACTPrepGet800

INTRODUCTION
STUDYING FOR SUCCESS

*T*his book was written specifically for the student currently scoring more than 25 in ACT math. Results will vary, but if you are such a student and you work through the lessons in this book, then you will see a substantial improvement in your score.

If your current ACT math score is below 25 or you discover that you have weaknesses in applying more basic techniques (such as the ones reviewed in the first lesson from this book), you may want to use *320 ACT Math Problems* until your score improves up to this level.

The book you are now reading is self-contained. Each lesson was carefully created to ensure that you are making the most effective use of your time while preparing for the ACT. It should be noted that a score of 30 can usually be attained without ever attempting a Level 5 problem. Readers currently scoring below a 30 on practice tests should not feel obligated to work on Level 5 problems the first time they go through this book.

The optional material in this book contains what I refer to as "Challenge" questions. Challenge questions may be more theoretical in nature and are much more difficult than anything that will ever appear on an ACT. These questions are for those students that really want an ACT math score of 36.

1. Using this book effectively

- Begin studying at least three months before the ACT.
- Practice ACT math problems twenty minutes each day.
- Choose a consistent study time and location.

You will retain much more of what you study if you study in short bursts rather than if you try to tackle everything at once. So try to choose about a twenty-minute block of time that you will dedicate to ACT math each day. Make it a habit. The results are well worth this small time commitment. Some students will be able to complete each lesson within this twenty-minute block of time. If it takes you longer than twenty minutes to complete a lesson, you can stop when twenty minutes are up and then complete the lesson the following day. At the very least, take a nice long break, and then finish the lesson later that same day.

- Every time you get a question wrong, **mark it off, no matter what your mistake**.
- Begin each lesson by first redoing the problems from previous lessons on the same topic that you have marked off.
- If you get a problem wrong again, **keep it marked off**.

As an example, before you begin the third Number Theory lesson (Lesson 9), you should redo all the problems you have marked off from the first two Number Theory lessons (Lessons 1 and 5). Any question that you get right you can "unmark" while leaving questions that you get wrong marked off for the next time. If this takes you the full twenty minutes, that is okay. Just begin the new lesson the next day.

Note that this book often emphasizes solving each problem in more than one way. Please listen to this advice. The same question is never repeated on any ACT, and so the important thing is learning as many techniques as possible. Being able to solve any specific problem is of minimal importance. The more ways you have to solve a single problem, the more prepared you will be to tackle a problem you have never seen before, and the quicker you will be able to solve that problem. Also, if you have multiple methods for solving a single problem, then on the actual ACT when you "check over" your work you will be able to redo each problem in a different way. This will eliminate all "careless" errors on the actual exam. In this book the quickest solution to any problem will always be marked with an asterisk (*).

2. Calculator use.

- Use a TI-84 or comparable calculator if possible when practicing and during the ACT.
- Make sure that your calculator has fresh batteries on test day.

- You may have to switch between DEGREE and RADIAN modes during the test. If you are using a TI-84 (or equivalent) calculator press the MODE button and scroll down to the third line when necessary to switch between modes.

Below are the most important things you should practice on your graphing calculator.

- Practice entering complicated computations in a single step.
- Know when to insert parentheses:
  - Around numerators of fractions
  - Around denominators of fractions
  - Around exponents
  - Whenever you actually see parentheses in the expression

Examples:

We will substitute a 5 in for x in each of the following examples.

Expression	Calculator computation
$\dfrac{7x+3}{2x-11}$	(7*5 + 3)/(2*5 − 11)
$(3x-8)^{2x-9}$	(3*5 − 8)^(2*5 − 9)

- Clear the screen before using it in a new problem. The big screen allows you to check over your computations easily.
- Press the **ANS** button (**2ND (-)**) to use your last answer in the next computation.
- Press **2ND ENTER** to bring up your last computation for editing. This is especially useful when you are plugging in answer choices, or guessing and checking.
- You can press **2ND ENTER** over and over again to cycle backwards through all the computations you have ever done.
- Know where the $\sqrt{\ }$, π, and ^ buttons are so you can reach them quickly.
- Change a decimal to a fraction by pressing **MATH ENTER ENTER**.
- Press the **MATH** button - in the first menu that appears you can take cube roots and nth roots for any n. Scroll right to **NUM** and you have **lcm(** and **gcd(**. Scroll right to **PRB** and you have **nPr**, **nCr**, and **!** to compute permutations, combinations and factorials very quickly.

- Know how to use the **SIN**, **COS** and **TAN** buttons as well as **SIN^{-1}**, **COS^{-1}** and **TAN^{-1}**.

You may find the following graphing tools useful.

- Press the **Y=** button to enter a function, and then hit **ZOOM 6** to graph it in a standard window.
- Practice using the **WINDOW** button to adjust the viewing window of your graph.
- Practice using the **TRACE** button to move along the graph and look at some of the points plotted.
- Pressing **2ND TRACE** (which is really **CALC**) will bring up a menu of useful items. For example, selecting **ZERO** will tell you where the graph hits the x-axis, or equivalently where the function is zero. Selecting **MINIMUM** or **MAXIMUM** can find the vertex of a parabola. Selecting **INTERSECT** will find the point of intersection of 2 graphs.

3. Tips for taking the ACT

Each of the following tips should be used whenever you take a practice ACT as well as on the actual exam.

Check your answers properly: When you go back to check your earlier answers for careless errors *do not* simply look over your work to try to catch a mistake. This is usually a waste of time.

- When "checking over" problems you have already done, **always redo the problem from the beginning** without looking at your earlier work.
- If possible, use a different method than you used the first time.

For example, if you solved the problem by picking numbers the first time, try to solve it algebraically the second time, or at the very least pick different numbers. If you do not know, or are not comfortable with a different method, then use the same method, but do the problem from the beginning and do not look at your original solution. If your two answers do not match up, then you know that this is a problem you need to spend a little more time on to figure out where your error is.

This may seem time consuming, but that is okay. It is better to spend more time checking over a few problems, than to rush through a lot of problems and repeat the same mistakes.

Take a guess whenever you cannot solve a problem: There is no guessing penalty on the ACT. Whenever you do not know how to solve a problem take a guess. Ideally you should eliminate as many answer choices as possible before taking your guess, but if you have no idea whatsoever do not waste time overthinking. Simply put down an answer and move on. You should certainly mark it off and come back to it later if you have time.

Pace yourself: After you have been working on a question for about 30 seconds you need to make a decision. If you understand the question and think that you can get the answer in another 30 seconds or so, continue to work on the problem. If you still do not know how to do the problem or you are using a technique that is going to take a long time, mark it off and come back to it later if you have time.

If you have eliminated at least one answer choice, or it is a grid-in, feel free to take a guess. But you still want to leave open the possibility of coming back to it later. Remember that every problem is worth the same amount. Do not sacrifice problems that you may be able to do by getting hung up on a problem that is too hard for you.

Now, after going through the test once, you can then go through each of the questions you have marked off and solve as many of them as you can. You should be able to spend 5 to 7 minutes on this, and still have 7 minutes left to check your answers. If there are one or two problems that you just cannot seem to get, let them go for a while. You can come back to them intermittently as you are checking over other answers.

LESSON 1
NUMBER THEORY

In this lesson we will be reviewing four very basic strategies that can be used to solve a wide range of ACT math problems in all topics and all difficulty levels. Throughout this book you should practice using these four strategies whenever it is possible to do so. You should also try to solve each problem in a more straightforward way.

Start with the Middle Answer Choice

In many ACT math problems, you can get the answer simply by trying each of the answer choices until you find the one that works. Unless you have some intuition as to what the correct answer might be, then you should always start with the middle answer choice (C or H) as your first guess (an exception will be detailed in the next strategy below). The reason for this is simple. Answers are very often (but not always) given in increasing or decreasing order. So if the middle choice fails you can sometimes eliminate two of the other choices as well.

Try to answer the following question using this strategy. **Do not** check the solution until you have attempted this question yourself.

LEVEL 2: NUMBER THEORY

1. Seven consecutive integers are listed in increasing order. If their sum is 350, what is the third integer in the list?

    A. 45
    B. 46
    C. 47
    D. 48
    E. 49

12

Solution

Begin by looking at choice C. If the third integer is 47, then the seven integers are 45, 46, 47, 48, 49, 50, and 51. Add these up in your calculator to get 336. This is too small. So we can eliminate choices A, B and C.

Since 336 is pretty far from 350 let's try choice E next. If the third integer is 49, then the seven integers are 47, 48, 49, 50, 51, 52, and 53. Add these up in your calculator to get 350. Therefore, the answer is choice **E**.

Before we go on, try to solve this problem in two other ways.

(1) Algebraically (the way you would do it in school).
(2) With a quick computation.

Hint for (2): In a set of consecutive integers, the average (arithmetic mean) and median are equal (see the optional material at the end of Lesson 20 for a proof of this).

Solutions

(1) Algebraic solution: If we name the least integer x, then the seven integers are $x, x + 1, x + 2, x + 3, x + 4, x + 5$, and $x + 6$. So we have

$$x + (x + 1) + (x + 2) + (x + 3) + (x + 4) + (x + 5) + (x + 6) = 350$$
$$7x + 21 = 350$$
$$7x = 329$$
$$x = 47$$

The third integer is $x + 2 = 49$, choice **E**.

Important: Always remember to check what the question is asking for before choosing your answer. Many students would accidently choose choice C here as soon as they discovered that $x = 47$.

It is not a bad idea to underline the word *"third"* as you read the question. This may help you to avoid this kind of error.

* (2) Quick solution: Divide 350 by 7 to get that the fourth integer is 50. Thus, the third integer is 49, choice **E**.

Justification for the last solution: Recall from the algebraic solution above that $7x + 21 = 350$. Thus, $7(x + 3) = 350$, and therefore $x + 3 = \frac{350}{7} = 50$. Finally, we have $x + 2 = 50 - 1 = 49$.

Note that $x + 3$ is the median of the seven integers (the fourth integer in the list), $\frac{350}{7}$ is the average of the seven integers, and these two quantities are equal. See Lesson 20 for more details.

When NOT to Start with the Middle Answer Choice

If the word **least** appears in the problem, then start with the smallest number as your first guess. Similarly, if the word **greatest** appears in the problem, then start with the largest number as your first guess.

Try to answer the following question using this strategy. **Do not** check the solution until you have attempted this question yourself.

LEVEL 3: NUMBER THEORY

2. What is the largest positive integer value of k for which 7^k divides 147^{15} ?

    F. 3
    G. 7
    H. 15
    J. 28
    K. 30

Solution

*Pull out your calculator. Since the question has the word **"largest"** in it, we will start with the largest answer choice which is choice E, and we divide 147^{15} by 7^{30}. We type 147^15 / 7^30 into our calculator and the output is 14,348,907. Since this is an integer, the answer is choice **K**.

Note that all five answer choices give an integer, but 30 is the largest positive integer that works.

Before we go on, try to solve this problem directly (without using the answer choices).

Solution

The prime factorization of 147 is $147 = 3 \cdot 7^2$. Therefore,
$$147^{15} = (3 \cdot 7^2)^{15} = 3^{15}(7^2)^{15} = 3^{15}\, 7^{30}.$$
So 7^{30} divides 147^{15}, but 7^{31} does not. Thus, the answer is choice **E**.

Note: Prime factorizations will be reviewed in Lesson 5.

Take a Guess

Sometimes the answer choices themselves cannot be substituted in for the unknown or unknowns in the problem. But that does not mean that you cannot guess your own numbers. Try to make as reasonable a guess as possible, but do not over think it. Keep trying until you zero in on the correct value.

Try to answer the following question using this strategy. **Do not** check the solution until you have attempted this question yourself.

LEVEL 3: NUMBER THEORY

3. Dana has pennies, nickels and dimes in her pocket. The number of dimes she has is three times the number of nickels, and the number of nickels she has is 2 more than the number of pennies. Which of the following could be the total number of coins in Dana's pocket?

    A. 14
    B. 15
    C. 16
    D. 17
    E. 18

Solution

* Let's take a guess and say that Dana has 3 pennies. It follows that she has $3 + 2 = 5$ nickels, and $(3)(5) = 15$ dimes. So the total number of coins is $3 + 5 + 15 = 23$. This is too many. So let's guess that Dana has 2 pennies. Then she has $2 + 2 = 4$ nickels, and $(3)(4) = 12$ dimes for a total of $2 + 4 + 12 = 18$ coins. Thus, the answer is choice **E**.

15

Before we go on, try to solve this problem the way you might do it in school.

Solution

If we let x represent the number of pennies, then the number of nickels is $x + 2$, and the number of dimes is $3(x + 2)$. Thus, the total number of coins is

$$x + (x + 2) + 3(x + 2) = x + x + 2 + 3x + 6 = 5x + 8.$$

So some possible totals are 13, 18, 23,... which we get by substituting 1, 2, 3,... for x. Substituting 2 in for x gives 18 which is answer choice **E**.

Warning: Many students incorrectly interpret "three times the number of nickels" as $3x + 2$. This is not right. The number of nickels is $x + 2$, and so "three times the number of nickels" is $3(x + 2) = 3x + 6$.

Pick a Number

A problem may become much easier to understand and to solve by substituting a specific number in for a variable. Just make sure that you choose a number that satisfies the given conditions.

Here are some guidelines when picking numbers.

(1) Pick a number that is simple but not too simple. In general, you might want to avoid picking 0 or 1 (but 2 is usually a good choice).

(2) Try to avoid picking numbers that appear in the problem.

(3) When picking two or more numbers try to make them all different.

(4) Most of the time picking numbers only allows you to eliminate answer choices. So do not just choose the first answer choice that comes out to the correct answer. If multiple answers come out correct you need to pick a new number and start again. But you only have to check the answer choices that have not yet been eliminated.

(5) If there are fractions in the question a good choice might be the least common denominator (lcd) or a multiple of the lcd.

(6) In percent problems choose the number 100.

(7) If your first attempt does not eliminate 4 of the 5 choices, try to choose a number that's of a different "type." Here are some examples of types:

16

(a) A positive integer greater than 1.
(b) A positive fraction (or decimal) between 0 and 1.
(c) A negative integer less than -1.
(d) A negative fraction (or decimal) between -1 and 0.

(8) If you are picking pairs of numbers, try different combinations from (7). For example, you can try two positive integers greater than 1, two negative integers less than -1, or one positive and one negative integer, etc.

Remember that these are just guidelines and there may be rare occasions where you might break these rules. For example, sometimes it is so quick and easy to plug in 0 and/or 1 that you might do this even though only some of the answer choices get eliminated.

Try to answer the following question using this strategy. **Do not** check the solution until you have attempted this question yourself.

LEVEL 4: NUMBER THEORY

4. n is a two-digit number whose units digit is 3 times its tens digit, which of the following statements must be true?

   F. n is less than 15
   G. n is greater than 30
   H. n is a multiple of 3
   J. n is a multiple of 10
   K. n is a multiple of 13

Solution

Let's choose a value for n, say $n = 13$. Notice that we chose a number whose units digit is 3 times its tens digit.

Now let's check if each answer choice is true or false.

   F. True
   G. False
   H. False
   J. False
   K. True

17

Since G, H, and J are each false we can eliminate them. Let's choose a new value for n, say $n = 26$. Let's check if each of choices F and K is true or false with this new value for n.

> **F.** False
> **K.** True

Choice F does not give the correct answer this time so we can eliminate it. Thus, the answer is choice **K**.

Notes: (1) When we chose our first number we needed to check **every** answer choice. A common mistake would be to choose answer choice F because it was the first one to come out true. When we choose our second number we only have to check the answer choices that haven't yet been eliminated.

(2) There are only 3 possibilities for n: 13, 26, and 39. Note that each of these 3 numbers is a multiple of 13.

You're doing great! Let's just practice a bit more. Try to solve each of the following problems by using one of the four strategies you just learned. Then, if possible, solve each problem another way. The answers to these problems, followed by full solutions are at the end of this lesson. **Do not** look at the answers until you have attempted these problems yourself. Please remember to mark off any problems you get wrong.

LEVEL 1: NUMBER THEORY

5.   Which of the following numbers has the greatest value?

> **A.** $0.\overline{7}$
> **B.** 0.7
> **C.** 0.77
> **D.** 0.777
> **E.** 0.7777

6.   The square root of a specific number is approximately 7.6315. The specific number is between what 2 integers?

> **F.** 2 and 3
> **G.** 3 and 5
> **H.** 7 and 15
> **J.** 14 and 29
> **K.** 49 and 63

18

LEVEL 2: NUMBER THEORY

7. What is the least common denominator of the fractions $\frac{3}{10}$, $\frac{2}{45}$, and $\frac{5}{27}$?

   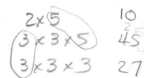

   A.   54
   B.   270
   C.   450
   D.   2430
   E.   12,150

LEVEL 3: NUMBER THEORY

8. What positive number when divided by its reciprocal has a result of $\frac{9}{16}$?

   F. $\frac{8}{3}$

   G. $\frac{3}{8}$

   H. $\frac{4}{3}$

   J. $\frac{3}{16}$

   K. $\frac{3}{4}$

9. A group of friends will rent out a hotel for $1800 for a party. The cost of the hotel will be equally distributed among the friends who plan to attend the party. The current cost per person will increase by $15 if 6 of the friends decide not to attend the party. How many friends are currently planning to attend the party?

   A. 10
   B. 20
   C. 24
   D. 30
   E. 42

LEVEL 4: NUMBER THEORY

10. If c is a positive odd integer and d is a positive even integer, then $[(+7)(-7)]^{cd}$

    F. negative and even
    G. negative and odd
    H. positive and even
    J. positive and odd
    K. zero

11. For every negative real value of a, all of the following are true EXCEPT:

    A. $|3a| > 0$
    B. $a^7 < 0$
    C. $5a < 0$
    D. $a - |a| = 0$
    E. $4a - 2a^2 < 0$

12. A ball is dropped from 567 centimeters above the ground and after the fourth bounce it rises to a height of 7 centimeters. If the height to which the ball rises after each bounce is always the same fraction of the height reached on its previous bounce, what is this fraction?

    F. $\dfrac{1}{81}$

    G. $\dfrac{1}{27}$

    H. $\dfrac{1}{9}$

    J. $\dfrac{1}{3}$

    K. $\dfrac{1}{2}$

Answers

1. E	5. A	9. D
2. K	6. K	10. J
3. E	7. B	11. D
4. K	8. K	12. J

20

Full Solutions

8.

Solution by starting with choice H: Let's start with $\frac{4}{3}$ as our first guess. The reciprocal of $\frac{4}{3}$ is $\frac{3}{4}$, and when we divide $\frac{4}{3}$ by $\frac{3}{4}$, we get $\frac{16}{9}$. This is not correct, but it is the reciprocal of what we are trying to get. So the answer is the reciprocal of $\frac{4}{3}$, which is $\frac{3}{4}$, choice **K**.

Notes: (1) The **reciprocal** of the fraction $\frac{a}{b}$ is the fraction $\frac{b}{a}$. In other words, we get the reciprocal of the fraction by interchanging the number on top (the **numerator**) with the number on bottom (the **denominator**).

(2) We can divide $\frac{4}{3}$ by $\frac{3}{4}$ right in our TI-84 calculator by typing

(4 / 3) / (3 / 4) ENTER MATH ENTER ENTER

The output will be $\frac{16}{9}$.

Pressing MATH ENTER ENTER at the end changes the decimal to a fraction.

(3) We can also do the computation by hand as follows:

$$\frac{4}{3} \div \frac{3}{4} = \frac{4}{3} \cdot \frac{4}{3} = \frac{4 \cdot 4}{3 \cdot 3} = \frac{16}{9}$$

(4) Let's also just confirm that choice K is the answer. I'll use the hand method, but you can also feel free to use your calculator.

$$\frac{3}{4} \div \frac{4}{3} = \frac{3}{4} \cdot \frac{3}{4} = \frac{3 \cdot 3}{4 \cdot 4} = \frac{9}{16}$$

* Algebraic solution: Let x be the positive number. We are given that

$$x \div \frac{1}{x} = \frac{9}{16}$$
$$x \cdot \frac{x}{1} = \frac{9}{16}$$
$$x \cdot x = \frac{9}{16}$$
$$x^2 = \frac{9}{16}$$
$$x = \pm\sqrt{\frac{9}{16}} = \pm\frac{\sqrt{9}}{\sqrt{16}} = \pm\frac{3}{4}$$

21

Since we are given that x is a positive number, $x = \frac{3}{4}$, choice **K**.

9.
* Solution by starting with choice C: Let's start with choice C and guess that 24 friends are planning to attend the party. Then they are each paying $\frac{1800}{24} = 75$ dollars. If 6 friends decide not to go, then there will be $24 - 6 = 18$ friends attending the party, and they would each have to pay $\frac{1800}{18} = 100$ dollars. The increase is $100 - 75 = 25$ dollars, too big.

Let's try choice D next and guess that 30 friends are planning to attend the party. Then they are each paying $\frac{1800}{30} = 60$ dollars. If 6 friends decide not to go, then there will be $30 - 6 = 24$ friends attending the party, and they would each have to pay $\frac{1800}{24} = 75$ dollars. The increase is $75 - 60 = 15$ dollars. This is correct, and so the answer is choice D.

Algebraic solution: Let n be the number of friends planning to attend the party. Then each friend will be paying $\frac{1800}{n}$ dollars. If 6 friends were to decide not to attend the party, then the number of friends remaining would be $n - 6$, and each remaining friend would pay $\frac{1800}{n-6}$ dollars. We are also given that the current cost would increase by \$15 in this case, and so we have

$$\frac{1800}{n-6} = \frac{1800}{n} + 15$$

If we multiply each side of the equation by $n(n-6)$, we get

$$1800n = 1800(n-6) + 15n(n-6)$$
$$1800n = 1800n - 10{,}800 + 15n^2 - 60n$$
$$15n^2 - 60n - 10{,}800 = 0$$
$$n^2 - 4n - 720 = 0$$
$$(n-30)(n+24) = 0$$
$$n - 30 = 0 \text{ or } n + 24 = 0$$
$$n = 30 \text{ or } n = -24$$

So $n = 30$, choice **D**.

Note: Do not worry too much if you have trouble understanding this algebraic solution. We will be reviewing all of this algebra later in this book.

10.

* Solution by picking numbers: Let's let $c = 1$ and $d = 2$. It follows that

$$[(+7)(-7)]^{cd} = [(+7)(-7)]^2 = 2{,}401$$

We now check if each answer choice is true or false:

F.	negative and even	False
G.	negative and odd	False
H.	positive and even	False
J.	positive and odd	True
K.	zero	False

Since only choice J is true, the answer is **J**.

Notes: (1) The following describes what happens when you add and multiply various combinations of even and odd integers.

$$
\begin{array}{ll}
e + e = e & ee = e \\
e + o = o & eo = e \\
o + e = o & oe = e \\
o + o = e & oo = o
\end{array}
$$

For example, the product of two odd integers is odd ($oo = o$).

(2) Observe that the behavior described in note (1) is independent of the choices of the integers themselves. All that matters is whether the integers are even or odd. It follows that we can choose *any* positive odd integer for c, and *any* positive even integer for d.

Direct solution: Since c is positive and odd, and d is positive and even, it follows that cd is positive and even.

So we are raising -49 to a positive even power.

When we raise an integer to a positive even power, the result is always positive. So this narrows down the answer to choice H or J.

When we multiply two odd numbers together, the result is always odd. In particular, multiplying an odd number by itself over and over again will always give an odd result. So the answer is choice **J**.

11.

Solution by picking numbers and starting with choice C: We need to find a negative real value of a that makes one of the statements false.

23

Let's try $a = -2$ and start with choice C. We have $5(-2) = -10 < 0$. So for this value of a, C is true.

Let's try D next. We have $-2 - |-2| = -2 - 2 = -4 \neq 0$. So D is false for this choice of a, and therefore the answer is **D**.

Note: (1) Let's plug $a = -2$ into each answer choice just to see that the remaining answer choices are true.

A.	$|3(-2)| = |-6| = 6 > 0$	True
B.	$(-2)^7 = -128 < 0$	True
C.	$5(-2) = -10 < 0$	True
D.	$-2 - |-2| = -2 - 2 = -4 = 0$	False
E.	$4(-2) - 2(-2)^2 = -8 - 2 \cdot 4 < 0$	True

(2) Normally picking numbers can be used only for eliminating answer choices. In this case however the wording of the question allows us to choose the first choice that fails for a specific value of a.

Solution by process of elimination: The absolute value of any nonzero number is always positive. Since a is nonzero (it's negative), it follows that $3a$ is nonzero, and so $|3a| > 0$. This eliminates A.

A negative number raised to an odd power is negative. This eliminates B.

The product of a positive number and a negative number is negative. Since 5 is positive and a is negative, $5a < 0$. This eliminates C.

$4a - 2a^2 = 2a(2 - a)$. Since a is negative, $2a$ is negative (by reasoning in last paragraph) and $2 - a$ is positive (pos − neg =pos + pos = pos), and so the product satisfies $2a(2 - a) < 0$ (again by the reasoning in the last paragraph). This eliminates E.

So the answer is **D**.

* Direct solution: Let a be negative. Then, since $a \neq 0$, $|a|$ is positive. So $a - |a|$ is negative (a negative number minus a positive number is the same as adding two negative numbers, and therefore the result is negative). In particular, $a - |a| \neq 0$. So the answer is **D**.

Note: We needed to find a single negative number a that makes choice D false. We actually just showed something much stronger than this. We showed that D is false for *all* negative values of a.

12.

* Solution by starting with choice H: Let's begin with choice H. We divide 567 by 9 four times and get 0.0864197531 which is much too small. So we can eliminate choices F, G, and H. We next try choice J. If we divide 567 by 3 four times we get 7 so that the correct answer is **J**.

Note: We could have also multiplied 7 by 3 four times to get 567.

An algebraic solution: We want to solve the following equation.

$$567x^4 = 7$$
$$x^4 = \frac{1}{81}$$
$$x = \frac{1}{3}$$

Thus, the answer is choice **J**.

Download additional solutions for free here:

www.satprepget800.com/28LesAdv

LESSON 2
ALGEBRA

Systems of Linear Equations

There are many different ways to solve a system of linear equations. We will use an example to demonstrate several different methods.

LEVEL 5: ALGEBRA

1. If $2x = 7 - 3y$ and $5y = 5 - 3x$, what is the value of x?

    A. -10
    B. -5
    C. 10
    D. 20
    E. 25

* Method 1 – elimination: We begin by making sure that the two equations are "lined up" properly. We do this by adding $3y$ to each side of the first equation, and adding $3x$ to each side of the second equation.

$$2x + 3y = 7$$
$$3x + 5y = 5$$

We will now multiply each side of the first equation by 5, and each side of the second equation by -3.

$$5(2x + 3y) = (7)(5)$$
$$-3(3x + 5y) = (5)(-3)$$

Do not forget to distribute correctly on the left. Add the two equations.

$$10x + 15y = 35$$
$$\underline{-9x - 15y = -15}$$
$$x \qquad = 20$$

This is choice **D**.

Remarks: (1) We chose to use 5 and -3 because multiplying by these numbers makes the y column "match up" so that when we add the two equations in the next step the y term vanishes. We could have also used -5 and 3.

(2) If we wanted to find y instead of x we would multiply the two equations by 3 and -2 (or -3 and 2). In general, if you are looking for only one variable, try to eliminate the one you are **not** looking for.

(3) We chose to multiply by a negative number so that we could add the equations instead of subtracting them. We could have also multiplied the first equation by 5, the second by 3, and subtracted the two equations, but a computational error is more likely to occur this way.

Method 2 – Gauss-Jordan reduction: As in method 1, we first make sure the two equations are "lined up" properly.

$$2x + 3y = 7$$
$$3x + 5y = 5$$

Begin by pushing the MATRIX button (which is 2ND x^{-1}). Scroll over to EDIT and then select [A] (or press 1). We will be inputting a 2 × 3 matrix, so press 2 ENTER 3 ENTER. We then begin entering the numbers 2, 3, and 7 for the first row, and 3, 5, and 5 for the second row. To do this we can simply type 2 ENTER 3 ENTER 7 ENTER 3 ENTER 5 ENTER 5 ENTER.

Note: What we have just done was create the **augmented matrix** for the system of equations. This is simply an array of numbers which contains the coefficients of the variables together with the right hand sides of the equations.

Now push the QUIT button (2ND MODE) to get a blank screen. Press MATRIX again. This time scroll over to MATH and select rref((or press B). Then press MATRIX again and select [A] (or press 1) and press ENTER.

Note: What we have just done is put the matrix into **reduced row echelon form**. In this form we can read off the solution to the original system of equations.

Warning: Be careful to use the rref(button (2 r's), and not the ref(button (which has only one r).

The display will show the following.

$$[\,[1\ 0\ 20]$$
$$[0\ 1-11]\,]$$

The first line is interpreted as $x = 20$ and the second line as $y = -11$. In particular, $x = 20$, choice **D**.

Method 3 – substitution: We solve the second equation for y and substitute into the first equation.

$5y = 5 - 3x$ implies $y = \frac{5-3x}{5} = \frac{5}{5} - \frac{3x}{5} = 1 - \frac{3x}{5}$. So now using the first equation we have

$$2x = 7 - 3y = 7 - 3\left(1 - \frac{3x}{5}\right) = 7 - 3 + \frac{9x}{5} = 4 + \frac{9x}{5}.$$

Multiply each side of this equation by 5 to get rid of the denominator on the right. So we have $10x = 20 + 9x$, and therefore, $x = 20$, choice **D**.

Remark: If we wanted to find y instead of x we would solve the first equation for x and substitute into the second equation.

Method 4 – graphical solution: We begin by solving each equation for y.

$$2x = 7 - 3y \qquad\qquad 5y = 5 - 3x$$
$$2x - 7 = -3y \qquad\qquad y = 1 - \frac{3x}{5}$$
$$y = -\frac{2x}{3} + \frac{7}{3}$$

In your graphing calculator press the Y= button, and enter the following.

$$Y1 = -2X/3 + 7/3$$
$$Y2 = 1 - 3X/5$$

Now press ZOOM 6 to graph these two lines in a standard window. It looks like the point of intersection of the two lines is off to the right. So we will need to extend the viewing window. Press the WINDOW button, and change Xmax to 50 and Ymin to -20. Then press 2nd TRACE (which is CALC) 5 (or select INTERSECT). Then press ENTER 3 times. You will see that the x-coordinate of the point of intersection of the two lines is 20, choice **D**.

Remark: The choices made for Xmax and Ymin were just to try to ensure that the point of intersection would appear in the viewing window. Many other windows would work just as well.

Method 5 – plugging in answer choices: We can substitute each answer choice (starting with C) into each equation for x, and solve for y. When we get the same y value, we have found the answer. I leave the details of this solution to the reader.

Matrices

A **matrix** is simply an array of numbers. Here are some examples:

$$A = \begin{bmatrix} 0 & 1 \\ 3 & 2 \end{bmatrix} \quad B = \begin{bmatrix} 1 & -2 \\ 2 & 3 \\ 0 & -1 \end{bmatrix} \quad C = \begin{bmatrix} 1 & 2 & 0 \\ 0 & 3 & 6 \end{bmatrix}$$

A is a 2 × 2 matrix because it has 2 rows and 2 columns. Similarly, B is a 3 × 2 matrix and C is a 2 × 3 matrix.

Two matrices are **equal** if they have the same size, and all of their entries are equal. For example, if $\begin{bmatrix} x & y \\ z & w \end{bmatrix} = \begin{bmatrix} 0 & 1 \\ 3 & 2 \end{bmatrix}$, then $x = 0$, $y = 1$, $z = 3$, and $w = 2$.

We add two matrices of the same size by adding entry by entry. For example,

$$\begin{bmatrix} 1 & -2 \\ 2 & 3 \\ 0 & -1 \end{bmatrix} + \begin{bmatrix} 2 & 1 \\ 3 & 0 \\ 5 & -2 \end{bmatrix} = \begin{bmatrix} 3 & -1 \\ 5 & 3 \\ 5 & -3 \end{bmatrix}$$

We multiply a matrix by a real number (called a **scalar**) by multiplying each entry by that number. For example,

$$3\begin{bmatrix} 2 & -5 & 3 \\ 1 & -1 & -2 \end{bmatrix} = \begin{bmatrix} 6 & -15 & 9 \\ 3 & -3 & -6 \end{bmatrix}$$

Example:

$$2\begin{bmatrix} 2 & 3 \\ 5 & -2 \end{bmatrix} + 5\begin{bmatrix} 1 & 0 \\ 2 & 2 \end{bmatrix} = \begin{bmatrix} 4 & 6 \\ 10 & -4 \end{bmatrix} + \begin{bmatrix} 5 & 0 \\ 10 & 10 \end{bmatrix} = \begin{bmatrix} 9 & 6 \\ 20 & 6 \end{bmatrix}$$

We can multiply two matrices together if the number of columns of the first matrix is equal to the number of rows of the second matrix. For example, if we consider the matrices A, B, and C above, we can multiply A times C because A has 2 columns and C has 2 rows. Here are the products we **can** form:

$$AA \quad AC \quad BC \quad BA$$

And here are the products we **cannot** form:

$$AB \quad CB \quad CA \quad BB \quad CC$$

29

Now how do we actually multiply two matrices? This is a bit complicated and requires just a little practice. For each row of the first matrix and each column of the second matrix, we add up the products entry by entry. Let's compute the product AC as an example.

$$AC = \begin{bmatrix} 0 & 1 \\ 3 & 2 \end{bmatrix} \cdot \begin{bmatrix} 1 & 2 & 0 \\ 0 & 3 & 6 \end{bmatrix} = \begin{bmatrix} x & y & z \\ u & v & w \end{bmatrix}$$

Since x is in the first row and first column, we use the first row of A and the first column of C to get $x = \begin{bmatrix} 0 & 1 \end{bmatrix} \begin{bmatrix} 1 \\ 0 \end{bmatrix} = 0 \cdot 1 + 1 \cdot 0 = 0 + 0 = 0.$

Since u is in the second row and first column, we use the second row of A and the first column of C to get $y = \begin{bmatrix} 3 & 2 \end{bmatrix} \begin{bmatrix} 1 \\ 0 \end{bmatrix} = 3 \cdot 1 + 2 \cdot 0 = 3.$

See if you can follow this procedure to compute the values of the remaining entries. The final product is

$$AC = \begin{bmatrix} 0 & 3 & 6 \\ 3 & 12 & 12 \end{bmatrix}$$

Note: The product of a **2 × 2** matrix and a 2 × 3 matrix is a 2 × 3 matrix.

More generally, the product of an $m \times n$ matrix and an $n \times p$ marix is an $m \times p$ matrix. Observe that the inner most numbers (both n) must agree, and the resulting product has dimensions given by the outermost numbers (m and p).

The **determinant** of the 2 × 2 matrix $\begin{bmatrix} a & b \\ c & d \end{bmatrix}$ is

$$\begin{vmatrix} a & b \\ c & d \end{vmatrix} = ad - bc$$

For example, let's compute the determinant of matrix A above.

$$|A| = \begin{vmatrix} 0 & 1 \\ 3 & 2 \end{vmatrix} = 0 \cdot 2 - 1 \cdot 3 = 0 - 3 = -3$$

Consider the following system of equations:

$$ax + by = c$$
$$dx + ey = f$$

The **augmented matrix** of this system is the matrix

$$\left[\begin{array}{cc|c} a & b & c \\ d & e & f \end{array}\right]$$

In other words, the entries of the matrix are the **coefficients** in the equations. We simply disregard the variables.

LEVEL 2: ALGEBRA

2. Which of the following augmented matrices represents the system of linear equations below?

$$4x - y = 7$$
$$3x + 2y = -5$$

F. $\begin{bmatrix} 4 & -1 & | & -7 \\ 3 & 2 & | & 5 \end{bmatrix}$

G. $\begin{bmatrix} 4 & -1 & | & 7 \\ 3 & 2 & | & -5 \end{bmatrix}$

H. $\begin{bmatrix} 4 & 0 & | & 7 \\ 3 & 2 & | & -5 \end{bmatrix}$

J. $\begin{bmatrix} 4 & 1 & | & 7 \\ 3 & 2 & | & -5 \end{bmatrix}$

K. $\begin{bmatrix} 4 & 3 & | & 7 \\ -1 & 2 & | & -5 \end{bmatrix}$

* Solution: It should be clear that the answer is choice **G**.

Note: $-y = -1y$. So the coefficient of y in the first equation is -1.

Systems of Linear Inequalities

Let's use an example to see how to solve a system of linear inequalities.

LEVEL 5: ALGEBRA

$$y \le 2x + 2$$
$$y \ge -3x - 3$$

3. A system of inequalities is shown above, and a graph is shown to the right. Which section or sections of the graph could represent all of the solutions to the system?

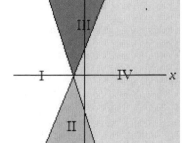

    A. Section I
    B. Section IV
    C. Sections II and III
    D. Sections II and IV
    E. Sections I, II, and IV

* **Quick solution:** The line $y = 2x + 2$ has a slope of $2 > 0$, and therefore the graph is the line that moves upwards as it is drawn from left to right.

The point $(0,0)$ satisfies the inequality $y \leq 2x + 2$ since $0 \leq 2(0) + 2$, or equivalently $0 \leq 2$ is true.

It follows that the graph of $y \leq 2x + 2$ consists of sections II and IV.

The line $y = -3x - 3$ has a slope of $-3 < 0$, and therefore the graph is a line that moves downwards as it is drawn from left to right.

$(0,0)$ satisfies the inequality $y \geq -3x - 3$ since $0 \geq -3(0) - 3$, or equivalently $0 \geq -3$ is true.

It follows that the graph of $y \geq -3x - 3$ consists of sections III and IV.

The intersection of the two solution graphs is section IV, choice **B**.

Complete algebraic solution: Let's sketch each inequality, one at a time, starting with $y \leq 2x + 2$. We first sketch the line $y = 2x + 2$. There are several ways to do this. A quick way is to plot the two intercepts. We get the y-intercept by setting $x = 0$. In this case we get $y = 2 \cdot 0 + 2 = 2$. So the point $(0,2)$ is on the line. We get the x-intercept by setting $y = 0$. In this case we get $0 = 2x + 2$, so that $-2 = 2x$, and $x = -\frac{2}{2} = -1$. So the point $(-1,0)$ is on the line. This line is shown in the figure on the left below.

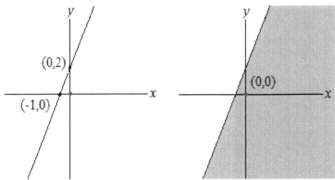

Now we need to figure out which direction to shade. To do this we plug any point *not on the line* into the inequality. For example, we can use $(0,0)$. Substituting this point into $y \leq 2x + 2$ gives $0 \leq 2$. Since this expression is true, we shade the region that includes $(0,0)$ as shown above in the figure on the right.

We now do the same thing for the second inequality. The intercepts of $y = -3x - 3$ are $(0,-3)$ and $(-1,0)$. When we test $(0,0)$ we get the true statement $0 \geq -3$.

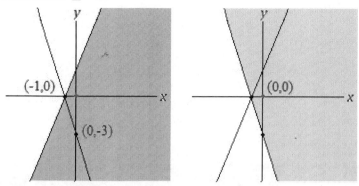

The figure on the above left shows the graph of $y = -3x - 3$ with the intercepts plotted, and the graph on the right shows the solution set of $y \geq -3x - 3$ (the shaded part).

The intersection of the two shaded regions in both figures above is the solution of the system of inequalities. This is region IV, choice **B**.

You're doing great! Let's just practice a bit more. Try to solve each of the following problems. The answers to these problems, followed by full solutions are at the end of this lesson. **Do not** look at the answers until you have attempted these problems yourself. Please remember to mark off any problems you get wrong.

LEVEL 2: ALGEBRA

4. The system of equations below has one solution (a, b). What is the value of b ?

$$x + y = 1$$
$$2x + y = 3$$

      F. -2
      G. -1
      H. 0
      J. 3
      K. 7

LEVEL 3: ALGEBRA

5. What value of z satisfies the matrix equation below?

$$3\begin{bmatrix}1 & 1 & 3\\2 & 2 & 0\end{bmatrix} - 2\begin{bmatrix}1 & 3 & 1\\1 & z & 3\end{bmatrix} = \begin{bmatrix}1 & -3 & 7\\4 & 4 & -6\end{bmatrix}$$

    A. -2
    B. -1
    C. 0
    D. 1
    E. 2

LEVEL 4: ALGEBRA

6. The *determinant* of a matrix $\begin{bmatrix}a & b\\c & d\end{bmatrix}$ is equal to $ad - bc$. What must be the value of z for the matrix $\begin{bmatrix}z & z\\z & 6\end{bmatrix}$ to have a determinant of 9 ?

    F. -6
    G. -3
    H. $-\dfrac{12}{5}$
    J. $\dfrac{12}{7}$
    K. 3

7. Which of the following (x, y) pairs is the solution for the system of equations $\frac{1}{3}x - \frac{1}{6}y = 7$ and $\frac{1}{5}y - \frac{1}{5}x = 8$?

    A. $(-36, -57)$
    B. $(12, 43)$
    C. $(\frac{101}{5}, \frac{307}{5})$
    D. $(82, 122)$
    E. $(122, 82)$

8. Given that $\begin{bmatrix} a & b \\ c & 7 \end{bmatrix} = k\begin{bmatrix} 1 & 2 \\ 3 & 4 \end{bmatrix}$ for some real number k, what is $2ab$?

    F. $\dfrac{7}{4}$

    G. $\dfrac{7}{2}$

    H. $\dfrac{49}{4}$

    J. $\dfrac{49}{2}$

    K. 49

LEVEL 5: ALGEBRA

9. Three matrices are given below.

$$A = \begin{bmatrix} 1 & 3 \\ 2 & 4 \end{bmatrix} \quad B = \begin{bmatrix} 4 & 7 \\ 2 & 3 \\ 0 & 1 \end{bmatrix} \quad C = \begin{bmatrix} 1 & 2 & 5 \\ 8 & 4 & 6 \end{bmatrix}$$

Which of the following matrix products is undefined?

    A. AB
    B. AC
    C. BC
    D. BA
    E. BAC

10. If the system of inequalities $y < 4x + 1$ and $y \geq -\frac{1}{2}x - 2$ is graphed in the xy-plane below, which quadrant contains no solutions to the system?

    F. Quadrant I
    G. Quadrant II
    H. Quadrant III
    J. Quadrant IV
    K. There are solutions in all four quadrants.

35

11. Which of the following matrices is equal to the matrix product
$$\begin{bmatrix} -3 & 1 \\ 4 & -2 \end{bmatrix} \cdot \begin{bmatrix} 1 \\ -2 \end{bmatrix}$$

    A. $\begin{bmatrix} -3 & -2 \\ 4 & 4 \end{bmatrix}$

    B. $\begin{bmatrix} -2 & 2 \\ 2 & -4 \end{bmatrix}$

    C. $\begin{bmatrix} -3 & 4 \\ -2 & 4 \end{bmatrix}$

    D. $\begin{bmatrix} -1 \\ 0 \end{bmatrix}$

    E. $\begin{bmatrix} -5 \\ 8 \end{bmatrix}$

12. If $6x = 2 + 4y$ and $7x = 3 - 3y$, what is the value of x?

    F. $\dfrac{9}{23}$

    G. $\dfrac{10}{23}$

    H. $\dfrac{11}{23}$

    J. $\dfrac{12}{23}$

    K. $\dfrac{13}{23}$

Answers

1. D	5. D	9. A
2. G	6. K	10. K
3. B	7. D	11. E
4. G	8. H	12. F

Full Solutions

5.

* Quick solution: We need only find the entry in the second row and second column.

$$3 \cdot 2 - 2z = 4$$
$$6 - 2z = 4$$
$$-2z = -2$$
$$z = 1$$

This is choice **D**.

Note: For completeness, let's do the whole computation on the left:

$$3\begin{bmatrix} 1 & 1 & 3 \\ 2 & 2 & 0 \end{bmatrix} - 2\begin{bmatrix} 1 & 3 & 1 \\ 1 & z & 3 \end{bmatrix} = \begin{bmatrix} 3 & 3 & 9 \\ 6 & 6 & 0 \end{bmatrix} - \begin{bmatrix} 2 & 6 & 2 \\ 2 & 2z & 6 \end{bmatrix}$$

$$= \begin{bmatrix} 1 & -3 & 7 \\ 4 & 6-2z & -6 \end{bmatrix}$$

So we have

$$\begin{bmatrix} 1 & -3 & 7 \\ 4 & 6-2z & -6 \end{bmatrix} = \begin{bmatrix} 1 & -3 & 7 \\ 4 & 4 & -6 \end{bmatrix}$$

In particular, we must have $6 - 2z = 4$. So $z = 1$, choice **D**.

6.

$$\begin{vmatrix} z & z \\ z & 6 \end{vmatrix} = (z)(6) - (z)(z) = 6z - z^2$$

We can now proceed in two ways.

Solution by plugging in answer choices: Normally we would start with choice H, but in this case there is no real advantage to doing so. We might as well start with choice K since it is the easiest to plug in. If $z = 3$, then $6z - z^2 = 6(3) - 3^2 = 18 - 9 = 9$. This is correct. So the answer is choice **K**.

* Algebraic solution: We need to solve the equation $6z - z^2 = 9$. Bringing everything over to the right gives $0 = z^2 - 6z + 9$. We can factor on the right to get $0 = (z-3)^2$. So $z - 3 = 0$ and therefore $z = 3$, choice **K**.

7.
* Solution using the elimination method: Let's begin by multiplying the first equation by 6 and the second equation by 5 to get rid of the denominators. So we have

$$2x - y = 42$$
$$y - x = 40$$

Let's rewrite $y - x$ as $-x + y$ and add the two equations.

$$2x - y = 42$$
$$\underline{-x + y = 40}$$
$$x = 82$$

Let's substitute $x = 82$ into the second equation in the solution to get $y - 82 = 40$. Adding 82 gives $y = 40 + 82 = 122$.

So the answer is (82,122), choice **D**.

37

Solution by plugging in the points: Let's begin plugging the answer choices into the given equations. Choice C looks to be difficult, so let's start with choice B.

$$\frac{1}{3}x - \frac{1}{6}y = \frac{1}{3}(12) - \frac{1}{6}(43) = 4 - \frac{43}{6} \neq 7$$

So we can eliminate choice B.

Let's try D next.

$$\frac{1}{3}x - \frac{1}{6}y = \frac{1}{3}(82) - \frac{1}{6}(122) = \frac{2 \cdot 82}{6} - \frac{122}{6} = \frac{164 - 122}{6} = \frac{42}{6} = 7$$

$$\frac{1}{5}y - \frac{1}{5}x = \frac{1}{5}(122) - \frac{1}{5}(82) = \frac{122 - 82}{5} = \frac{40}{5} = 8$$

So the answer is choice **D**.

8.
*

$$\begin{bmatrix} a & b \\ c & 7 \end{bmatrix} = k \begin{bmatrix} 1 & 2 \\ 3 & 4 \end{bmatrix} = \begin{bmatrix} k & 2k \\ 3k & 4k \end{bmatrix}$$

Equating the entries in row 2, column 2, we have $7 = 4k$, and so $k = \frac{7}{4}$.

It follows that $a = k = \frac{7}{4}$, $b = 2k = \frac{7}{2}$, and so $2ab = 2\left(\frac{7}{4}\right)\left(\frac{7}{2}\right) = \frac{49}{4}$, choice **H**.

9.
* In order for a matrix product to be defined, the number of columns of the first matrix must be equal to the number of rows of the second matrix. Since A has two columns and B has three rows, AB is undefined. This is choice **A**.

10.
* **Complete algebraic solution:** Let's sketch each inequality, one at a time, starting with $y < 4x + 1$. We first sketch the line $y = 4x + 1$ by plotting the two intercepts. We get the y-intercept by setting $x = 0$. In this case we get $y = 4 \cdot 0 + 1 = 1$. So the point $(0,1)$ is on the line. We get the x-intercept by setting $y = 0$. In this case we get $0 = 4x + 1$, so that $-1 = 4x$, and $x = -\frac{1}{4}$. So the point $\left(-\frac{1}{4}, 0\right)$ is on the line. This line is shown in the figure on the left below. Note that we draw a dotted line because the strict inequality $<$ tells us that points on this line are not actually solutions to the inequality $y < 4x + 1$.

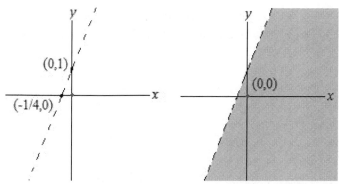

Now we need to figure out which direction to shade. To do this we plug any point *not on the line* into the inequality. For example, we can use (0,0). Substituting this point into $y < 4x + 1$ gives $0 < 1$. Since this expression is true, we shade the region that includes (0,0) as shown above in the figure on the right.

We now do the same thing for the second inequality. The intercepts of $y = -\frac{1}{2}x - 2$ are $(0,-2)$ and $(-4,0)$. When we test (0,0) we get the true statement $0 \geq -2$.

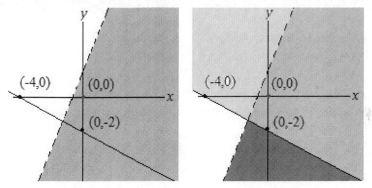

The figure on the above left shows the graph of $y = -\frac{1}{2}x - 2$ with the intercepts plotted, and the graph on the right shows three different shadings. The rightmost shading is the solution set of the given system.

Note that there are solutions in all four quadrants, choice **K**.

11.

$$\begin{bmatrix} -3 & 1 \\ 4 & -2 \end{bmatrix} \cdot \begin{bmatrix} 1 \\ -2 \end{bmatrix} = \begin{bmatrix} (-3)(1) + (1)(-2) \\ (4)(1) + (-2)(-2) \end{bmatrix} = \begin{bmatrix} -5 \\ 8 \end{bmatrix}$$

This is choice **E**.

12.

* Solution using the elimination method: Since we are trying to find x, we want to make y go away. So we make the two coefficients of y "match up" by multiplying by the appropriate numbers. We will multiply the first equation by 3 and the second equation by 4.

$$3(6x) = (2 + 4y)(3)$$
$$4(7x) = (3 - 3y)(4)$$

Don't forget to distribute on the right. Then add the two equations.

$$18x = 6 + 12y$$
$$\underline{28x = 12 - 12y}$$
$$46x = 18$$

Now divide each side by 46 to get $x = \frac{9}{23}$, choice **F**.

OPTIONAL MATERIAL

CHALLENGE QUESTIONS

1. If x and y are positive integers with $x^8 = \frac{z^3}{16}$ and $x^{12} = \frac{z^7}{y^4}$, what is the value of $\frac{xy}{z}$?

2. If $2x + 3y - 4z = 2$, $x - y + 5z = 6$ and $3x + 2y - z = 4$, what is the value of y?

Solutions

1.

$$* \ x^4 = \frac{x^{12}}{x^8} = \frac{z^7}{y^4} \div \frac{z^3}{16} = \frac{z^7}{y^4} \cdot \frac{16}{z^3} = \frac{16z^4}{y^4}. \text{ So } x = \frac{2z}{y}, \text{ and therefore } \frac{xy}{z} = 2.$$

2.

* Solution using Gauss-Jordan reduction: Push the MATRIX button, scroll over to EDIT and then select [A] (or press 1). We will be inputting a 3×4 matrix, so press 3 ENTER 4 ENTER. Then enter the numbers $2, 3, -4$ and 2 for the first row, $1, -1, 5$ and 6 for the second row, and $3, 2, -1$ and 4 for the third row. Now push the QUIT button (2ND MODE) to get a blank screen. Press MATRIX again. This time scroll over to MATH and select rref((or press B). Then press MATRIX again and select [A] (or press 1) and press ENTER. We see that $y = 3.6$.

40

LESSON 3
GEOMETRY

Computation of Slopes

You should make sure that you know the following.

$$\text{Slope} = m = \frac{rise}{run} = \frac{y_2 - y_1}{x_2 - x_1}$$

Note: Lines with positive slope have graphs that go upwards from left to right. Lines with negative slope have graphs that go downwards from left to right. If the slope of a line is zero, it is horizontal. Vertical lines have **no** slope (this is different from zero slope).

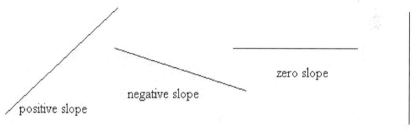

The **slope-intercept form of an equation of a line** is $y = mx + b$ where m is the slope of the line and b is the y-coordinate of the y-intercept, i.e. the point $(0, b)$ is on the line. Note that this point lies on the y-axis.

The **point-slope form of an equation of a line** is $y - y_0 = m(x - x_0)$ where m is the slope of the line and (x_0, y_0) is any point on the line.

Try to answer the following question using this strategy together with the strategy of picking numbers from Lesson 1. **Do not** check the solution until you have attempted this question yourself.

41

LEVEL 4: GEOMETRY

1. If $a > 1$, what is the slope of the line in the xy-plane that passes through the points (a^2, a^4) and (a^3, a^6)?

   A. $-a^3 + 6a^2$
   B. $-a^3 + a^2$
   C. $-a^3 - a^2$
   D. $a^3 - a^2$
   E. $a^3 + a^2$

Solution

Let's pick a number for a, say $a = 2$. So the two points are $(4,16)$ and $(8,64)$. The slope of the line passing through these two points is

$$m = \frac{64-16}{8-4} = \frac{48}{4} = 12.$$

Put a nice big circle around the number 12. We now plug $a = 2$ into each answer choice.

   A. $-8 + 6(4) = 16$
   B. $-8 + 4 = -4$
   C. $-8 - 4 = -12$
   D. $8 - 4 = 4$
   E. $8 + 4 = 12$

Since choices A, B, C, and D all came out incorrect, the answer is **E**.

Remark: We could have also gotten the slope geometrically by plotting the two points, and noticing that to get from $(4,16)$ to $(8,64)$ we need to travel up 48 units and right 4 units. So the slope is

$$m = \frac{rise}{run} = \frac{48}{4} = 12.$$

Before we go on, try to solve this problem directly (without plugging in numbers).

Solution

Note: Do not worry if you have trouble following this solution. The algebra performed here will be reviewed in Lesson 14.

* Using the slope formula we have

$$m = \frac{a^6-a^4}{a^3-a^2} = \frac{a^4(a^2-1)}{a^2(a-1)} = \frac{a^2(a+1)(a-1)}{a-1} = a^2(a+1) = a^3 + a^2.$$

This is choice **E**.

Plug in the Given Point

If the graph of a function or other equation passes through certain points, plug those points into the equation to eliminate answer choices.

Try to answer the following question using this strategy. **Do not** check the solution until you have attempted this question yourself.

LEVEL 4: GEOMETRY

2. Which of the following is an equation of the line in the xy-plane that passes through the point $(4, -2)$ and is perpendicular to the line $y = -4x + 7$?

    F. $y = -4x - 6$

    G. $y = -4x - 3$

    H. $y = -4x + 3$

    J. $y = \frac{1}{4}x - 3$

    K. $y = \frac{1}{4}x + 6$

Solution

* Since the point $(4, -2)$ lies on the line, if we substitute 4 in for x, we should get -2 for y. Let's substitute 4 in for x in each answer choice.

    F. $-4 * 4 - 6 = -16 - 6 = -22$
    G. $-4 * 4 - 3 = -16 - 3 = -19$
    H. $-4 * 4 + 3 = -16 + 3 = -13$
    J. $(1/4) * 4 - 3 = 1 - 3 = -2$
    K. $(1/4) * 4 + 6 = 1 + 6 = 7$

We can eliminate choices F, G, H and K because they did not come out to -2. The answer is therefore choice **J**.

Important note: J is **not** the correct answer simply because y came out to -2. It is correct because all 4 of the other choices did **not** give -2 for y.

Before we go on, try to solve this problem using geometry.

Solution

Note that the given line has a slope of -4. Since **perpendicular lines have slopes that are negative reciprocals of each other**, $m = \frac{1}{4}$. Also, we are given that the point $(x_0, y_0) = (4, -2)$ is on the line. We use the point-slope form for an equation of a line $y - y_0 = m(x - x_0)$ to get $y - (-2) = \frac{1}{4}(x - 4)$. Let's solve this equation for y.

$$y - (-2) = \frac{1}{4}(x - 4)$$
$$y + 2 = \frac{1}{4}(x - 4)$$
$$y + 2 = \frac{1}{4}x - 1$$
$$y = \frac{1}{4}x - 3$$

Therefore, the answer is choice **J**.

Note: To get the reciprocal of a number we interchange the numerator and denominator. The number -4 has a "hidden" denominator of 1, so the reciprocal of -4 is $-\frac{1}{4}$. Now to get the negative reciprocal, we simply change the sign of the reciprocal. So the negative reciprocal of -4 is $\frac{1}{4}$.

Now try to solve each of the following problems. The answers to these problems, followed by full solutions are at the end of this lesson. **Do not** look at the answers until you have attempted these problems yourself. Please remember to mark off any problems you get wrong.

LEVEL 1: GEOMETRY

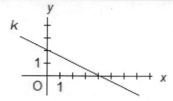

3. What is the equation of line k in the figure above?

    A. $y = -2x + 2$
    B. $y = -2x + 4$
    C. $y = -\frac{1}{2}x + 2$
    D. $y = -\frac{1}{2}x + 4$
    E. $y = 2x + 2$

LEVEL 2: GEOMETRY

4. In the standard xy-coordinate plane, what is the slope of the line $7x - 3y = 5$?

    F. -7
    G. $\frac{7}{5}$
    H. $\frac{7}{3}$
    J. 5
    K. 7

LEVEL 3: GEOMETRY

5. In the standard (x, y) coordinate plane, which of the following lines is perpendicular to the line $2x + y = 5$?

    A. $y = -2x - \frac{1}{5}$
    B. $y = -\frac{1}{2}x + 3$
    C. $y = \frac{1}{2}x - 5$
    D. $y = 2x - 5$
    E. $y = -2x + 5$

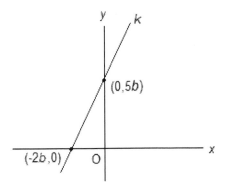

6. In the figure above, what is the slope of line k ?

    F. $-\dfrac{5}{2}$

    G. $-\dfrac{2b}{5}$

    H. $\dfrac{2}{5}$

    J. $\dfrac{2b}{5}$

    K. $\dfrac{5}{2}$

7. In the xy-coordinate plane, line n passes through the points $(0,5)$ and $(-2,0)$. If line m is perpendicular to line n, what is the slope of line m?

    A. $-\dfrac{5}{2}$

    B. $-\dfrac{2}{5}$

    C. 1

    D. $\dfrac{2}{5}$

    E. $\dfrac{5}{2}$

46

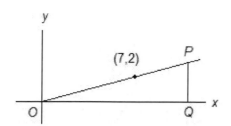

8. Line k (not shown) passes through O and intersects $\overline{PQ}$ midway between P and Q. What is the slope of line k?

    F. -7

    G. $-\dfrac{1}{7}$

    H. $\dfrac{1}{7}$

    J. 7

    K. Cannot be determined from the given information

LEVEL 4: GEOMETRY

9. Which of the following is the equation of a line in the xy-plane that is perpendicular to the line with equation $y = 3$?

    A. $y = -3$
    B. $y = -\dfrac{1}{3}$
    C. $x = -2$
    D. $y = -3x$
    E. $y = -\dfrac{1}{3}x$

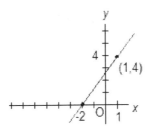

10. The line in the xy-plane above has equation $y = mx + b$, where m and b are constants. What is the value of b?

    F.   1

    G. $\dfrac{3}{4}$

    H. $\dfrac{4}{3}$

    J. $\dfrac{8}{3}$

    K.   4

11. What are all real values of a, if any, such that any line through the points $(5, 2)$ and $(a, 2)$ will be horizontal when graphed in the standard (x, y) coordinate plane?

    A. -5
    B.   2
    C.   All real numbers except 5 satisfy this condition.
    D.   All real numbers satisfy this condition.
    E.   No real numbers satisfy this condition.

LEVEL 5: GEOMETRY

12. In the xy-plane, the points $(5, e)$ and $(f, 7)$ are on a line that is perpendicular to the graph of the line $y = -\dfrac{1}{5}x + 12$. Which of the following represents e in terms of f?

    F. $5f + 32$
    G. $-5f + 32$
    H. $5f + 25$
    J. $-\dfrac{1}{5}f + 32$
    K. $\dfrac{1}{5}f + 32$

Answers

1. E	5. C	9. C
2. J	6. K	10. J
3. C	7. B	11. C
4. H	8. H	12. G

Full Solutions

5.

* We first solve the given equation for y to get $y = -2x + 5$. The slope of this line is -2. Therefore, the slope of a line perpendicular to the given one is $\frac{1}{2}$. It follows that the answer is choice **C**.

Notes: (1) Recall that the **slope-intercept form of an equation of a line** is $y = mx + b$, where m is the slope of the line.

For example, the equation $y = -2x + 5$ is an equation of a line in slope-intercept form, and the line has slope $m = -2$.

(2) Perpendicular lines have slopes that are negative reciprocals of each other.

(3) The reciprocal of -2 is $-\frac{1}{2}$, and the negative reciprocal of -2 is $-\left(-\frac{1}{2}\right) = \frac{1}{2}$.

(4) The slope-intercept form of an equation of a line with slope $\frac{1}{2}$ is

$$y = \frac{1}{2}x + b$$

for some real number b. Only choice C has this form.

6.

Solution by picking a number: Let's choose a value for b, say $b = 3$. Then the two points are $(-6, 0)$ and $(0, 15)$. Therefore, the slope of line k is $\frac{15-0}{0-(-6)} = \frac{15}{6} = 2.5$. Let's now substitute $b = 3$ into each answer choice.

49

F. $-\dfrac{5}{2} = -2.5$

G. $-\dfrac{6}{5} = -1.2$

H. $\dfrac{2}{5} = 0.4$

J. $\dfrac{6}{5} = 1.2$

K. $\dfrac{5}{2} = 2.5$

Since F, G, H, and J all came out incorrect, the answer is choice **K**.

Remarks: (1) Here we have used the slope formula $m = \dfrac{y_2 - y_1}{x_2 - x_1}$.

(2) $0 - (-6) = 0 + 6 = 6$

(3) We could have also found the slope graphically by plotting the two points and observing that to get from $(-6, 0)$ to $(0, 15)$ we need to move up 15 and right 6. Thus, the slope is $m = \dfrac{rise}{run} = 2.5$.

* Solution using just the slope formula: $\dfrac{5b - 0}{0 - (-2b)} = \dfrac{5b}{2b} = \dfrac{5}{2}$, choice **K**.

7.
* We first compute the slope of line n. We can do this by plotting the two points, and computing $\dfrac{rise}{run} = \dfrac{5}{2}$ (to get from $(-2, 0)$ to $(0, 5)$ we go up 5 and right 2). Since line m is perpendicular to line n, the slope of line m is the negative reciprocal of the slope of line n. So the answer is $-\dfrac{2}{5}$, choice **B**.

Remark: We can also find the slope of line n by using the slope formula $m = \dfrac{y_2 - y_1}{x_2 - x_1} = \dfrac{5 - 0}{0 - (-2)} = \dfrac{5}{2}$.

8.
* Line k passes through $(0,0)$ and $(7,1)$. Now plug these two points into the slope formula to get $\dfrac{1 - 0}{7 - 0} = \dfrac{1}{7}$, choice **H**.

Remark: If the line j passes through the origin (the point $(0, 0)$) and the point (a, b) with $a \neq 0$, then the slope of line j is simply $\dfrac{b}{a}$.

Alternate solution: The slope of line $\overline{OP}$ is $\dfrac{2}{7}$ (see the Remark above) and the slope of line $\overline{OQ}$ is 0. Therefore, the slope of line k is $\dfrac{1}{2}\left(\dfrac{2}{7}\right) = \dfrac{1}{7}$, choice **H**.

9.

* Any equation of the form $y = a$ for some real number a is a horizontal line. Any equation of the form $x = c$ for some real number c is a vertical line. Vertical lines are perpendicular to horizontal lines. Therefore, the answer is choice **C**.

10.

* From the graph we can see that the line passes through $(-2,0)$ and $(1,4)$ so that the slope of the line is $\frac{4}{3}$. Let's use the point $(1,4)$ and write an equation of the line in point slope form.

$$y - 4 = \frac{4}{3}(x - 1)$$

We now solve for y to get the line into slope-intercept form. We have that $y - 4 = \frac{4}{3}x - \frac{4}{3}$, or equivalently $y = \frac{4}{3}x + \frac{8}{3}$. From the last equation we see that $b = \frac{8}{3}$, choice **J**.

Notes: (1) To get the last equation we had to add 4 to $-\frac{4}{3}$.

$$4 - \frac{4}{3} = \frac{12}{3} - \frac{4}{3} = \frac{12-4}{3} = \frac{8}{3}.$$

(2) You can also just enter $4 - \frac{4}{3}$ into your calculator and then press MATH ENTER ENTER to get the fraction $\frac{8}{3}$.

11.

* Since the y-coordinates of both points are 2, the equation of the line passing through $(5, 2)$ and $(a, 2)$ is $y = 2$ as long as $a \neq 5$ (if $a = 5$, there is only one point, and therefore infinitely many lines passing through this point, only one of which is horizontal). As stated in the solution to problem 9, this is a horizontal line. So the answer is choice **C**.

12.

* The given line has a slope of $-\frac{1}{5}$. Since **perpendicular lines have slopes that are negative reciprocals of each other**, we have that the slope of the line containing points $(5, e)$ and $(f, 7)$ is 5 or $\frac{5}{1}$. So $\frac{e-7}{5-f} = \frac{5}{1}$. Cross multiplying (or simply multiplying by $5 - f$) yields

$$e - 7 = 5(5 - f) = 25 - 5f = -5f + 25.$$

Adding 7 to each side of this equation gives $e = -5f + 32$, choice **G**.

51

LESSON 4
COMPLEX NUMBERS

Complex Numbers

A **complex number** has the form $a + bi$ where a and b are real numbers and $i = \sqrt{-1}$.

Example: The following are complex numbers:

$$2 + 3i \quad \frac{3}{2} + (-2i) = \frac{3}{2} - 2i \quad -\pi + 2.6i \quad \sqrt{-9} = 3i$$

$0 + 5i = 5i$ This is called a **pure imaginary** number.

$17 + 0i = 17$ This is called a **real number.**

$0 + 0i = 0$ This is **zero**.

Powers of i: Since $i = \sqrt{-1}$, we have the following:

$$i^2 = \sqrt{-1}\,\sqrt{-1} = -1$$

$$i^3 = i^2 i = -1i = -i$$

$$i^4 = i^2 i^2 = (-1)(-1) = 1$$

$$i^5 = i^4 i = 1i = i$$

Notice that the pattern begins to repeat.

Starting with $i^0 = 1$, we have

$i^0 = 1$	$i^1 = i$	$i^2 = -1$	$i^3 = -i$
$i^4 = 1$	$i^5 = i$	$i^6 = -1$	$i^7 = -i$
$i^8 = 1$	$i^9 = i$	$i^{10} = -1$	$i^{11} = -i$

$$\cdots$$

In other words, when we raise i to a nonnegative integer, there are only four possible answers:

$$1, i, -1, \text{ or } -i$$

To decide which of these values is correct, we can find the remainder upon dividing the exponent by 4.

Example: $i^{73} = i^1 = i$ because when we divide 73 be 4 we get a remainder of 1.

Notes: (1) To get the remainder upon dividing 73 by 4, you **cannot** simply divide 73 by 4 in your calculator. This computation produces the answer 18.75 which does not tell you anything about the remainder.

To find a remainder you must either do the division by hand, or use the Calculator Algorithm below.

(2) This computation can also be done quickly in your calculator, but be careful. Your calculator may sometimes "disguise" the number 0 with a tiny number in scientific notation. For example, when we type i ^ 73 ENTER into our TI-84, we get an output of $-2.3E-12 + i$. The expression $-2.3E-12$ represents a tiny number in scientific notation which is essentially 0. So this should be read as $0 + i = i$.

(3) **Calculator Algorithm for computing a remainder:** Although performing division in your calculator never produces a remainder, there is a simple algorithm you can perform which mimics long division. Let's find the remainder when 73 is divided by 4 using this algorithm.

Step 1: Perform the division in your calculator: 73/4 = 18.75
Step 2: Multiply the integer part of this answer by the divisor: 18*4 = 72
Step 3: Subtract this result from the dividend to get the remainder:

$$73 - 72 = 1.$$

Addition and subtraction: We add two complex numbers simply by adding their real parts, and then adding their imaginary parts.

$$(a + bi) + (c + di) = (a + c) + (b + d)i$$

LEVEL 1: COMPLEX NUMBERS

1. For $i = \sqrt{-1}$, the sum $(2 - 3i) + (-5 + 6i)$ is

    A. $-7 + 3i$
    B. $-7 + 9i$
    C. $-3 - 3i$
    D. $-3 + 3i$
    E. $-3 - 18i$

* **Solution:** $(2 - 3i) + (-5 + 6i) = (2 - 5) + (-3 + 6)i = -3 + 3i$, choice **D**.

Multiplication: We can multiply two complex numbers by formally taking the product of two binomials and then replacing i^2 by -1.

$$(a + bi)(c + di) = (ac - bd) + (ad + bc)i$$

LEVEL 3: COMPLEX NUMBERS

2. Which of the following complex numbers is equivalent to $(2 - 3i)(-5 + 6i)$? (Note: $i = \sqrt{-1}$)

  F. $-7 + 3i$
  G. $-7 + 9i$
  H. $-3 - 3i$
  J. $-10 - 18i$
  K. $8 + 27i$

* **Solution:** $(2 - 3i)(-5 + 6i) = (-10 + 18) + (12 + 15)i = 8 + 27i$, choice **K**.

The **conjugate** of the complex number $a + bi$ is the complex number $a - bi$.

Example: The conjugate of $-5 + 6i$ is $-5 - 6i$.

Note that when we multiply conjugates together we always get a real number. In fact, we have

$$(a + bi)(a - bi) = a^2 + b^2$$

Division: We can put the quotient of two complex numbers into standard form by multiplying both the numerator and denominator by the conjugate of the denominator. This is best understood with an example.

LEVEL 4: COMPLEX NUMBERS

$$\frac{1 + 5i}{2 - 3i}$$

3.   If the expression above is rewritten in the form $a + bi$, where a and b are real numbers, what is the value of $b - a$?

    A.   0
    B.   1
    C.   2
    D.   3
    E.   4

Solution: We multiply the numerator and denominator of $\frac{1+5i}{2-3i}$ by $(2 + 3i)$ to get

$$\frac{(1 + 5i)}{(2 - 3i)} \cdot \frac{(2 + 3i)}{(2 + 3i)} = \frac{(2 - 15) + (3 + 10)i}{4 + 9} = \frac{-13 + 13i}{13}$$

$$= -\frac{13}{13} + \frac{13}{13}i = -1 + i$$

So $a = -1$, $b = 1$, and $b - a = 1 - (-1) = 1 + 1 = 2$, choice **C**.

Absolute Value: The **absolute value** of the complex number $a + bi$, written $|a + bi|$ is the nonnegative real number $\sqrt{a^2 + b^2}$.

Examples: $|2 + 3i| = \sqrt{2^2 + 3^2} = \sqrt{4 + 9} = \sqrt{13}$

$|3i| = |0 + 3i| = \sqrt{0^2 + 3^2} = \sqrt{9} = 3$

$|-5| = |-5 + 0i| = \sqrt{(-5)^2 + 0^2} = \sqrt{25} = 5$

Geometrically, we can plot the complex number $a + bi$ as the point (a, b), and $|a + bi|$ is the distance from the origin to (a, b).

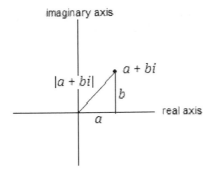

Example: Here is a picture of the complex number $3 + 4i$ and its absolute value.

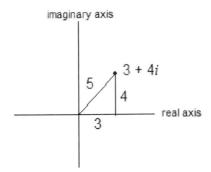

From the figure above, we see that $|3 + 4i| = 5$.

Remark: To get $|3 + 4i| = 5$ we can also use the definition

$$|3 + 4i| = \sqrt{3^2 + 4^2} = \sqrt{9 + 16} = \sqrt{25} = 5$$

or we can simply use the Pythagorean triple $3 - 4 - 5$.

LEVEL 2: COMPLEX NUMBERS

4. When we subtract $2 - 3i$ from $-5 + 6i$ we get which of the following complex numbers?

    F. $-10 - 18i$
    G. $-7 + 3i$
    H. $-7 + 9i$
    J. $-3 - 3i$
    K. $-3 + 3i$

LEVEL 3: COMPLEX NUMBERS

5. For $i = \sqrt{-1}, \frac{1}{1-i} \cdot \frac{1+i}{1+i} = ?$

    A. $1 + i$
    B. $1 - i$
    C. $i - 1$
    D. $\frac{1+i}{2}$
    E. $\frac{1-i}{2}$

LEVEL 4: COMPLEX NUMBERS

6. After solving a quadratic equation by completing the square, it was found that the equation had solutions, $x = -3 \pm \sqrt{-16b^2}$ where b is a positive real number. Which of the following gives the solutions as complex numbers?

    F. $-3 \pm \quad bi$
    G. $-3 \pm \quad 4bi$
    H. $-3 \pm \quad 8bi$
    J. $-3 \pm 16bi$
    K. $-3 \pm 256bi$

7. In the complex numbers, where $i^2 = -1, (3 - 5i)^2 =$

    A. -16
    B. 34
    C. $9 - 25i$
    D. $9 + 25i$
    E. $-16 - 30i$

8. If $i = \sqrt{-1}$, and $\frac{(3+4i)}{(-5-2i)} = a + bi$, where a and b are real numbers, then what is the value of $|b|$ to the nearest tenth?

    F. 0.5
    G. 1.2
    H. 1.7
    J. 2.0
    K. 2.1

9. If u and v are real numbers, $i = \sqrt{-1}$, and

$$(u - v) + 3i = 7 + vi,$$

then what is $u + v$?

  A. 3
  B. 10
  C. 13
  D. 17
  E. 23

10. If $(x - 3i)(5 + yi) = 28 - 3i$ then what is one possible value of $x + y$? (Note: $i = \sqrt{-1}$)

  F. 2
  G. 6
  H. 7
  J. 8
  K. 28

LEVEL 5: COMPLEX NUMBERS

11. For the complex number i and an integer k, which of the following is a possible value of i^{2k+1} ?

  A. -1
  B. 0
  C. 1
  D. $1 - i$
  E. $-i$

12. If $|z| = 5$, then z CANNOT be which of the following?

  F. -5
  G. $4 - 3i$
  H. $-2 - \sqrt{21}i$
  J. $\sqrt{22} - 3i$
  K. $\sqrt{24} + i$

Answers

1. D	5. D	9. C
2. K	6. G	10. J
3. C	7. E	11. E
4. H	8. F	12. J

Full Solutions

5.

* $(1 - i)(1 + i) = 1^2 + 1^2 = 2$. So $\frac{1}{1-i} \cdot \frac{1+i}{1+i} = \frac{1+i}{2}$, choice **D**.

6.

Since both the question and answer choices all begin with -3, it suffices to evaluate $\sqrt{-16b^2}$.

Since $4^2 = 16$, choice B looks like it should be the answer. Indeed, we have $(4bi)^2 = (4bi)(4bi) = 16b^2i^2 = 16b^2(-1) = -16b^2$. It follows that $\sqrt{-16b^2} = 4bi$, and so the answer is choice **G**.

* **Quick solution:** $\sqrt{-16b^2} = \sqrt{-16}\sqrt{b^2} = 4i \cdot b = 4bi$, choice **G**.

Technical Remark: If a and b are nonnegative real numbers, then it is always true that $\sqrt{ab} = \sqrt{a}\sqrt{b}$, but this rule is NOT always true when dealing with complex numbers.

For example, if a, b are both -2, then $\sqrt{ab} = \sqrt{(-2)(-2)} = \sqrt{4} = 2$, but $\sqrt{a}\sqrt{b} = \sqrt{-2}\sqrt{-2} = \sqrt{2}i\sqrt{2}i = 2i^2 = -2$.

So we need to be extra careful with the above reasoning. In this problem we do get the correct answer.

7.

* $(3 - 5i)^2 = (3 - 5i)(3 - 5i) = (9 - 25) + i(-15 - 15)$

$$= -16 - 30i, \text{ choice } \mathbf{E}.$$

8.

* $\frac{(3+4i)}{(-5-2i)} = \frac{(3+4i)}{(-5-2i)} \cdot \frac{(-5+2i)}{(-5+2i)} = \frac{(-15-8)+(6-20)i}{25+4} = \frac{-23-14i}{29} = -\frac{23}{29} - \frac{14}{29}i$

So $b = -\frac{14}{29}$. Therefore, $|b| = \frac{14}{29} \approx .4827586207$. To the nearest tenth this is 0.5, choice **F**.

9.

* Two complex numbers are equal if their real parts are equal and their imaginary parts are equal. So we have $u - v = 7$ and $3 = v$.

Since $v = 3$ (from the second equation), we have that $u - 3 = 7$. Thus, $u = 7 + 3 = 10$. Finally, $u + v = 10 + 3 = 13$, choice **C**.

10.

* $(x - 3i)(5 + yi) = (5x + 3y) + (-15 + xy)i$. So $5x + 3y = 28$ and $-15 + xy = -3$. So $xy = 12$. We need to solve the following system of equations:

$$5x + 3y = 28$$
$$xy = 12$$

There are several ways to solve this formally, but we can also just try guessing. We are looking for two numbers that multiply to 12. If we try $x = 2, y = 6$, we see that $5x + 3y = 5(2) + 3(6) = 10 + 18 = 28$.

So a possible solution to the system is $x = 2$, $y = 6$, and in this case $x + y = 8$, choice **J**.

11.

* **Solution by picking numbers:** If $k = 0$, then $i^{2k+1} = i^1 = i$. But i is not an answer choice.

If $k = 1$, then $i^{2k+1} = i^3 = i^2 \cdot i = (-1) \cdot i = -i$. So the answer is choice **E**.

Notes: (1) When i is raised to an integer power, the only possible results are $1, i, -1$ and $-i$. This eliminates choices B and D.

(2) If k is an integer, then $2k + 1$ always represents an odd integer. When i is raised to an odd power, the only possible results are i and $-i$.

12.

Solution by starting with choice H: Letting $z = x + iy$, by the definition of absolute value, we need $x^2 + y^2 = 25$.

Starting with choice H, we have $x = -2$ and $y = \sqrt{21}$. It follows that $x^2 + y^2 = (-2)^2 + \left(\sqrt{21}\right)^2 = 4 + 21 = 25$. So we can eliminate H.

Trying J next, we have $\left(\sqrt{22}\right)^2 + (-3)^2 = 22 + 9 = 31$. Since we did not get 25, the answer is **J**.

LESSON 5
NUMBER THEORY

Reminder: Before beginning this lesson remember to redo the problems from Lesson 1 that you have marked off. Do not "unmark" a question unless you get it correct.

Remainders in Disguise

To solve a problem that asks to find or use a remainder always begin with a number that is evenly divisible.

LEVEL 4: NUMBER THEORY

1. Vincent must inspect 9 electronic components that are arranged in a line and labeled numerically from 1 to 9. He must start with component 1 and proceed in order, returning to the beginning and repeating the process after inspecting component 9, stopping when he encounters a defective component. If the first defective component he encounters is component 6, which of the following could be the total number of components that Vincent inspects (counting repetition), including the defective one?

   A. 103
   B. 105
   C. 107
   D. 109
   E. 111

Solution

* We have a sequence which repeats in cycles of 9. Component 6 is in the 6th position in this cycle. So we are looking for a number that gives a remainder of 6 when divided by 9. Well, 99 is evenly divisible by 9. Therefore, $99 + 6 = 105$ gives a remainder of 6 when divided by 9. So the answer is choice **B**.

Before we go on, try to solve this problem by "Starting with choice (C)" (see Lesson 1).

61

Solution

Let's compute the remainder when 107 is divided by 9. We do the long division by hand (or by using the Calculator Algorithm below). 9 goes into 107 eleven times with a remainder 0f 8. So if we just subtract 2 from 107 we will get a number that gives a remainder of 6 when divided by 9. So the answer is $107 - 2 = 105$, choice **B**.

Remarks: (1) Notice that remainders have a very nice, cyclical pattern. The remainders when you divide $..., 97, 98, 99, 100, 101, 102, ..$ by 9 are $..., 7, 8, 0, 1, 2, 3, ..$

(2) See the beginning of Lesson 4 for a calculator algorithm for computing a remainder. Here is the algorithm applied to this problem:

Step 1: Perform the division in your calculator: $\frac{105}{9} \approx 11.67$

Step 2: Multiply the integer part of this answer by the divisor:
$$11 * 9 = 99$$
Step 3: Subtract this result from the dividend to get the remainder:
$$105 - 99 = \mathbf{6}.$$

Prime Factorization

The Fundamental Theorem of Arithmetic: Every integer greater than 1 can be written "uniquely" as a product of primes.

The word "uniquely" is written in quotes because prime factorizations are only unique if we agree to write the primes in increasing order.

For example, 6 can be written as $2 \cdot 3$ or as $3 \cdot 2$. But these two factorizations are the same except that we changed the order of the factors. To make things as simple as possible we always agree to use the **canonical representation**. The word "canonical" is just a fancy name for "natural," and the most natural way to write a prime factorization is in increasing order of primes. So the canonical representation of 6 is $2 \cdot 3$.

As another example, the canonical representation of 18 is $2 \cdot 3 \cdot 3$. We can tidy this up a bit by rewriting $3 \cdot 3$ as 3^2. So the canonical representation of 18 is $2 \cdot 3^2$.

If you are new to factoring, you may find it helpful to draw a factor tree.

62

For example, here is a factor tree for 18:

To draw this tree, we started by writing 18 as the product $2 \cdot 9$. We put a box around 2 because 2 is prime, and does not need to be factored anymore. We then proceeded to factor 9 as $3 \cdot 3$. We put a box around each 3 because 3 is prime. We now see that we are done, and the prime factorization can be found by multiplying all of the boxed numbers together. Remember that we will usually want the canonical representation, so write the final product in increasing order of primes.

By the Fundamental Theorem of Arithmetic above it does not matter how we factor the number – we will always get the same canonical form. For example, here is a different factor tree for 18:

GCD and LCM

The **greatest common divisor (gcd)** of a set of positive integers is the largest positive integer that each integer in the set is divisible by. The **least common multiple (lcm)** of a set of positive integers is the smallest positive integer that is divisible by each integer in the set.

Example 1: Find the gcd and lcm of $\{9, 15\}$.

Method 1: The factors of 9 are 1, 3 and 9. The factors of 15 are 1, 3, 5 and 15. So the common factors of 9 and 15 are 1 and 3. So gcd(9,15) = **3**.

The multiples of 9 are 9, 18, 27, 36, 45, 54, 63,... and the multiples of 15 are 15, 30, 45,.. We can stop at 45 because 45 is also a multiple of 9. So lcm(9,15) = **45**.

Method 2: The prime factorizations of 9 and 15 are $9 = 3^2$ and $15 = 3 \cdot 5$. To find the gcd we multiply together the smallest powers of each prime from both factorizations, and for the lcm we multiply the highest powers of each prime. So $\gcd(9,15) = 3$ and $\text{lcm}(9,15) = 3^2 \cdot 5 = 45$.

Note: If you have trouble seeing where the gcd and lcm are coming from here, it may help to insert the "missing" primes. In this case, 5 is missing from the factorization of 9. So it might help to write $9 = 3^2 \cdot 5^0$. Now we can think of the gcd as $3^1 \cdot 5^0 = 3$.

Method 3: On your TI-84 calculator press MATH, scroll right to NUM. For the gcd press 9, type 9, 15 and press ENTER. You will see an output of **3**. For the lcm press 8, type 9, 15 and press ENTER for an output of **45**.

Example 2: Find the gcd and lcm of $\{100, 270\}$.

The prime factorizations of 100 and 270 are $100 = 2^2 \cdot 5^2$ and $270 = 2 \cdot 3^3 \cdot 5$. So,

$\gcd(100, 270) = 2 \cdot 5 = \mathbf{10}$ and $\text{lcm}(100, 270) = 2^2 \cdot 3^3 \cdot 5^2 = \mathbf{2700}$.

Note: If we insert the "missing" primes in the prime factorization of 100 we get $100 = 2^2 \cdot 3^0 \cdot 5^2$. So we can think of the gcd as

$$2^1 \cdot 3^0 \cdot 5^1 = 10.$$

Now try to solve each of the following problems. The answers to these problems, followed by full solutions are at the end of this lesson. **Do not** look at the answers until you have attempted these problems yourself. Please remember to mark off any problems you get wrong.

LEVEL 2: NUMBER THEORY

2.   What is the least common multiple of 100, 70, and 30?

      F. 210,000
      G.   2,100
      H.   210
      J.   180
      K.   60

3. Given that k is a positive integer and j is 7 times k, what is the least common denominator, in terms of k, for the addition of $\frac{1}{k}$ and $\frac{1}{j}$?

    A. $\frac{k}{7}$
    B. $7k$
    C. $7k^2$
    D. $k + 7$
    E. $k(k + 7)$

LEVEL 3: NUMBER THEORY

4. Let p be a prime number greater than 500,000 and let $z = \frac{1}{\sqrt{p}}$. Which of the following expressions represents a rational number?

    F. $z + 2$
    G. $2z$
    H. $\frac{z}{2}$
    J. $\sqrt{z}$
    K. $3z^2$

                STACKSTAC...

5. In the pattern above, the first letter is S and the letters S, T, A, C, and K repeat continually in that order. What is the 97th letter in the pattern?

    A. S
    B. T
    C. A
    D. C
    E. K

6. Maggie is making a bracelet. She starts with 3 yellow beads, 5 purple beads, and 4 white beads, in that order, and repeats the pattern until there is no more room on the bracelet. If the last bead is purple, which of the following could be the total number of beads on the bracelet?

    F. 81
    G. 85
    H. 87
    J. 88
    K. 93

7. If an integer n is divisible by 3, 7, 21, and 49, what is the next larger integer divisible by these numbers?

    A. $n + 21$
    B. $n + 49$
    C. $n + 73$
    D. $n + 147$
    E. $n + 294$

LEVEL 4: NUMBER THEORY

8. What is the least positive integer greater than 7 that leaves a remainder of 6 when divided by both 9 and 15?

    F. 51
    G. 52
    H. 53
    J. 54
    K. 55

9. Cards numbered from 1 through 2012 are distributed, one at a time, into nine stacks. The card numbered 1 is placed on stack 1, card number 2 on stack 2, card number 3 on stack 3, and so on until each stack has one card. If this pattern is repeated, the card numbered 2012 will be placed on the nth stack. What is the value of n?

    A. 1
    B. 2
    C. 3
    D. 4
    E. 5

10. When the positive integer k is divided by 12 the remainder is 3. When the positive integer m is divided by 12 the remainder is 7. What is the remainder when the product km is divided by 6?

    F. 1
    G. 2
    H. 3
    J. 4
    K. 5

LEVEL 5: NUMBER THEORY

11. Consider the fractions $\frac{1}{p}, \frac{1}{q}, \frac{1}{r}$, and $\frac{1}{t}$, where p and q are distinct prime numbers greater than 7, $r = 5p$, and $t = 7q$. Suppose that $p \cdot q \cdot r \cdot t$ is used as the common denominator when finding the sum of these fractions. In order for the sum to be in lowest terms, its numerator and denominator must be reduced by a factor of which of the following?

    A. 35
    B. pq
    C. rt
    D. $pqrt$
    E. $35pqrt$

12. In the repeating decimal

$$0.\overline{7654321} = 0.765432176543217654321\ldots$$

where the digits 7654321 repeat, which digit is in the 2012th place to the right of the decimal?

    F. 3
    G. 4
    H. 5
    J. 6
    K. 7

Answers

1. B	5. B	9. E
2. G	6. J	10. H
3. B	7. D	11. B
4. K	8. F	12. H

Full Solutions

4.

* $z^2 = \left(\frac{1}{\sqrt{p}}\right)^2 = \frac{1^2}{(\sqrt{p})^2} = \frac{1}{p}$, and so $3z^2 = 3\left(\frac{1}{p}\right) = \frac{3}{p}$. Since 3 and p are both integers, $\frac{3}{p}$ is a rational number. Thus, the answer is choice **K**.

5.

* We first find an integer as close as possible to 97 that is divisible by 5 (there are five letters in the pattern). We find that 95 is divisible by 5. Thus, the 96th letter is S. So the 97th letter is T, choice **B**.

Remark: Note that the remainder upon dividing 97 by 5 is 2. Therefore, the 97th letter in the sequence is the same as the 2nd letter in the sequence, which is T.

Caution: If the remainder is 0, you get the 5th letter in the sequence (there is no 0th letter). For example, the 95th letter in the sequence is K.

6.

* There are 12 beads before the sequence begins repeating. The 4th, 5th, 6th, 7th and 8th bead are each purple. So when we divide the total number of beads by 12 the remainder should be a number between 4 and 8, inclusive. Since 84 is divisible by 12, 88 gives a remainder of 4 when divided by 12. So the answer is choice **J**.

7.

Solution by starting with choice A and picking numbers: Let's choose a value for n satisfying the given condition. If we multiply the given numbers together, then we get $n = \mathbf{24,696}$. Starting with choice A, plug in 24,696 for n, and divide the result by each of the given four numbers.

 A. $24,696 + 21 = 24,717$ (not divisible by 49: $\frac{24,717}{49} \approx 504.4$)

 B. $24,696 + 49 = 24,745$ (not divisible by 3: $\frac{24,745}{3} \approx 8248.33$)

 C. $24,696 + 73 = 24,769$ (not divisible by 3: $\frac{24,769}{3} \approx 8256.33$)

 D. $24,696 + 147 = 24,843$ (divisible by all three)

Since D works we can stop here and choose answer choice **D**.

Notes: (1) We only need to check divisibility by 3 and $7^2 = 49$ since these are the highest powers of primes that are factors of the given numbers.

(2) 21 and 49 would work as well (since together they contain the factors 3 and $7^2 = 49$).

(3) A better choice for n is the **least common multiple** of the four given numbers which is $3 \cdot 7^2 = 147$. In this case we get the following:

  A. $147 + 21 = 168$ (not divisible by 49: $168/49 \approx 3.4$)
  B. $147 + 49 = 196$ (not divisible by 3: $196/3 \approx 65.33$)
  C. $147 + 73 = 220$ (not divisible by 3: $220/3 \approx 73.33$)
  D. $147 + 147 = 294$ (divisible by all three)

Advanced Method: As stated in note (3) above, the least common multiple of the given numbers is 147. We can therefore add any multiple of 147 to n and maintain divisibility by each of the four given numbers. So the correct answer is choice **D**.

Note: Choice E also always gives an integer divisible by the given four numbers. It is not correct because it is not the **next** larger integer.

Remarks: (1) Note that if n is divisible by 147 it can be written as $147k$ for some integer k. Thus, $n + 147 = 147k + 147 = 147(k + 1)$. So $n + 147$ is divisible by 147, and thus by any factor of 147 including 3, 7, 21 and 49.

(2) Now that we know the above theory we see that we can get the next larger number divisible by the given numbers by adding the lcm of the given numbers.

* Quick Solution: lcm $= 3 \cdot 7^2 = 147$. So the answer is $n + 147$, choice **D**.

    8.
* The lcm of 9 and 15 is 45 (this was done in Example 1 toward the beginning of this lesson). We now simply add the remainder:

$$45 + 6 = 51.$$

This is choice **F**.

9.

We first find an integer as close as possible to 2012 that is divisible by 9. We can check this in our calculator.

$2012/9 \approx 223.56$ $2011/9 \approx 223.44$ $2010/9 \approx 223.33$
$2009/9 \approx 223.22$ $2008/9 \approx 223.11$ $2007/9 = 223$

The last computation gave an integer. Therefore 2007 is divisible by 9. So card number 2007 will go on the 9th stack. Card 2008 will go on the 1st stack, card 2009 will go on the 2nd stack, card 2010 will go on the 3rd stack, card 2011 will go on the 4th stack, and card 2012 will go on the 5th stack. Thus, the answer is 5, choice **E**.

* Solution using the calculator algorithm: Divide 2012 by 9 to get $2012/9 \approx 223.56$. Now take the integer part of the answer and multiply by 9. We get $223 * 9 = 2007$. Subtract this result from 2012 to get the remainder: $2012 - 2007 = 5$, choice **E**.

10.

Solution by picking numbers: Let's choose a positive integer k whose remainder is 3 when it is divided by 12. A simple way to find such a k is to add 12 and 3. So let $k = 15$. Similarly, let's let $m = 12 + 7 = 19$. Then we have $km = 15 \cdot 19 = 285$. 6 goes into 285 forty-seven times with a remainder of 3, choice **H**.

Important: To find a remainder you must perform division **by hand**, or by using the calculator algorithm given toward the beginning of Lesson 4. Dividing in your calculator does **not** give you a remainder!

* Note: A slightly simpler choice for k is $k = 3$. Indeed, when 3 is divided by 12 we get 0 with 3 left over. Similarly, we can choose $m = 7$. Then $km = 3 \cdot 7 = 21$, and the remainder when km is divided by 6 is 3, choice **H**.

Note that in general we can get a value for k by starting with any multiple of 12 and adding 3. So $k = 12n + 3$ for some integer n. Similarly, $m = 12r + 3$ for some integer r.

Remark: The answer to this problem is independent of our choices for k and m (assuming that k and m satisfy the given condition, of course). The method just described does **not** show this. The next method does.

Algebraic solution: Here is a complete algebraic solution that actually demonstrates the independence of choice for k and m. This solution is quite sophisticated and I do not recommend using it on the actual ACT.

The given condition means that we can write k as $k = 12n + 3$ and $m = 12r + 7$ for some integers n and r. Then

$$km = (12n + 3)(12r + 7) = 144nr + 84n + 36r + 21$$
$$= 144nr + 84n + 36r + 18 + 3 = 6(24nr + 14n + 6r + 3) + 3$$
$$= 6z + 3$$

where z is the integer $24nr + 14n + 6r + 3$. This shows that when km is divided by 6 the remainder is 3, choice **H**.

11.

*

$$\frac{1}{p} + \frac{1}{q} + \frac{1}{r} + \frac{1}{t} = \frac{qrt + prt + pqt + pqr}{pqrt} = \frac{q \cdot 5p \cdot 7q + p \cdot 5p \cdot 7q + pq \cdot 7q + pq \cdot 5p}{pq \cdot 5p \cdot 7q}$$
$$= \frac{pq(35q + 35p + 7q + 5p)}{pq(35pq)}$$

So we see that we must reduce the numerator and denominator by pq, choice **B**.

12.
* Since there are exactly 7 digits before repeating we look for the remainder when 2012 is divided by 7. Using one of our standard methods we see that this remainder is 3. So the digit in the 2012th place is the same as the digit in the third place to the right of the decimal point. This is 5, choice **H**.

OPTIONAL MATERIAL

CHALLENGE QUESTIONS

1.   The integer n is equal to k^3 for some integer k. Suppose that n is divisible by 45 and 400. What is the smallest possible value of n ?

2. If a and b are positive integers, $\left(a^{\frac{1}{2}}b^{\frac{1}{3}}c^{\frac{1}{5}}\right)^{30} = 41{,}472$, and $abc = 1$, what is the value of ab?

3. Find the smallest positive integer k such that $\frac{k}{2}$ is a perfect square and $\frac{k}{3}$ is a perfect cube.

Solutions

1.

* We are looking for the smallest perfect cube that is divisible by the least common multiple of 45 and 400. We begin by getting the prime factorizations of 45 and 400 as follows: $45 = 3^2 \cdot 5$, and $400 = 2^4 \cdot 5^2$. So $\text{lcm}(45{,}400) = 2^4 \cdot 3^2 \cdot 5^2$. The least perfect cube divisible by this number is $2^6 \cdot 3^3 \cdot 5^3 = \mathbf{216{,}000}$.

2.

* $\left(a^{\frac{1}{2}}b^{\frac{1}{3}}c^{\frac{1}{5}}\right)^{30} = a^{15}b^{10}c^6 = (abc)^6(ab)^4a^5 = (ab)^4a^5$. So we have that $(ab)^4a^5 = 41{,}472$. Since a and b are positive integers, ab must be a positive integer. So let's begin trying positive integer values for ab.

If $ab = 1$, then $a^5 = 41{,}472$. So $a = (41{,}472)^{\frac{1}{5}}$ which is not an integer. Let's try $ab = 2$ next. Then $a^5 = \frac{41{,}472}{2^4} = 2592$. So $a = 2592^{\frac{1}{2}}$ which is also not an integer. Setting ab equal to 3, 4, and 5 also do not work. But if we let $ab = 6$, then $a^5 = \frac{41{,}472}{6^4} = 32$. So $a = 2$, and thus, $b = 3$. So a and b are both integers. Therefore, $ab = \mathbf{6}$.

Note: It turns out that c is not an integer ($c = \frac{1}{6}$).

3.

Since k is divisible by 2 and 3 and we want the smallest such k, there are positive integers a and b with $k = 2^a3^b$. We have $\frac{k}{2} = 2^{a-1}3^b$ and $\frac{k}{3} = 2^a3^{b-1}$. Since $\frac{k}{2}$ is a perfect square, $a - 1$ and b must be even. Since $\frac{k}{3}$ is a perfect cube, a and $b - 1$ must each be a multiple of 3. So a must be an odd multiple of 3 and b must be even and 1 more than a multiple of 3. The least values of a and b satisfying these conditions are $a = 3$ and $b = 4$. So $k = 2^33^4 = \mathbf{648}$.

LESSON 6
ALGEBRA AND FUNCTIONS

Reminder: Before beginning this lesson remember to redo the problems from Lesson 2 that you have marked off. Do not "unmark" a question unless you get it correct.

The Distributive Property

The **distributive property** says that for all real numbers a, b, and c

$$a(b + c) = ab + ac$$

More specifically, this property says that the operation of multiplication distributes over addition. The distributive property is very important as it allows us to multiply and factor algebraic expressions.

Numeric example: Show that $2(3 + 4) = 2 \cdot 3 + 2 \cdot 4$

Solution: $2(3 + 4) = 2 \cdot 7 = 14$ and $2 \cdot 3 + 2 \cdot 4 = 6 + 8 = 14$.

Geometric Justification: The following picture gives a physical representation of the distributive property for this example.

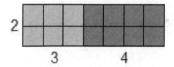

Note that the area of the light grey rectangle is $2 \cdot 3$, the area of the dark grey rectangle is $2 \cdot 4$, and the area of the whole rectangle is $2(3 + 4)$.

Algebraic examples: Use the distributive property to write each algebraic expression in an equivalent form.

   (1) $2(x + 1)$ (2) $x(y - 3)$ (3) $-(x - y)$

Solutions: (1) $2(x + 1) = 2x + 2$

(2) $x(y - 3) = xy - 3x$

(3) $-(x - y) = -x + y$

Factoring

When we use the distributive property in the opposite direction, we usually call it **factoring**.

Examples: (1) $2x + 4y = 2(x + 2y)$

(2) $3x + 5xy = x(3 + 5y)$

(3) $6xy + 9yz = 3y(2x + 3z)$

Here are some more sophisticated techniques for factoring:

The Difference of Two Squares: $a^2 - b^2 = (a - b)(a + b)$

Examples: (1) $x^2 - 9 = (x - 3)(x + 3)$
(2) $4x^2 - 25y^2 = (2x - 5y)(2x + 5y)$
(3) $36 - 49x^2y^2 = (6 - 7xy)(6 + 7xy)$

Trinomial Factoring: $x^2 - (a + b)x + ab = (x - a)(x - b)$

Examples: (1) $x^2 - 5x + 6 = (x - 2)(x - 3)$

(2) $x^2 - 2x - 35 = (x - 7)(x + 5)$

(3) $x^2 + 14x + 33 = (x + 3)(x + 11)$

Square Root Property

The **square root property** says that if $x^2 = a^2$, then $x = \pm a$.

For example, the equation $x^2 = 9$ has the two solutions $x = 3$ and $x = -3$.

Important note: Using the square root property is different from taking a square root. We apply the square root property to an equation of the form $x^2 = a^2$ to get two solutions, whereas when we take the positive square root of a number we get just one answer.

For example, when we take the positive square root of 9 we get 3, i.e. $\sqrt{9} = 3$. But when we apply the square root property to the equation $x^2 = 9$, we have seen that we get the two solutions $x = 3$ and $x = -3$.

Example: Solve the equation $(x - 3)^2 = 2$ using the square root property.

74

Solution: When we apply the square root property we get $x - 3 = \pm\sqrt{2}$. We then add 3 to each side of this last equation to get the two solutions $x = 3 \pm \sqrt{2}$.

Completing the Square

Completing the square is a technique with many useful applications. We complete the square on an expression of the form

$$x^2 + bx$$

To complete the square, we simply take half of b, and then square the result. In other words, we get $\left(\frac{b}{2}\right)^2$.

The expression $x^2 + bx + \left(\frac{b}{2}\right)^2$ is always a perfect square. In fact,

$$x^2 + bx + \left(\frac{b}{2}\right)^2 = \left(x + \frac{b}{2}\right)^2$$

For example, let's complete the square in the expression $x^2 + 6x$.

Well half of 6 is 3, and when we square 3 we get 9. So the new expression is $x^2 + 6x + 9$ which factors as $(x + 3)^2$.

Important notes: (1) When we complete the square we usually get an expression that is <u>not</u> equal to the original expression. For example, $x^2 + 6x \neq x^2 + 6x + 9$.

(2) The coefficient of x^2 <u>must</u> be 1 before we complete the square. So, for example, we cannot complete the square on the expression $2x^2 + 32x$.

But we can first factor out the 2 to get $2(x^2 + 16x)$, and then complete the square on the expression $x^2 + 16x$ to get $2(x^2 + 16x + 64)$.

Note that we increased the expression by $2 \cdot 64 = 128$.

Solving Quadratic Equations

A quadratic equation has the form $ax^2 + bx + c = 0$.

Let's use a simple example to illustrate the various methods for solving such an equation.

Example: In the quadratic equation $x^2 - 2x = 15$, find the positive solution for x.

75

Solution by guessing: We plug in guesses for x until we find the answer. For example, if we guess that $x = 3$, then $3^2 - 2 \cdot 3 = 9 - 6 = 3$. This is too small.

Let's try $x = 5$ next. We get $5^2 - 2 \cdot 5 = 25 - 10 = 15$. This is correct. So the answer is **5**.

Solution by factoring: We bring everything to the left hand side of the equation to get $x^2 - 2x - 15 = 0$. We then factor the left hand side to get $(x - 5)(x + 3) = 0$. So $x - 5 = 0$ or $x + 3 = 0$. It follows that $x = 5$ or $x = -3$. Since we want the positive solution for x, the answer is **5**.

Solution by using the quadratic formula: As in the last solution we bring everything to the left hand side of the equation to get

$$x^2 - 2x - 15 = 0.$$

We identify $a = 1$, $b = -2$, and $c = -15$.

$$x = \frac{-b \pm \sqrt{b^2 - 4ac}}{2a} = \frac{2 \pm \sqrt{4 + 60}}{2} = \frac{2 \pm \sqrt{64}}{2} = \frac{2 \pm 8}{2} = 1 \pm 4.$$

So we get $x = 1 + 4 = 5$ or $x = 1 - 4 = -3$. Since we want the positive solution for x, the answer is **5**.

Solution by completing the square: For this solution we leave the constant on the right hand side: $x^2 - 2x = 15$.

We take half of -2, which is -1, and square this number to get 1. We then add 1 to each side of the equation to get $x^2 - 2x + 1 = 15 + 1$. This is equivalent to $(x - 1)^2 = 16$. We now apply the square root property to get $x - 1 = \pm 4$. So $x = 1 \pm 4$. This yields the two solutions $1 + 4 = 5$, and $1 - 4 = -3$. Since we want the positive solution for x, the answer is **5**.

Graphical solution: In your graphing calculator press the Y= button, and enter the following.

$$Y1 = X^2 - 2X - 15$$

Now press ZOOM 6 to graph the parabola in a standard window. Then press 2nd TRACE (which is CALC) 2 (or select ZERO), move the cursor just to the left of the second x-intercept and press ENTER. Now move the cursor just to the right of the second x-intercept and press ENTER again. Press ENTER once more, and you will see that the x-coordinate of the second x-intercept is **5**.

Functions

A function is simply a rule that for each "input" assigns a specific "output." Functions may be given by equations, tables or graphs.

Note about the notation $f(x)$: The variable x is a placeholder. We evaluate the function f at a specific value by substituting that value in for x.

For example, if $f(x) = x^3 + 2x$, then $f(-2) = (-2)^3 + 2(-2) = -12$

LEVEL 4: ALGEBRA AND FUNCTIONS

x	$p(x)$	$q(x)$	$r(x)$
−2	−3	4	−3
−1	2	1	2
0	5	−1	−6
1	−7	0	−5

1. The functions p, q and r are defined for all values of x, and certain values of those functions are given in the table above. What is the value of $p(-2) + q(0) - r(1)$?

    A. 0
    B. 1
    C. 2
    D. 3
    E. 4

Solution

* To evaluate $p(-2)$, we look at the row corresponding to $x = -2$, and the column corresponding to $p(x)$. We see that the entry there is −3. Therefore, $p(-2) = -3$. Similarly, $q(0) = -1$ and $r(1) = -5$. Finally, we have that $p(-2) + q(0) - r(1) = -3 - 1 - (-5) = -4 + 5 = 1$, choice **B**.

Try to solve each of the following problems. The answers to these problems, followed by full solutions are at the end of this lesson. **Do not** look at the answers until you have attempted these problems yourself. Please remember to mark off any problems you get wrong.

LEVEL 2: ALGEBRA AND FUNCTIONS

2. A function f is defined as $f(x, y, z) = xy^2 - x^2z + yz$. What is $f(-1, -2, 3)$?

   F. -13
   G. -7
   H. -5
   J. -1
   K. 1

$$ax - bx + cx - dx$$

3. For all real numbers a, b, c, and d, the expression above can be written as the product of x and which of the following?

   A. $-a + b - c + d$
   B. $-a + b - c - d$
   C. $-a - b - c - d$
   D. $a - b + c - d$
   E. $a + b + c + d$

LEVEL 3: ALGEBRA AND FUNCTIONS

4. Which of the following expressions is a factor of the polynomial $x^2 - x - 110$?

   F. $x - 7$
   G. $x - 8$
   H. $x - 9$
   J. $x - 10$
   K. $x - 11$

5. For all real numbers x, let the function f be defined as $f(x) = 5x - 10$. Which of the following is equal to $f(3) + f(5)$?

   A. $f(4)$
   B. $f(6)$
   C. $f(7)$
   D. $f(12)$
   E. $f(20)$

78

6. Which of the following expressions is equivalent to $\frac{1}{3}b^3(12a^2 - 5b^4 + 6a^2 + 5b^4)$?

    F. $6a^2b^3$
    G. $18a^2b^4$
    H. $4a^2b^3 + 6a^2$
    J. $6a^2b^3 + 6a^2$
    K. $4a^2b^3 + 6a^2 - 5b^2 + 5b^4$

LEVEL 4: ALGEBRA AND FUNCTIONS

7. For all nonzero values of b, $\frac{15b^8 - 20b^5}{5b^2} = ?$

    A. $3b^6 - 4b^3$
    B. $3b^6 - 4b^4$
    C. $3b^6 - 20b^5$
    D. $3b^4 - 4b^3$
    E. $-b^4$

8. Which of the following expressions is the greatest monomial factor of $54x^2y^3z - 126xy^2z^2$?

    F. $18xyz$
    G. $18xy^2z$
    H. $18x^2y^3z^2$
    J. $378x^2y^3z^3$
    K. $378x^3y^5z^3$

$$P(x) = \frac{20x}{98 - x}$$

9. The function P above models the monthly profit, in thousands of dollars, for a company that sells x percent of their inventory for the month. If \$90,000 is earned in profit during the month of April, what percent of April's inventory, to the nearest whole percent, has been sold?

    A. 25%
    B. 42%
    C. 56%
    D. 80%
    E. 90%

LEVEL 5: ALGEBRA AND FUNCTIONS

10. Which of the following is a quadratic equation that has $-\frac{5}{7}$ as its only solution?

F. $49x^2 - 70x + 25 = 0$
G. $49x^2 + 70x + 25 = 0$
H. $49x^2 + 35x + 25 = 0$
J. $49x^2 + 25 = 0$
K. $49x^2 - 25 = 0$

11. For all positive integers x, the function f is defined by $f(x) = (\frac{1}{b^5})^x$, where b is a constant greater than 1. Which of the following is equivalent to $f(3x)$?

A. $\sqrt[3]{f(x)}$
B. $(f(x))^3$
C. $3f(x)$
D. $\frac{1}{3}f(x)$
E. $\frac{1}{9}f(x)$

12. The domain of $\frac{17}{x^3 - 16x}$ is the set of all real numbers EXCEPT:

F. $-\frac{17}{16}$
G. 4
H. -4 and 4
J. 0 and 4
K. -4, 0, and 4

Answers

1. B	5. B	9. D
2. F	6. F	10. G
3. D	7. A	11. B
4. K	8. G	12. K

Full Solutions

4.

* Quick solution: $x^2 - x - 110 = (x - 11)(x + 10)$. So $x - 11$ is a factor and the answer is choice **K**.

Solution using the factor theorem: $11^2 - 11 - 110 = 121 - 121 = 0$. So $x - 11$ is a factor of $x^2 - x - 110$, choice **K**.

Note: The **factor theorem** says that r is a root of the polynomial $p(x)$ if and only if $x - r$ is a factor of the polynomial.

In this question, the polynomial is $p(x) = x^2 - x - 110$, and we saw that $p(11) = 0$. So 11 is a root of the polynomial, and therefore by the factor theorem, $x - 11$ is a factor of the polynomial.

5.

Solution by starting with choice C: First note that

$$f(3) = 5(3) - 10 = 5 \text{ and } f(5) = 5(5) - 10 = 15.$$

So $f(3) + f(5) = 5 + 15 = \textbf{20}$.

Now, beginning with choice C we see that $f(7) = 5(7) - 10 = 25$. This is a bit too big. So let's try choice B. We have $f(6) = 5(6) - 10 = 20$. This is correct. Thus, the answer is choice **B**.

Warning: Many students will compute $f(3) + f(5) = 20$ and immediately choose choice E. Do not fall into this trap!

* Algebraic solution: As in the previous solution, direct computation gives $f(3) + f(5) = 20$. Setting $f(x) = 20$ yields $5x - 10 = 20$, so that $5x = 30$, and so $x = \frac{30}{5} = 6$, i.e., $f(6) = 20 = f(3) + f(5)$, choice **B**.

6.

* First note that $-5b^4$ cancels with $5b^4$, and $12a^2 + 6a^2 = 18a^2$ to get

$$\frac{1}{3}b^3(12a^2 - 5b^4 + 6a^2 + 5b^4) = \frac{1}{3}b^3(18a^2).$$

So we have $\frac{1}{3}b^3(18a^2) = \frac{1}{3} \cdot 18 \cdot b^3 a^2 = 6a^2 b^3$, choice **F**.

7.
* Algebraic solution:

$$\frac{15b^8 - 20b^5}{5b^2} = \frac{5b^5(3b^3 - 4)}{5b^2} = b^3(3b^3 - 4) = 3b^6 - 4b^3.$$

This is choice **A**.

Note: See Lesson 14 for the laws of exponents used here.

For example, we have $b^8 = b^{5+3} = b^5 b^3$. It follows that

$$15b^8 - 20b^5 = 15b^5 b^3 - 20b^5 = b^5(15b^3 - 20).$$

We can now also factor out 5 because 15 and 20 are both divisible by 5.

As another example, we have $\frac{b^5}{b^2} = b^{5-2} = b^3$.

Alternate solution: $\frac{15b^8 - 20b^5}{5b^2} = \frac{15b^8}{5b^2} - \frac{20b^5}{5b^2} = 3b^6 - 4b^3$, choice **A**.

Note: This problem can also be solved by picking numbers. This isn't a very efficient way to solve this problem, but it can be used as a last resort.

8.
* Solution using the distributive property:

$$54x^2 y^3 z - 126xy^2 z^2 = 18xy^2 z(3xyz - 7z).$$

So the answer is choice **G**.

Note: A **monomial** is a polynomial with just one term. A **binomial** is a polynomial with two terms, and a **trinomial** is a polynomial with three terms.

In this problem, $18xy^2 z$ is a monomial and $3xyz - 7z$ is a binomial.

9.
Solution by starting with choice C: We are given that $P(x) = 90$, and we are being asked to approximate x. So we have $\frac{20x}{98 - x} = 90$. Let's begin with choice C and plug in 56 for x. $20(56)/(98 - 56) \approx 26.67$, too small.

Let's try choice D next. So $20(80)/(98 - 80) \approx 88.89$. This is close, so the answer is probably choice D. To be safe we should check the other answer choices.

A. $20(25)/(98 - 25) \approx 6.85$
B. $20(42)/(98 - 42) = 15$
E. $20(90)/(98 - 90) = 225$

So the answer must be choice **D**.

* **Algebraic solution:**

$$\frac{20x}{98 - x} = 90$$
$$20x = 90(98 - x)$$
$$20x = 8820 - 90x$$
$$110x = 8820$$
$$x = \frac{8820}{110} \approx 80.18$$

The final answer, to the nearest percent, is 80%, choice **D**.

10.

* If $-\frac{5}{7}$ is the only solution, then $x + \frac{5}{7}$ is the only factor (by the factor theorem). So we have

$$\left(x + \frac{5}{7}\right)\left(x + \frac{5}{7}\right) = 0$$
$$x^2 + \frac{5}{7}x + \frac{5}{7}x + \left(\frac{5}{7}\right)^2 = 0$$
$$x^2 + \frac{10}{7}x + \frac{25}{49} = 0$$
$$49x^2 + 70x + 25 = 0$$

This is choice **G**.

Notes: (1) See the note following the explanation to problem 4 for the factor theorem. The words "solution," "root," and "zero" all mean the same thing.

(2) In factored form, a quadratic equation always has two factors. Since $x + 5/7$ is the only factor in this problem, it must appear twice.

(3) In going from the first equation to the second equation, we multiplied the two polynomials ($x + \frac{5}{7}$ times itself). To do this you can use FOIL or any other method you like for multiplying polynomials.

(4) In going from the second equation to the third equation, we simply added $\frac{5}{7}x + \frac{5}{7}x = \frac{10}{7}x$.

(5) In going from the third equation to the last equation, we multiplied both sides of the equation by the least common denominator, which is 49. More precisely, on the left hand side we have

$$49\left(x^2 + \frac{10}{7}x + \frac{25}{49}\right) = 49x^2 + 49\left(\frac{10}{7}x\right) + 49\left(\frac{25}{49}\right)$$
$$= 49x^2 + 7(10x) + 25 = 49x^2 + 70x + 25.$$

11.

Solution by picking a number: Let's let $b = 2$. Then $f(x) = \left(\frac{1}{32}\right)^x$. Now let's plug in a value for x, say $x = 1$. Then we have $f(3x) = f(3) = \left(\frac{1}{32}\right)^3 \approx .00003$. Put a nice, big, dark circle around this number, and now plug $x = 1$ into each answer choice.

A. $\sqrt[3]{f(1)} = \sqrt[3]{\frac{1}{32}} \approx .315$

B. $(f(1))^3 = \left(\frac{1}{32}\right)^3 \approx .00003$

C. $3f(1) = 3\left(\frac{1}{32}\right) = .09375$

D. $\frac{1}{3}(f(1)) = \frac{1}{3}\left(\frac{1}{32}\right) \approx .0104.$

E. $\frac{1}{9}(f(1)) = \frac{1}{9}\left(\frac{1}{32}\right) \approx .0035$

We can eliminate choices A, C, D, and E, and therefore the answer is choice **B**.

* Algebraic solution: $f(3x) = \left(\frac{1}{b^5}\right)^{3x} = \left(\left(\frac{1}{b^5}\right)^x\right)^3 = (f(x))^3$, choice **B**.

12.
Solution by plugging in: We need to find all x-values that make the denominator zero. The answer choices can help us decide which numbers to try:

$x = 4$: $x^3 - 16x = 4^3 - 16(4) = 0$

$x = -4$: $(-4)^3 - 16(-4) = -4^3 + 64 = 0$

$x = 0: 0^3 - 16(0) = 0$

So the answer is choice **K**.

* Solution by factoring: $x^3 - 16x = x(x^2 - 16) = x(x - 4)(x + 4)$.

This expression is zero when each factor is zero, and so the numbers that make the denominator zero are 0, 4, and −4, choice **K**.

Remark: We used the factor theorem for this solution. See problem 4 for more information on the factor theorem.

OPTIONAL MATERIAL

CHALLENGE QUESTION

1. Let f be a linear function such that $f(5) = -2$ and $f(11) = 28$. What is the value of $\frac{f(9)-f(7)}{2}$?

Solution

1.

* The graph of f is a line with slope

$$\frac{f(11)-f(5)}{11-5} = \frac{28-(-2)}{6} = \frac{30}{6} = 5.$$

But the slope of the line is also $\frac{f(9)-f(7)}{9-7} = \frac{f(9)-f(7)}{2}$. So the answer is **5**.

Download additional solutions for free here:

www.satprepget800.com/28LesAdv

LESSON 7
GEOMETRY

Reminder: Before beginning this lesson remember to redo the problems from Lesson 3 that you have marked off. Do not "unmark" a question unless you get it correct.

The Triangle Rule

The triangle rule states that the length of the third side of a triangle is between the sum and difference of the lengths of the other two sides.

Example: If a triangle has sides of length 2, 5, and x, then we have that $5 - 2 < x < 5 + 2$. That is, $3 < x < 7$.

LEVEL 3: GEOMETRY

1. Which of the following lists of numbers could be the side lengths, in centimeters, of a triangle?

    A. $2, 3, 4$
    B. $4, 5, 9$
    C. $7, 10, 17$
    D. $8, 12, 19$
    E. $10, 13, 22$

Solution

* We use the Triangle Rule together with process of elimination. Since $2 + 3 = 5 > 4$, we can eliminate choice A. Similarly, since $4 + 5 = 9$, $7 + 10 = 17$, and $8 + 12 = 20 > 19$, we can eliminate choices B, C, and D. The answer is therefore choice **E**.

Notes: (1) When checking to see if a list of numbers could be the side lengths of a triangle, we need check only if the largest number is between the sum and difference of the other two.

(2) For completeness, let's check that choice E satisfies the Triangle Rule. By note (1) we need only check that $13 - 10 < 22 < 13 + 10$. But this is equivalent to $3 < 22 < 23$, which is true.

The Pythagorean Theorem and its Converse

The Pythagorean Theorem says that if a right triangle has legs of length a and b, and a hypotenuse of length c, then $c^2 = a^2 + b^2$.

The converse of the Pythagorean Theorem is also true: If a triangle has sides with length a, b, and c satisfying $c^2 = a^2 + b^2$, then the triangle is a right triangle.

More specifically, we have the following.

$c^2 > a^2 + b^2$ if and only if the angle opposite the side of length c is greater than 90 degrees.

$c^2 < a^2 + b^2$ if and only if the angle opposite the side of length c is less than 90 degrees.

Example: Let's find the possibilities for the length of $\overline{PQ}$ in the following triangle.

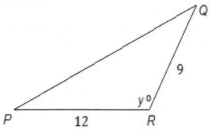

Solution: We have $12 - 9 = 3$ and $12 + 9 = 21$. So by the **Triangle Rule**, $3 < PQ < 21$.

Using the **converse of the Pythagorean Theorem**, we have $(PQ)^2 > (PR)^2 + (RQ)^2$. Thus, $(PQ)^2 > 12^2 + 9^2 = 144 + 81 = 225$, and therefore $PQ > 15$.

Putting the two rules together we have $\mathbf{15 < PQ < 21}$.

Distance

There are two methods for finding the distance between two points.

Method 1: Plot the two points, draw a right triangle, and use the Pythagorean Theorem.

87

Method 2: Use the **distance formula**:

The distance between the two points (a, b) and (c, d) is given by

$d = \sqrt{(c - a)^2 + (d - b)^2}$, or equivalently, $d^2 = (c - a)^2 + (d - b)^2$

Example: Let's find the distance between the points $(2, -4)$ and $(-4, 4)$.

Solution using a right triangle: Let's plot the two points and form a right triangle.

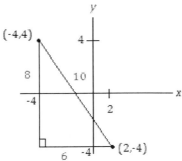

We got the length of the left leg by subtracting $4 - (-4) = 4 + 4 = 8$, and we got the bottom leg by subtracting $2 - (-4) = 2 + 4 = 6$. We now use the Pythagorean Theorem: $c^2 = 6^2 + 8^2 = 36 + 64 = 100$. So $c = 10$.

Remarks: (1) If you recognize that 6, 8, 10 is a multiple of the **Pythagorean triple** 3, 4, 5 (just multiply each number by 2), then you do not need to use the Pythagorean Theorem.

(2) 3, 4, 5 and 5, 12, 13 are the two most common Pythagorean triples.

* Solution using the distance formula:

$$d = \sqrt{(-4 - 2)^2 + \left(4 - (-4)\right)^2} = \sqrt{(-6)^2 + 8^2} = \sqrt{36 + 64} = \sqrt{100} = 10.$$

The Generalized Pythagorean Theorem

The length d of the long diagonal of a rectangular solid is given by

$$d^2 = a^2 + b^2 + c^2$$

where a, b and c are the length, width and height of the rectangular solid.

Example: Find the length of the longest line segment with endpoints on a cube with side length 11.

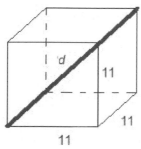

* In this example, our rectangular solid is a cube with a, b and c all equal to 11. So $d^2 = a^2 + b^2 + c^2 = 11^2 + 11^2 + 11^2 = 11^2 \cdot 3$. Therefore, $d = \mathbf{11\sqrt{3}}$.

Now try to solve each of the following problems. The answers to these problems, followed by full solutions are at the end of this lesson. **Do not** look at the answers until you have attempted these problems yourself. Please remember to mark off any problems you get wrong.

LEVEL 3: GEOMETRY

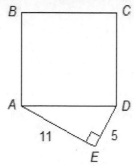

2.   In the figure above, what is the area of square *ABCD* ?

    F. $2\sqrt{21}$
    G. $\sqrt{146}$
    H. 84
    J. 146
    K. Cannot be determined from the given information.

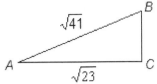

3. In right triangle ABC above, what is the length of side $\overline{BC}$?

    A. $\sqrt{18}$
    B. $\sqrt{41} - \sqrt{23}$
    C. 8
    D. 18
    E. 64

LEVEL 4: GEOMETRY

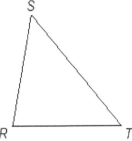

4. In the triangle above, $RS = RT = 10$ and $ST = 12$. What is the area of the triangle?

    F. 24
    G. 30
    H. 48
    J. 60
    K. 80

LEVEL 5: GEOMETRY

5. If x is an integer less than 6, how many different triangles are there with sides of length 5, 9 and x ?

    A. One
    B. Two
    C. Three
    D. Four
    E. Five

90

6. A cube with volume 343 cubic inches is inscribed in a sphere so that each vertex of the cube touches the sphere. What is the length of the radius, in inches, of the sphere?

    F. $\dfrac{\sqrt{3}}{2}$

    G. $\sqrt{3}$

    H. $\dfrac{7\sqrt{3}}{2}$

    J. $7\sqrt{3}$

    K. $14\sqrt{3}$

7. The lengths of the sides of a triangle are x, 16 and 31, where x is the shortest side. If the triangle is not isosceles, which of the following are possible values of x?

    I. 14
    II. 15
    III. 16

    A. None
    B. II only
    C. III only
    D. II and III only
    E. I, II, and III

8. Points Q, R and S lie in a plane. If the distance between Q and R is 18 and the distance between R and S is 11, which of the following could be the distance between Q and S ?

    I. 7
    II. 28
    III. 29

    F. I only
    G. II only
    H. III only
    J. I and III only
    K. I, II, and III

91

9. The lengths of the sides of an isosceles triangle are 22, m, and m. If m is an integer, what is the smallest possible perimeter of the triangle?

    A. 30
    B. 31
    C. 32
    D. 34
    E. 46

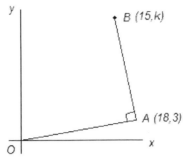

10. In the xy-plane above $OA = AB$. What is the value of k?

    F. 18
    G. 19
    H. 20
    J. 21
    K. 22

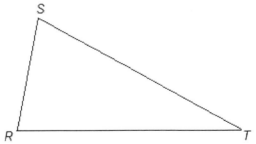

11. In the triangle above, $RS = 6$ and $ST = 9$. Point U lies on RT between R and T so that $SU \perp RT$. Which of the following cannot be the length of SU?

    A. 1
    B. 2
    C. 3
    D. 5
    E. 7

12. A cube is inscribed in a sphere of radius 5 centimeters so that each vertex of the cube touches the sphere. What is the length, in centimeters, of a side of the cube?

    F. 5

    G. $\frac{10\sqrt{3}}{3}$

    H. $\frac{10\sqrt{2}}{2}$

    J. $10\sqrt{2}$

    K. $10\sqrt{3}$

Answers

1. E	5. A	9. E
2. J	6. H	10. J
3. A	7. A	11. E
4. H	8. K	12. G

Full Solutions

2.

* Solution using the Pythagorean Theorem: Let x be the length of a side of the square. So $AD = x$. By the Pythagorean Theorem,

$$x^2 = 11^2 + 5^2 = 121 + 25 = 146.$$

But x^2 is precisely the area of the square. Therefore, the answer is 146, choice **J**.

3.

* Solution using the Pythagorean Theorem:

$$c^2 = a^2 + b^2$$
$$AB^2 = AC^2 + BC^2$$
$$\left(\sqrt{41}\right)^2 = \left(\sqrt{23}\right)^2 + BC^2$$
$$41 = 23 + BC^2$$

Therefore, $BC^2 = 41 - 23 = 18$, and so $BC = \sqrt{18}$, choice **A**.

4.

* We choose ST as the base, and draw altitude RP from vertex R to base ST.

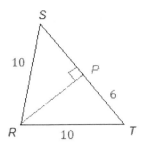

In an isosceles triangle the altitude is equal to the median. It follows that $TP = \frac{1}{2}ST = \frac{1}{2}(12) = 6$. Note that $6 = 2 \cdot 3$ and $10 = 2 \cdot 5$. Using the Pythagorean triple 3, 4, 5, we have that $RP = 2 \cdot 4 = 8$.

Area $= \frac{1}{2}bh = \frac{1}{2} \cdot 12 \cdot 8 = 48$, choice **H**.

Remarks: (1) An **altitude** of a triangle is perpendicular to the base. A **median** of a triangle splits the base into two equal parts. In an isosceles triangle, the altitude and median are equal (when you choose the base that is **not** one of the equal sides).

(2) We chose ST to be the base because it is the side that is not one of the equal sides.

(3) If you do not remember the Pythagorean triple used here it is no big deal. Just use the Pythagorean Theorem. In this case,

$$6^2 + b^2 = 10^2$$
$$36 + b^2 = 100$$
$$b^2 = 100 - 36 = 64$$
$$b = 8$$

5.

* **Solution using the triangle rule:** By the triangle rule, we have $9 - 5 < x < 9 + 5$. That is, $4 < x < 14$. Since x is an integer less than 6, x can only be 5. So there is **one** possibility, choice **A**.

6.

* The diameter of the sphere is the long diagonal of the cube.

Since the volume of the cube is 343, the length of a side of the cube is 7 (we get this by taking the cube root of 343).

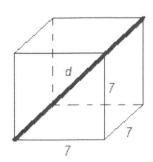

94

Thus, the diameter of the sphere is given by

$$d^2 = a^2 + b^2 + c^2 = 7^2 + 7^2 + 7^2 = 49 \cdot 3.$$

So $d = 7\sqrt{3}$, and the radius is $r = \frac{d}{2} = \frac{7}{2}\sqrt{3}$, choice **H**.

7.

* Solution using the triangle rule: By the triangle rule, x lies between $31 - 16 = 15$ and $31 + 16 = 47$. That is, we have $15 < x < 47$.

But we are also given that x is the length of the shortest side of the triangle. So $x < 16$. Therefore, we have $15 < x < 16$, and the answer is choice **A**.

8.

* Solution using the triangle rule: In this case, if Q, R and S form a triangle, then the length of QS is between $18 - 11 = 7$ and $18 + 11 = 29$. The extreme cases 7 and 29 form straight lines. In this problem that is fine, so the distance between Q and S is between 7 and 29, inclusive. Thus, the answer is choice **K**.

9.

Solution using the triangle rule: Using the triangle rule we have that $m - m < 22 < m + m$. That is, $0 < 22 < 2m$. So $m > \frac{22}{2} = 11$. Therefore, the smallest integer that m can be is $m = 12$, and so the smallest perimeter of the triangle is $22 + 12 + 12 = 46$, choice **E**.

* A slightly quicker solution: For this particular question we actually only need that the third side of the triangle is less than the sum of the other two sides. So we have $22 < m + m = 2m$, and so $m > \frac{22}{2} = 11$. Once again, it follows that we should let $m = 12$, and thus the perimeter is $22 + 12 + 12 = 46$, choice **E**.

10.

* Geometric solution using slopes: To get from O to A we go up 3 units, right 18 units. So the slope of OA is $\frac{3}{18} = \frac{1}{6}$. Since AB is perpendicular to OA, we have that the slope of AB is $-6 = -\frac{6}{1}$. Thus, for every unit we move right along AB, we must move down 6 units. Equivalently, for every unit we move left along AB, we must move up 6 units. To get from 18 to 15 we must move left 3 units. Therefore, we must move up $3 \cdot 6 = 18$ units. Since we are starting at 3, $k = 3 + 18 = 21$, choice **J**.

Algebraic solution using slopes: We can do all of this algebraically using the slope formula as follows.

The slope of OA is $\frac{3}{18} = \frac{1}{6}$ (see the remark at the end of the first solution to problem 8 from Lesson 3). So the slope of AB is -6 because OA and AB are perpendicular. We can also compute the slope of AB using the slope formula as follows.

$$m_{AB} = \frac{k - 3}{15 - 18} = \frac{k - 3}{-3}$$

Now set these equal to each other and solve for k (or guess and check).

$$\frac{k - 3}{-3} = -6$$
$$k - 3 = 18$$
$$k = 21$$

This is choice **J**.

A solution using two applications of the Pythagorean Theorem: We form two right triangles and use the given points to write down three lengths as shown in the picture below.

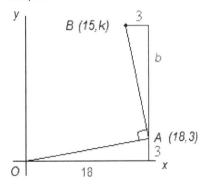

We can now find OA using the Pythagorean Theorem.

$$OA^2 = 18^2 + 3^2 = 333.$$

So $OA = \sqrt{333}$, and therefore $AB = \sqrt{333}$ also since $OA = AB$ is given. Finally, we can use the Pythagorean Theorem one more time to find b.

$$3^2 + b^2 = AB^2$$
$$9 + b^2 = 333$$
$$b^2 = 324$$
$$b = 18$$

So $k = 3 + 18 = 21$, choice **J**.

11.
*Let's draw SU.

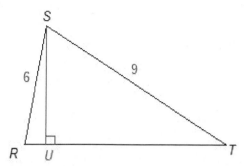

Now just note that RS is the hypotenuse of triangle RSU. Thus, SU must be less than 6. So SU cannot be 7, and the answer is choice **E**.

12.
* The diameter of the sphere is $d = 2r = 2 \cdot 5 = 10$, and this length is also the long diagonal of the cube. (You may want to draw a picture similar to that in problem 6).

If we let x be the length of a side of the cube, then we have

$$x^2 + x^2 + x^2 = 10^2$$
$$3x^2 = 100$$
$$x^2 = \frac{100}{3}$$
$$x = \sqrt{\frac{100}{3}} = \frac{\sqrt{100}}{\sqrt{3}} = \frac{10}{\sqrt{3}} = \frac{10\sqrt{3}}{3}$$

This is choice **G**.

Notes: (1) If you do not know how to get that $\frac{10}{\sqrt{3}}$ is equal to $\frac{10\sqrt{3}}{3}$, you can simply put $\frac{10}{\sqrt{3}}$ into your calculator, followed by the answer choices until you see which choice matches up. In this case, both $\frac{10}{\sqrt{3}}$ and $\frac{10\sqrt{3}}{3}$ give the decimal approximation 5.7735 when we use our calculator.

(2) We can rationalize the denominator of $\frac{10}{\sqrt{3}}$ by multiplying both the numerator and denominator by $\sqrt{3}$: $\frac{10}{\sqrt{3}} = \frac{10}{\sqrt{3}} \cdot \frac{\sqrt{3}}{\sqrt{3}} = \frac{10\sqrt{3}}{3}$

LESSON 8
TRIGONOMETRY

Reminder: Before beginning this lesson remember to redo the problems from Lesson 4 that you have marked off. Do not "unmark" a question unless you get it correct.

Right Triangle Trigonometry

Let's consider the following right triangle, and let's focus our attention on angle A.

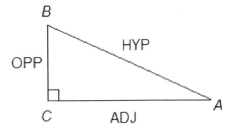

Note that the **hypotenuse** is ALWAYS the side opposite the right angle.

The other two sides of the right triangle, called the **legs**, depend on which angle is chosen. In this picture we chose to focus on angle A. Therefore, the opposite side is BC, and the adjacent side is AC.

It's worth memorizing how to compute the six trig functions:

$$\sin A = \frac{\text{OPP}}{\text{HYP}} \qquad \csc A = \frac{\text{HYP}}{\text{OPP}}$$

$$\cos A = \frac{\text{ADJ}}{\text{HYP}} \qquad \sec A = \frac{\text{HYP}}{\text{ADJ}}$$

$$\tan A = \frac{\text{OPP}}{\text{ADJ}} \qquad \cot A = \frac{\text{ADJ}}{\text{OPP}}$$

Here are a couple of tips to help you remember these:

(1) Many students find it helpful to use the word SOHCAHTOA. You can think of the letters here as representing sin, opp, hyp, cos, adj, hyp, tan, opp, adj.

98

(2) The three trig functions on the right are the reciprocals of the three trig functions on the left. In other words, you get them by interchanging the numerator and denominator. It's pretty easy to remember that the reciprocal of tangent is cotangent. For the other two, just remember that the "s" goes with the "c" and the "c" goes with the "s." In other words, the reciprocal of sine is cosecant, and the reciprocal of cosine is secant.

Example: Compute all six trig functions for each of the angles (except the right angle) in the triangle below.

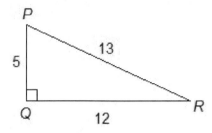

Solution:

$$\sin P = \frac{12}{13} \qquad \csc P = \frac{13}{12} \qquad \sin R = \frac{5}{13} \qquad \csc R = \frac{13}{5}$$

$$\cos P = \frac{5}{13} \qquad \sec P = \frac{13}{5} \qquad \cos R = \frac{12}{13} \qquad \sec R = \frac{13}{12}$$

$$\tan P = \frac{12}{5} \qquad \cot P = \frac{5}{12} \qquad \tan R = \frac{5}{12} \qquad \cot R = \frac{12}{5}$$

Now try to answer the following question. **Do not** check the solution until you have attempted this question yourself.

LEVEL 2: TRIGONOMETRY

1.   If $0 \leq x \leq 90°$ and $\cos x = \frac{5}{13}$, then $\tan x =$

   A. $\frac{5}{12}$

   B. $\frac{12}{13}$

   C. $\frac{13}{12}$

   D. $\frac{12}{5}$

   E. $\frac{13}{5}$

Solution

* Let's draw a picture. We begin with a right triangle and label one of the angles x.

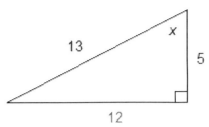

Since $\cos x = \frac{\text{ADJ}}{\text{HYP}}$, we label the leg adjacent to x with a 5 and the hypotenuse with 13. We can use the Pythagorean triple 5, 12, 13 to see that the other side is 12.

Finally, $\tan x = \frac{\text{OPP}}{\text{ADJ}} = \frac{12}{5}$, choice **D**.

Notes: (1) The most common Pythagorean triples are 3, 4, 5 and 5, 12, 13. Two others that may come up are 8, 15, 17 and 7, 24, 25.

(2) If you don't remember the Pythagorean triple 5, 12, 13, you can use the Pythagorean Theorem:

Here we have $5^2 + b^2 = 13^2$. Therefore $25 + b^2 = 169$. Subtracting 25 from each side of this equation gives $b^2 = 169 - 25 = 144$. So $b = 12$.

(3) The equation $b^2 = 144$ would normally have two solutions: $b = 12$ and $b = -12$. But the length of a side of a triangle cannot be negative, and so we reject -12.

Inverse Trigonometric Functions

If $0 \leq x \leq 90°$, then the following three equations are equivalent:

$$\sin x = y \qquad x = \sin^{-1} y \qquad x = \text{Arcsin}\, y$$

Similarly, we have five other inverse trigonometric functions.

For example, in the last problem we had $0 \leq x \leq 90°$ and $\cos x = \frac{5}{13}$. Another way to write this is $x = \cos^{-1} \frac{5}{13}$ or $x = \text{Arccos}\, \frac{5}{13}$.

Now try to answer the following question. **Do not** check the solution until you have attempted this question yourself.

LEVEL 3: TRIGONOMETRY

2. A 17 foot ladder rests against the side of a wall and reaches a point that is 11 feet above the ground. Which of the following expressions is closest to the angle of inclination between the bottom of the ladder and the horizontal floor?

    F. $\sin^{-1}\frac{11}{17}$

    G. $\sin^{-1}\frac{17}{11}$

    H. $\cos^{-1}\frac{11}{17}$

    J. $\cos^{-1}\frac{17}{11}$

    K. $\tan^{-1}\frac{11}{17}$

Solution

* Let's draw a picture.

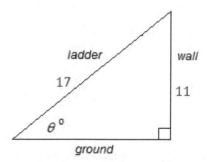

The angle of inclination is labeled $\theta°$ in the figure. Since the opposite side to θ and the hypotenuse are given, we have $\sin\theta° = \frac{11}{17}$. It follows that $\theta° = \sin^{-1}\frac{11}{17}$, choice **F**.

Special Right Triangles

It is very helpful on the ACT to know the following two special right triangles.

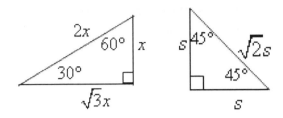

Now try to answer the following question. **Do not** check the solution until you have attempted this question yourself.

LEVEL 4: TRIGONOMETRY

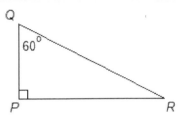

3.   In the triangle above, $QR = 8$. What is the area of $\triangle PQR$?

     A. $32\sqrt{3}$
     B. 32
     C. $16\sqrt{3}$
     D. 16
     E. $8\sqrt{3}$

* Solution using a 30, 60, 90 triangle: Using the special 30, 60, 90 triangle we can label each side with its length as follows.

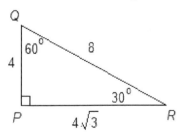

The area is then $A = \frac{1}{2}bh = \frac{1}{2}(4\sqrt{3})(4) = 8\sqrt{3}$, choice **E**.

Note: The hypotenuse of a 30, 60, 90 triangle is always twice the length of the side opposite the 30-degree angle.

Also, if we always think of a side as going with its opposite angle, there will never be any confusion, even if our picture were to change direction. This is actually good advice for any triangle problem. Always think of a side in terms of its opposite angle and vice versa.

Trigonometric solution: Let's label the sides of the triangle.

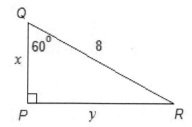

We have $\cos 60° = \dfrac{\text{ADJ}}{\text{HYP}} = \dfrac{x}{8}$. So $x = 8\cos 60°$.

We also have $\sin 60° = \dfrac{\text{OPP}}{\text{HYP}} = \dfrac{y}{8}$. So $y = 8\sin 60°$.

The area of the triangle is

$$\frac{1}{2}xy = \frac{1}{2} \cdot 8\cos 60° \cdot 8\sin 60° = 32 \cdot \frac{1}{2} \cdot \frac{\sqrt{3}}{2} = 8\sqrt{3}$$

This is choice **E**.

Notes: (1) We can do the computation $\frac{1}{2} \cdot 8\cos 60° \cdot 8\sin 60°$ right in our calculator to get approximately 13.8564.

We could then put the answer choices in our calculator to see which choice matches that decimal approximation. We see $8\sqrt{3} \approx 13.8564$. So the answer is choice E.

(2) We could use the special 30, 60, 90 triangle to get

$$\cos 60° = \frac{\text{ADJ}}{\text{HYP}} = \frac{1}{2} \qquad \text{and} \qquad \sin 60° = \frac{\text{OPP}}{\text{HYP}} = \frac{\sqrt{3}}{2}$$

So we have $\frac{1}{2} \cdot 8\cos 60° \cdot 8\sin 60° = \frac{1}{2} \cdot 8 \cdot \frac{1}{2} \cdot 8 \cdot \frac{\sqrt{3}}{2} = 8\sqrt{3}$, choice E.

(3) We can actually substitute any value for x in the picture of the 30, 60, 90 triangle that we like, because the x's always cancel when doing any trigonometric computation. For example, with $x = 1$, we have the following picture:

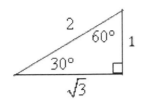

Trigonometric Identities

Here is a list of the trigonometric identities that are useful to know for the ACT:

Quotient Identity:

$$\tan x = \frac{\sin x}{\cos x}$$

Negative Identities:

$$\cos(-x) = \cos x \qquad \sin(-x) = -\sin x \qquad \tan(-x) = -\tan x$$

Cofunction Identities:

$$\sin(90° - x) = \cos x \qquad \cos(90° - x) = \sin x$$

Pythagorean Identity:

$$\cos^2 x + \sin^2 x = 1$$

LEVEL 3: TRIGONOMETRY

4. In a right triangle, one angle measures $x°$, where $\cos x° = \frac{2}{3}$. What is $\sin((90 - x)°)$?

    F. $\frac{2}{3}$

    G. $\frac{\sqrt{5}}{3}$

    H. $\frac{2\sqrt{5}}{5}$

    J. $\frac{3\sqrt{5}}{5}$

    K. $\frac{\sqrt{5}}{3}$

* Solution using a cofunction identity: $\sin((90-x)°) = \cos x° = \frac{2}{3}$, choice **F**.

If we were to encounter this problem, and we do not remember the cofunction identity, we can also solve this problem with a picture and some basic trigonometry.

Basic trig solution: Let's draw a picture:

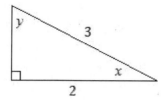

Notice that I labeled one of the angles with x, and used the fact that $\cos x = \frac{\text{ADJ}}{\text{HYP}}$ to label 2 sides of the triangle.

Now observe that $y° = (90-x)°$, so that

$$\sin((90-x)°) = \sin y° = \frac{\text{OPP}}{\text{HYP}} = \frac{2}{3}, \text{ choice } \mathbf{F}.$$

Radian Measure

One full rotation of a circle is 360°. All other rotations are in proportion to the full rotation. For example, half of a rotation of a circle is $\frac{360}{2} = 180°$.

In addition to degree measure, another way to measure rotations of a circle is to divide the arc length of the circle by the radius of the circle. This is called **radian** measure. For example, one full rotation of a circle is $\frac{2\pi r}{r} = 2\pi$ radians, and so half of a rotation of a circle is π radians.

So, we just showed that $180° = \pi$ radians.

We can convert between degree measure and radian measure by using the following simple ratio:

$$\frac{\text{degree measure}}{180°} = \frac{\text{radian measure}}{\pi}$$

Example 1: Convert 45° to radians.

Solution: $\frac{45°}{180°} = \frac{x}{\pi} \Rightarrow x = \frac{45\pi}{180} = \frac{\pi}{4}$ radians.

Shortcut: We can convert from degrees to radians by multiplying the given angle by $\frac{\pi}{180}$.

Example 2: Convert $\frac{\pi}{6}$ radians to degrees.

Solution: $\frac{x°}{180°} = \frac{\pi/6}{\pi} \Rightarrow x = \frac{180}{6} = 30°$.

Shortcut: We can convert from radians to degrees by multiplying the given angle by $\frac{180}{\pi}$.

If the angle has π in the numerator, we can simply replace π by 180.

LEVEL 4: TRIGONOMETRY

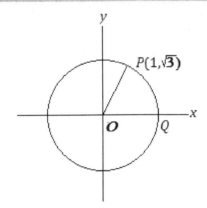

5. In the xy-plane above, O is the center of the circle, and the measure of $\angle POQ$ is $\frac{2\pi}{b}$ radians. What is the value of b ?

    A. 2
    B. 3
    C. 6
    D. 8
    E. 9

Solution

* We draw a right triangle inside the picture

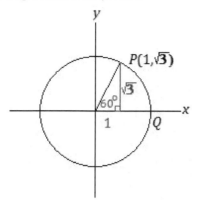

Observe that $\angle POQ$ measures $60°$. Converting to radians gives us

$$\frac{60\pi}{180} = \frac{\pi}{3} \text{ radians.}$$

So we have $\frac{2\pi}{b} = \frac{\pi}{3}$. Cross multiplying gives us $\pi b = 6\pi$, and so $b = 6$, choice **C**.

Note: If we had forgotten that the correct angle in that picture was $60°$, we could also use the TAN⁻¹ button (2ND TAN) to get $\tan^{-1}\frac{\sqrt{3}}{1} = 60$.

Make sure your calculator is in degree mode when doing this computation.

Polar Coordinates

The usual way we plot a point (in the rectangular coordinate system) is by using the first coordinate to move right or left from the origin, and the second coordinate to move up or down. For example, to plot the point $(2, 3)$, we start at the origin, move right 2 units, and then up 3 units.

In the polar coordinate system, the coordinates are (r, θ) where r is the distance from the origin to the point, and θ is the angle made with the positive x-axis and the ray starting at the origin and passing through the given point.

Here is a picture showing how a point is plotted using both methods, and the relationships between the two types of points.

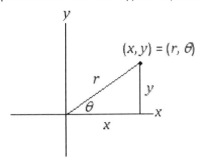

From the picture above, basic trigonometry, and the Pythagorean Theorem, we have the following:

$$x = r\cos\theta \qquad\qquad r^2 = x^2 + y^2$$
$$y = r\sin\theta \qquad\qquad \tan\theta = \frac{y}{x}$$

Example 1: Convert $(1, 1)$ from rectangular to polar coordinates.

Solution: $r^2 = x^2 + y^2 = 1^2 + (-1)^2 = 1 + 1 = 2$. So $r = \sqrt{2}$.

$\tan\theta = \frac{y}{x} = \frac{1}{1} = 1$. So $\theta = \tan^{-1} 1 = 45°$.

So the point in polar coordinates is $(\sqrt{2}, 45°)$.

Example 2: Convert $(3, 60°)$ from polar to rectangular coordinates.

Solution: $x = r\cos\theta = 3\cos 60° = 3 \cdot \frac{1}{2} = \frac{3}{2}$

$y = r\sin\theta = 3\sin 60° = 3 \cdot \frac{\sqrt{3}}{2} = \frac{3\sqrt{3}}{2}$.

So the point in rectangular is $(\frac{3}{2}, \frac{3\sqrt{3}}{2})$.

Coterminal Angles

Whenever we add $360°$ to an angle, we get an angle in the same exact position. For example, $45°$ and $405°$ are coterminal angles (<u>check</u>: $45 + 360 = 405$).

Similarly, if we subtract $360°$ from an angle, we also get an angle that is coterminal with the original. So $-315°$ is also coterminal with $45°$ (<u>check</u>: $45 - 360 = -315$).

If we are working in radians, then we use 2π in place of $360°$. For example, $\frac{\pi}{4} + 2\pi = \frac{\pi}{4} + \frac{8\pi}{4} = \frac{9\pi}{4}$. So $\frac{\pi}{4}$ and $\frac{9\pi}{4}$ are coterminal angles.

LEVEL 5: TRIGONOMETRY

6. Which of the following polar coordinates represents the same location as $(5, 30°)$?

    F. $(5, -330°)$
    G. $(5, -300°)$
    H. $(5, -30°)$
    J. $(5, 150°)$
    K. $(5, 330°)$

Solution

* $30 - 360 = -330$, and so the answer is choice **F**.

Now try to solve each of the following problems. The answers to these problems, followed by full solutions are at the end of this lesson. **Do not** look at the answers until you have attempted these problems yourself. Please remember to mark off any problems you get wrong.

LEVEL 2: TRIGONOMETRY

7. Right triangle $\triangle PQR$ is shown below. The side lengths are given in inches. What is $\cos R$?

    A. $\frac{5}{13}$

    B. $\frac{5}{12}$

    C. $\frac{12}{13}$

    D. $\frac{13}{12}$

    E. $\frac{13}{5}$

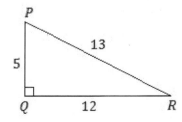

Level 4: Trigonometry

8. Which of the following is equal to $\cos\left(\frac{\pi}{5}\right)$?

    F. $-\cos\left(-\frac{\pi}{5}\right)$

    G. $-\sin\left(\frac{\pi}{5}\right)$

    H. $\sin\left(\frac{3\pi}{10}\right)$

    J. $-\sin\left(\frac{3\pi}{10}\right)$

    K. $-\cos\left(\frac{3\pi}{10}\right)$

Level 5: Trigonometry

9. In the standard (x, y) coordinate plane below, θ is the radian measure of any angle in standard position with the point (a, b) on the terminal side. Which of the following points is on the terminal side of the angle in standard position having radian measure $2\pi - \theta$?

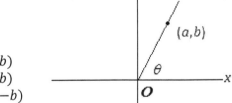

    A. $(a, -b)$
    B. $(-a, b)$
    C. $(-a, -b)$
    D. (b, a)
    E. $(b, -a)$

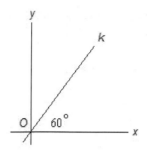

10. In the figure above, what is the equation of line k?

   F. $y = \frac{x}{2}$

   G. $y = \frac{x}{\sqrt{2}}$

   H. $y = \frac{x}{\sqrt{3}}$

   J. $y = \sqrt{2}x$

   K. $y = \sqrt{3}x$

11. A ladder rests against the side of a wall and reaches a point that is h meters above the ground. The angle formed by the ladder and the ground is $\theta°$. A point on the ladder is k meters from the wall. What is the vertical distance, in meters, from this point on the ladder to the ground?

   A. $(h - k)\tan\theta°$
   B. $(h - k)\cos\theta°$
   C. $h - k\sin\theta°$
   D. $h - k\cos\theta°$
   E. $h - k\tan\theta°$

12. It is given that $\cos x = k$, where x is the radian measure of an angle and $\pi < x < \frac{3\pi}{2}$. If $\cos z = -k$, which of the following could <u>not</u> be the value of z ?

   F. $x - \pi$
   G. $\pi - x$
   H. $2\pi - x$
   J. $3\pi - x$
   K. $x - 5\pi$

111

Answers

1. D	5. C	9. A
2. F	6. F	10. K
3. E	7. C	11. E
4. F	8. H	12. H

Full Solutions

8.

* Solution using a cofunction identity:

$$\cos\left(\frac{\pi}{5}\right) = \sin\left(\frac{\pi}{2} - \frac{\pi}{5}\right) = \sin\left(\frac{3\pi}{10}\right), \text{ choice } \mathbf{H}.$$

Notes: (1) A function f with the property that $f(-x) = f(x)$ for all x in the domain of f is called an **even** function.

$\cos x$ is an even function. It follows that $\cos(-A) = \cos A$. In particular, $\cos\left(-\frac{\pi}{5}\right) = \cos\left(\frac{\pi}{5}\right)$, and so $-\cos\left(-\frac{\pi}{5}\right) = -\cos\left(\frac{\pi}{5}\right) \neq \cos\left(\frac{\pi}{5}\right)$. This eliminates choice F.

(2) $\cos A$ and $\sin A$ are *not* negatives of each other in general. If $\cos A = -\sin A$, then $\frac{\cos A}{\sin A} = -1$. Taking reciprocals, $\frac{\sin A}{\cos A} = -1$, so that $\tan A = -1$. This happens only when $A = \pm\frac{3\pi}{4}, \pm\frac{7\pi}{4}, \pm\frac{11\pi}{4}, \dots$

This eliminates choice G.

(3) Since we know that choice H is the answer, we can use the same reasoning as in note (2) to show that $\cos\left(\frac{\pi}{5}\right)$ cannot be equal to $-\cos\left(\frac{3\pi}{10}\right)$. This eliminates choice K.

(4) We can also approximate the given expression and all the answer choices in our calculator to get the answer.

9.

* Let's draw a picture (see the picture to the right).

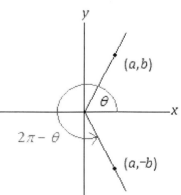

Now observe that the point $(a, -b)$ is on the terminal side, choice **A**.

Note: If θ is an angle in the first quadrant, then $\pi - \theta$ is in the second quadrant, $\pi + \theta$ is in the third quadrant, and $2\pi - \theta$ is in the fourth quadrant (as shown in the figure). See Lesson 24 for more details.

If (a, b) is a point on the terminal side of an angle θ in standard position, then $(-a, b)$ is on the terminal side of the angle $\pi - \theta$, $(-a, -b)$ is on the terminal side of the angle $\pi + \theta$, and $(a, -b)$ is on the terminal side of the angle $2\pi - \theta$. The last of these is shown in the figure. Try to draw pictures of the other two situations.

10.

* We begin by forming a 30, 60, 90 triangle. If we let $x = 1$ in the special triangle we get the following picture.

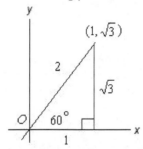

Note that we plotted the point by going right 1, then up $\sqrt{3}$. The slope of the line is $m = \frac{\sqrt{3}}{1} = \sqrt{3}$. Since the line passes through the origin, we have $b = 0$. Thus, the equation of the line in slope-intercept form is

$$y = mx + b = \sqrt{3}x + 0.$$

So $y = \sqrt{3}x$, choice **K**.

11.

* Let's draw a picture.

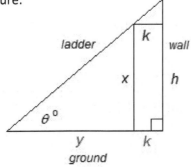

Note that there are two triangles in this picture. We will need to use both of them.

Also recall that for any angle A, $\tan A = \frac{\text{OPP}}{\text{ADJ}}$. Using the smaller triangle, we have $\tan \theta° = \frac{x}{y}$ and using the larger triangle we have $\tan \theta° = \frac{h}{y+k}$. The first equation gives us $y \tan \theta° = x$, and the second equation gives $(y + k) \tan \theta° = h$. Distributing this last equation on the left gives $y \tan \theta° + k \tan \theta = h$. Substituting from the first equation yields $x + k \tan \theta = h$. We subtract $k \tan \theta°$ from each side of this last equation to get $x = h - k \tan \theta$, choice **E**.

12.

* Solution using coterminal angles and a negative identity:

$$\cos(2\pi - x) = \cos(x - 2\pi) = \cos x = k \neq -k.$$

So $2\pi - x$ could not be the value of z, choice **H**.

Notes: (1) For the first equality we used the negative identity

$$\cos(-A) = \cos A,$$

together with the fact that $x - 2\pi = -(2\pi - x)$.

(2) In general we have $a - b = -(b - a)$. To see this simply distribute:

$$-(b - a) = -b + a = a - b.$$

(3) Using notes (1) and (2) together, we have

$$\cos(2\pi - x) = \cos(-(x - 2\pi)) = \cos(x - 2\pi).$$

(4) For the second equality we used the fact that x and $x - 2\pi$ are **coterminal angles**.

If a and b are coterminal angles, then $\cos a = \cos b$.

(5) Given an angle x, we get a coterminal angle by adding or subtracting any integer multiple of 2π. So the following are all coterminal with x:

$$\ldots x - 4\pi, x - 2\pi, x, x + 2\pi, x + 4\pi, \ldots$$

Solution using the cosine difference identity:

$$\cos(A - B) = \cos A \, \cos B + \sin A \, \sin B$$

Let's start with choice (C), and apply the difference identity:

$$\cos(2\pi - x) = \cos 2\pi \, \cos x + \sin 2\pi \, \sin x$$

$$= 1 \cdot \cos x + 0 \cdot \sin x = \cos x = k \neq -k.$$

So $2\pi - x$ could not be the value of z, choice **H**.

Notes: (1) The middle choice (in this case, choice H) is always a good choice to start with when plugging in (see Lesson 1).

(2) Let's apply the difference formula to the other answer choices as well:

$$\cos(x - \pi) = \cos x \, \cos \pi + \sin x \, \sin \pi$$

$$= \cos x \, (-1) + \sin x \, (0) = -\cos x = -k.$$

This shows that z can be $x - \pi$, and so we can eliminate choice F.

For $\pi - x$, we can use the difference identity again, or we can use the negative identity as we did in the last solution to get

$$\cos(\pi - x) = \cos(x - \pi) = -k$$

This shows that z can also be $\pi - x$, and so we can eliminate choice G.

$$\cos(3\pi - x) = \cos 3\pi \, \cos x + \sin 3\pi \, \sin x$$

$$= (-1) \cos x + 0 \cdot \sin x = -\cos x = -k.$$

This shows that z can also be $3\pi - x$, and we can eliminate choice J.

$$\cos(x - 5\pi) = \cos x \, \cos 5\pi + \sin x \, \sin 5\pi$$

$$= \cos x \, (-1) + \sin x \, (0) = -\cos x = -k.$$

This shows that z can be $x - 5\pi$, and so we can eliminate choice K.

(3) $3\pi = \pi + 2\pi$, and so π and 3π are coterminal angles. It follows that $\cos 3\pi = \cos \pi = -1$ and $\sin 3\pi = \sin \pi = 0$.

A similar computation can be made for 5π.

Solution using the unit circle: Since $\pi < x < \frac{3\pi}{2}$, when x is placed in standard position, its terminal side falls in the third quadrant, and $\cos x$ will be the x-coordinate of the point where the terminal side intersects the unit circle.

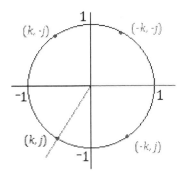

Since x is a third quadrant angle, it's reference angle is the first quadrant angle $x - \pi$, and so from the figure above we see $\cos(x - \pi) = -k$.

The corresponding second quadrant angle is $\pi - (x - \pi) = 2\pi - x$, and so we see from the figure that $\cos(2\pi - x) = k \neq -k$, and so z cannot equal $2\pi - k$, choice **H**.

Notes: (1) If θ is a first quadrant angle, then the corresponding angle in the second quadrant is $\pi - \theta$.

The corresponding angle in the third quadrant is $\pi + \theta$.

And the corresponding angle in the fourth quadrant is $2\pi - \theta$.

So in this problem, the first quadrant angle is $x - \pi$, the corresponding second quadrant angle is $\pi - (x - \pi) = \pi - x + \pi = 2\pi - x$, the corresponding third quadrant angle is $(x - \pi) + \pi = x$, and the fourth quadrant angle is $2\pi - (x - \pi) = 2\pi - x + \pi = 3\pi - x$.

(2) From the last note, and the picture above we have $\cos(x - \pi) = -k$, $\cos(2\pi - x) = k$, $\cos x = k$, and $\cos(3\pi - x) = -k$.

116

LESSON 9
NUMBER THEORY

Reminder: Before beginning this lesson remember to redo the problems from Lessons 1 and 5 that you have marked off. Do not "unmark" a question unless you get it correct.

Change Fractions to Decimals

Decimals are often easier to work with than fractions, especially since you have a calculator. To change a fraction to a decimal you simply perform the division in your calculator.

Try to answer the following question using this strategy. **Do not** check the solution until you have attempted this question yourself.

LEVEL 4: NUMBER THEORY

1. Which of the following numbers is between $\frac{5}{16}$ and $\frac{2}{5}$?

   A. $\frac{31}{100}$

   B. $\frac{39}{125}$

   C. $\frac{57}{160}$

   D. $\frac{101}{250}$

   E. $\frac{41}{100}$

Solution

We divide 5 by 16, and 2 by 5 in our calculator to get $\frac{5}{16} = 0.3125$ and $\frac{2}{5} = 0.4$. Now let's start with choice C and divide 57 by 160 in our calculator to get $\frac{57}{160} = 0.35625$. Since this number is between the other two, the answer is choice **C**.

Note: Using our calculator, we see that $\frac{31}{100} = 0.31$, $\frac{39}{125} = 0.312$, $\frac{101}{250} = 0.404$, and $\frac{41}{100} = 0.41$. None of these numbers are between 0.3125 and 0.4.

Change Fractional Parts to Wholes

We can often change fractional parts to wholes by making the total equal to some multiple of the least common denominator of the fractions involved. If the problem is multiple-choice use the denominators in the answer choices as a guide.

Try to answer the following question using this strategy. **Do not** check the solution until you have attempted this question yourself.

LEVEL 5: NUMBER THEORY

2. A business is owned by 1 man and 5 women, each of whom has an equal share. If one of the women sells $\frac{2}{5}$ of her share to the man, and another of the women keeps $\frac{1}{4}$ of her share and sells the rest to the man, what fraction of the business will the man own?

    F. $\frac{9}{40}$

    G. $\frac{37}{120}$

    H. $\frac{2}{3}$

    J. $\frac{43}{120}$

    K. $\frac{3}{8}$

Solution

Using the answer choices as a guide we will split the business into 120 parts, so that each person has $\frac{120}{6} = 20$ parts. We have $(\frac{2}{5})(20) = 8$ and $(\frac{3}{4})(20) = 15$. So after both sales the man has $20 + 8 + 15 = 43$ parts out of 120 parts total. Thus, the answer is choice **J**.

Remark: The number 120 comes from multiplying the least common denominator of the two fractions ($5 \cdot 4 = 20$) by the number of people (6).

Before we go on, try to solve this problem with a single computation.

Solution

* This is quick, but a bit tricky. Each of the 6 people begins with $\frac{1}{6}$ of the business. The first woman sells $(\frac{2}{5})(\frac{1}{6})$ of the business, and the second woman sells $(\frac{3}{4})(\frac{1}{6})$ of the business (if she keeps $\frac{1}{4}$, then she sells $\frac{3}{4}$). Therefore, we can get the answer by doing the following single computation in our calculator:

$$\frac{1}{6} + \left(\frac{2}{5}\right)\left(\frac{1}{6}\right) + \left(\frac{3}{4}\right)\left(\frac{1}{6}\right) = \frac{43}{120}, \text{ choice J.}$$

To Make Something Large Make Something Else Small (and Vice Versa)

Try to answer the following question using this strategy. **Do not** check the solution until you have attempted this question yourself.

LEVEL 5: NUMBER THEORY

3. If $14 \leq x \leq 18$ and $9 \leq y \leq 11$, what is the greatest possible value of $\frac{6}{x-y}$?

    A. $\frac{1}{11}$
    B. $\frac{2}{3}$
    C. $\frac{6}{7}$
    D. $\frac{6}{5}$
    E. 2

Solution

* To make a fraction as large as possible, we make the denominator of the fraction as small as possible (while keeping it positive). So we want to make $x - y$ as small as possible (but positive).

119

To make $x - y$ small, we make x as small as possible and y as large as possible. So we let $x = 14$ and $y = 11$. Then $x - y = 14 - 11 = 3$. Thus, $\dfrac{6}{x-y} = \dfrac{6}{3} = 2$, choice **E**.

If you ever get confused as to where the biggest and smallest numbers get plugged in, you can simply **try all the extremes**. Try to solve the problem this way as well.

Solution

We compute $\dfrac{6}{x-y}$ when x and y are equal to each of the extreme values in the given ranges. The extreme values for x are 14 and 18. The extreme values for y are 9 and 11.

x	y	$x - y$	$\dfrac{6}{x-y}$
14	9	5	$\dfrac{6}{5}$
14	11	3	$\dfrac{6}{3} = 2$
18	9	9	$\dfrac{6}{9} = \dfrac{2}{3}$
18	11	7	$\dfrac{6}{7}$

Notice that we tried all four possibilities using the extreme values for x and y. The last column shows that the greatest possible value of $\dfrac{6}{x-y}$ is 2, choice **E**.

The Pigeonhole Principle

If n pigeons are put into m pigeonholes with $n > m$, then at least one pigeonhole must contain more than one pigeon.

120

In the picture above there are $n = 5$ pigeons in $m = 4$ holes. Since $5 > 4$, the pigeonhole principle says that at least one hole has more than one pigeon.

Try to answer the following question using the pigeonhole principle. **Do not** check the solution until you have attempted this question yourself.

LEVEL 4: NUMBER THEORY

4. The integers 1 through 15 are written on each of fifteen boxes. A boy has placed 44 marbles into these boxes so that the 4th box has the greatest number of marbles. What is the <u>least</u> number of marbles that can be in the 4th box?

  F. 3
  G. 4
  H. 5
  J. 6
  K. 7

Solution

For the first 30 marbles we can place 2 in each box. We have 14 marbles left. If we place only 1 more in the 4th box for a total of 3, then at least one other box will have at least 3 as well, and the 4th box will <u>not</u> have the greatest number of marbles. So we must place 2 more marbles in the 4th box for a total of 4 marbles. We can now disperse the remaining 12 marbles evenly throughout 12 of the other boxes. Each of the other boxes will now have at most 3 marbles, while the 4th box has 4, choice **G**.

Now try to solve each of the following problems. The answers to these problems, followed by full solutions are at the end of this lesson. **Do not** look at the answers until you have attempted these problems yourself. Please remember to mark off any problems you get wrong.

LEVEL 1: NUMBER THEORY

5. Which of the following inequalities orders the numbers 0.1, 0.02, and $\frac{1}{8}$ from greatest to least?

    A. $0.1 > 0.02 > \frac{1}{8}$

    B. $0.02 > 0.1 > \frac{1}{8}$

    C. $0.02 > \frac{1}{8} > 0.1$

    D. $\frac{1}{8} > 0.02 > 0.1$

    E. $\frac{1}{8} > 0.1 > 0.02$

LEVEL 2: NUMBER THEORY

6. Given that $a \geq 3$ and $a + b \leq 5$, what is the GREATEST value that b can have?

    F. -8
    G. -2
    H. 0
    J. 2
    K. 8

LEVEL 4: NUMBER THEORY

7. Which of the following is the decimal equivalent to $\frac{3}{13}$? (Note: A bar indicates a digit pattern that is repeated.)

    A. $0.\overline{230769}$
    B. 0.23076923
    C. $0.23076\overline{23}$
    D. 0.2307692308
    E. $0.2307692\overline{307}$

122

8. What is the greatest total number of Sundays there could be in February and March of the same year? (Assume that it is not a leap year so that February has 28 days and March has 31 days).

    F. 8
    G. 9
    H. 10
    J. 11
    K. 12

9. There are 6 red, 6 brown, 6 yellow, and 6 gray scarves packaged in 24 identical, unmarked boxes, 1 scarf per box. What is the least number of boxes that must be selected in order to be sure that among the boxes selected 3 or more contain scarves of the same color?

    A. 6
    B. 7
    C. 8
    D. 9
    E. 10

10. The sum of 15 positive odd integers is 67. Some of these integers are equal to each other. What is the greatest possible value of one of these integers?

    F. 37
    G. 49
    H. 51
    J. 53
    K. 55

11. The set P consists of m integers, and the difference between the greatest integer in P and the least integer in P is 455. A new set of m integers, set Q, is formed by multiplying each integer in P by 5 and then adding 3 to the product. What is the difference between the greatest integer in Q and the least integer in Q?

    A. 455
    B. 457
    C. 2275
    D. 2278
    E. 2290

123

LEVEL 5: NUMBER THEORY

12. If $9 \leq x \leq 15$ and $3 \leq y \leq 5$, what is the greatest possible value of $\frac{7}{x-y}$?

F. $\frac{7}{12}$

G. $\frac{7}{10}$

H. $\frac{7}{9}$

J. $\frac{7}{6}$

K. $\frac{7}{4}$

Answers

1. C	5. E	9. D
2. J	6. J	10. J
3. E	7. A	11. C
4. G	8. G	12. K

Note: The full solution for question 12 has been omitted because its solution is very similar to the solution for question 3.

Full Solutions

7.

* **Solution by changing the fraction to a decimal:** When we divide 3 by 13 in our calculator, we get 0.2307692308. But that doesn't mean that choice D is the answer. It's actually a repeating decimal that our calculator rounded to the 10th digit. Note how the first six digits 230769 keep repeating, giving us choice **A**.

8.

* There are 59 days total. To maximize the number of Sundays, let's assume that day 1 is a Sunday. It follows that the Sundays are days $1, 8, 15, 22, 29, 36, 43, 50$, and 57. So there are 9 Sundays, choice **G**.

Remark: We listed all the values that give a remainder of 1 when divided by 7.

124

Warning: Dividing 59 by 7 gives approximately 8.4. This may lead you to believe that there can be at most 8 Sundays. But that is incorrect.

9.

* Solution using the pigeonhole principle: If you were to pick 4 boxes, then you COULD get 1 scarf of each color (this is the worst case scenario). If you were to pick 8 boxes, then you COULD get 2 scarfs of each color (again, worst case scenario). In other words, choosing 8 boxes will not GUARANTEE that you will get 3 scarves of the same color. But if you pick 9 boxes, then because there are only 4 colors, at least one of the three colors has to be selected 3 times. So the answer is 9, choice **D**.

10.

* To make one of the integers as large as possible we will make the other fourteen as small as possible. The smallest odd positive integer is 1, so we make 14 of the integers 1. Therefore, the 15th integer is $67 - 14 = 53$, choice **J**.

11.

* Solution by picking a number: The question implies that any choice for k will produce the same answer. So, let's choose $k = 2$, and let $P = \{0, 455\}$. Then $Q = \{3, 2278\}$, and the difference between the greatest and least integer in Q is $2278 - 3 = 2275$, choice **C**.

Algebraic solution: Let x and y be the least and greatest integers in set P, respectively. Then the least and greatest integers in set Q are $5x + 3$ and $5y + 3$. So the difference between the greatest and least integer in Q is

$$(5y + 3) - (5x + 3) = 5y + 3 - 5x - 3 = 5y - 5x$$
$$= 5(y - x) = 5(455) = 2275$$

So the answer is choice **C**.

Caution: A common mistake is to distribute the minus sign incorrectly. The following computation is **wrong**.

$$(5y + 3) - (5x + 3) = 5y + 3 - 5x + 3$$

OPTIONAL MATERIAL

CHALLENGE QUESTIONS

1. Given a list of 50 positive integers, each no bigger than 98, show that at least one integer in the list is divisible by another integer in the list.

2. Show that $\sqrt{5} - \sqrt{9 - 4\sqrt{5}}$ is an integer.

Solutions

1.

Any integer can be written as mn, where m is a power of 2 and n is odd. Let's call m the "even part" and n the "odd part" of the integer. There are $\frac{98}{2} = 49$ odd integers less than 98. By the pigeonhole principle, there must be two integers in the list with the same odd part n, let's call these two integers $j = 2^a n$, and $k = 2^b n$. If $a \leq b$, then k is divisible by j. Otherwise j is divisible by k.

2.

$$\sqrt{5} - \sqrt{9 - 4\sqrt{5}} = \sqrt{5} - \sqrt{5 - 4\sqrt{5} + 4} = \sqrt{5} - \sqrt{\left(\sqrt{5} - 2\right)^2}$$
$$= \sqrt{5} - \left(\sqrt{5} - 2\right) = \sqrt{5} - \sqrt{5} + 2 = 2$$

Download additional solutions for free here:

www.satprepget800.com/28LesAdv

126

LESSON 10
ALGEBRA

Reminder: Before beginning this lesson remember to redo the problems from Lessons 2 and 6 that you have marked off. Do not "unmark" a question unless you get it correct.

Absolute Value

Here are a few basic things you might want to know about absolute value for the ACT.

The **absolute value** of x, written $|x|$ is simply x if x is nonnegative, and $-x$ if x is negative. Put simply, $|x|$ just removes the minus sign if one is there.

Examples: $|3| = 3$, and $|-3| = 3$. Also, $|0| = 0$.

Geometrically, $|x - y|$ is the distance between x and y. In particular, $|x - y| = |y - x|$.

Examples: $|5 - 3| = |3 - 5| = 2$ because the distance between 3 and 5 is 2.

If $|x - 3| = 7$, then the distance between x and 3 is 7. So there are two possible values for x. They are $3 + 7 = 10$, and $3 - 7 = -4$. See the figure below for clarification.

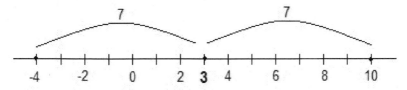

If $|x - 3| < 7$, then the distance between x and 3 is less than 7. If you look at the above figure you should be able to see that this is all x satisfying $-4 < x < 10$.

If $|x - 3| > 7$, then the distance between x and 3 is greater than 7. If you look at the above figure you should be able to see that this is all x satisfying $x < -4$ or $x > 10$

Algebraically, we have the following. For $c > 0$,

127

$|x| = c$ is equivalent to $x = c$ or $x = -c$

$|x| < c$ is equivalent to $-c < x < c$

$|x| > c$ is equivalent to $x < -c$ or $x > c$.

Let's look at the same examples as before algebraically.

Examples: If $|x - 3| = 7$, then $x - 3 = 7$ or $x - 3 = -7$.   So $x = 10$ or $x = -4$.

If $|x - 3| < 7$, then $-7 < x - 3 < 7$. So $-4 < x < 10$.

If $|x - 3| > 7$, then $x - 3 < -7$ or $x - 3 > 7$. So $x < -4$ or $x > 10$.

Try to answer the following question involving absolute value by "Starting with the middle answer choice" (see Lesson 1). **Do not** check the solution until you have attempted this question yourself.

LEVEL 3: ALGEBRA

1. If the exact weight of an item is X pounds and the estimated weight of the item is Y pounds, then the error, in pounds, is given by $|X - Y|$. Which of the following could be the exact weight, in pounds, of an object with an estimated weight of 6.2 pounds and with an error of less than 0.02 pounds?

   A. 6.215
   B. 6.221
   C. 6.23
   D. 6.3
   E. 6.33

Solution

Begin by looking at choice C. So we are assuming that the exact weight of the object is $X = 6.23$. It follows that $|X - Y| = |6.23 - 6.2| = 0.03$ which is too large. So we want X to be **closer** in value to Y.

Let's try choice B next. In this case $|X - Y| = |6.221 - 6.2| = 0.021$. This is still a bit too large.

Let's try choice A. So $|X - Y| = |6.215 - 6.2| = 0.015$. This is less than 0.02. Therefore, the answer is choice **A**.

128

Before we go on, try to solve this problem in two other ways.

(1) Algebraically
(2) Geometrically

Solutions

* **(1)** We are given $Y = 6.2$, so we have

$$|X - 6.2| < 0.02$$
$$-0.02 < X - 6.2 < 0.02$$
$$6.18 < X < 6.22$$

The only answer choice with a number that satisfies this inequality is choice **A**.

(2) We are given that the distance between X and 6.2 is less than 0.02. Let's draw a figure.

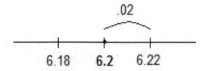

From this picture we see that 6.215 is in the given range, choice **A**.

Try to solve each of the following problems. The answers to these problems, followed by full solutions are at the end of this lesson. **Do not** look at the answers until you have attempted these problems yourself. Please remember to mark off any problems you get wrong.

LEVEL 1: ALGEBRA

2. If $|3c + 2| < 11$, which of the following cannot be equal to c?

    F. -4
    G. 0
    H. 1
    J. 2
    K. 3

LEVEL 3: ALGEBRA

3. What is the set of real solutions for $|x|^2 - |x| - 12 = 0$?

   A. $\{4\}$
   B. $\{-3, 4\}$
   C. $\{3, 4\}$
   D. $\{-4, 4\}$
   E. $\{-4, -3, 3, 4\}$

4. Let h be a function such that $h(x) = |5x| + c$ where c is a constant. If $h(4) = -2$, what is the value of $h(-9)$?

   F. -23
   G. -22
   H. 0
   J. 22
   K. 23

5. For all nonzero values of u, v and w, the value of which of the following expressions is *always* negative?

   A. $u - v - w$
   B. $-u - v - w$
   C. $|u| - |v| - |w|$
   D. $-|uv| + |-w|$
   E. $-|u| - |vw|$

LEVEL 4: ALGEBRA

6. If r and s are nonzero numbers, then which of the following is equivalent to the inequality $|r|\sqrt{7} < |s|\sqrt{2}$?

   F. $r^2 > \frac{2}{7}s^2$
   G. $r^2 < \frac{2}{7}s^2$
   H. $r > \frac{4}{49}s$
   J. $r > \frac{2}{7}s$
   K. $r < \frac{2}{7}s$

130

7. The number line graph below is the graph of which of the following inequalities?

-3   5

A. $|x| \geq 5$
B. $|x - 1| \geq 5$
C. $|x - 1| \geq 4$
D. $|x - 1| \leq 4$
E. $|x + 1| \geq 4$

8. In a certain game a player can attain a score that is a real number between 0 and 100. The player is said to be in scoring range D if his or her score is between 65 and 83. If John has a score of x, and John is in scoring range D, which of the following represents all possible values of x?

F. $|x + 74| < 9$
G. $|x - 74| < 9$
H. $|x + 74| = 9$
J. $|x - 74| > 9$
K. $|x - 74| = 9$

9. For all $k \neq 0$, $|x| + |y| = -k^2$ has how many (x, y) solutions?

A. 0
B. 1
C. 2
D. 3
E. 4

LEVEL 5: ALGEBRA

10. If $|-3a + 9| = 6$ and $|-2b + 10| = 20$, what is the greatest possible value of ab?

F. -25
G. -5
H. 15
J. 75
K. 77

131

11. On the number line, the distance between the point whose coordinate is s and the point whose coordinate is t is greater than 500. Which of the following must be true?

$$\text{I. } |s| \cdot |t| > 500$$
$$\text{II. } |s - t| > 500$$
$$\text{III. } t - s > 500$$

A. I only
B. II only
C. III only
D. I and II only
E. I, II, and III

12. If $f(x) = x^2 - 5$, which of the following is <u>not</u> true?

F. $f(-3) = |f(-3)|$
G. $f(-2) = -|f(2)|$
H. $f(1) < |f(-1)|$
J. $f(0) = |f(0)|$
K. $f(2) < |f(2)|$

Answers

1. A	5. E	9. A
2. K	6. G	10. J
3. D	7. C	11. B
4. K	8. G	12. J

Full Solutions

3.

* Solution by starting with choice C: Let's try $x = 3$ first. We have

$$|x|^2 - |x| - 12 = |3|^2 - |3| - 12 = 9 - 3 - 12 = -6$$

Since we did not get 0, $x = 3$ is NOT a solution, and we can eliminate choices C and E.

Let's try $x = 4$. Then we have $|4|^2 - |4| - 12 = 16 - 4 - 12 = 0$.

So $x = 4$ is a solution. A moment's thought should reveal that $x = -4$ will work as well (since we are taking absolute values). So the answer is choice **D**.

132

4.

* $h(4) = |5(4)| + c = |20| + c = 20 + c$. It is given that $h(4) = -2$. Thus, $20 + c = -2$, and so $c = -22$. Therefore, $h(x) = |5x| - 22$. Then $h(-9) = |5(-9)| - 22 = |-45| - 22 = 45 - 22 = 23$, choice **K**.

Calculator remark: You can take absolute values in your graphing calculator by pressing MATH, scrolling right to NUM and pressing ENTER (or 1). The display will say abs(. For example, in this problem to compute $h(-9)$ you can type abs(5 ∗ −9) − 22, and the output will read **23**.

5.

* **Direct solution:** The absolute value of a nonzero number is always positive. It follows that $|u|$ and $|vw|$ are both positive. So $-|u|$ and $-|vw|$ are negative. Therefore, $-|u| - |vw|$ is negative, choice **E**.

Solution by picking numbers and process of elimination: Let $u = 10$, $v = 1$ and $w = 1$. Then $u - v - w$ and $|u| - |v| - |w|$ are both 8, eliminating choices A and C.

Now, let $u = -10$, $v = 1$ and $w = 1$. Then $-u - v - w = 8$, eliminating choice B.

Finally, let $u = v = 1$ and $w = 10$. Then $-|uv| + |-w| = -1 + 10 = 9$, eliminating choice D.

The answer is therefore **E**.

6.

* Since $|r|$ and $|s|$ are positive (because r and s are nonzero), each side of the given inequality is positive. Therefore, if we square each side of the inequality, the order is maintained. Now $\left(|r|\sqrt{7}\right)^2 = r^2 \cdot 7$, and $\left(|s|\sqrt{2}\right)^2 = s^2 \cdot 2$. So we have $7r^2 < 2s^2$. We divide each side of this inequality by 7 to get $r^2 < \frac{2}{7}s^2$, choice **G**.

7.

Algebraic solution: The shaded part on the left represents all x-values less than or equal to −3, or equivalently, $x \leq -3$.

The shaded part on the right represents all x-values greater than or equal to 5, or equivalently $x \geq 5$.

If we subtract 1 from each side of these inequalities (using the answer choices as a guide), we get $x - 1 \leq -4$ and $x - 1 \geq 4$.

So x is on the graph precisely if $x - 1 \le -4$ or $x - 1 \ge 4$. This is equivalent to $|x - 1| \ge 4$, choice **C**.

* Geometric solution: The average of -3 and 5 is $\frac{-3+5}{2} = 1$. The numbers -3 and 5 are each 4 units away from 1. So the graph shows all real numbers x so that the distance between x and 1 is at least 4. So we get $|x - 1| \ge 4$, choice **C**.

8.

Solution by picking numbers: Let's pick a value for x that is in scoring range D and try to eliminate answer choices. A good choice is a number close to one of the extremes. So let's try $x = 66$, and substitute this value into each answer choice.

F. $|66 + 74| = |140| = 140$ and $140 < 9$ is False
G. $|66 - 74| = |-8| = 8$ and $8 < 9$ is True
H. $|66 + 74| = |140| = 140$ and $140 = 9$ is False
J. $|66 - 74| = |-8| = 8$ and $8 > 9$ is False
K. $|66 - 74| = |-8| = 8$ and $8 = 9$ is False

Since choices F, H, J, and K came out false we can eliminate them, and the answer is choice **G**.

* Algebraic solution: We are given that x is between 65 and 83. That is, $65 < x < 83$. Using the answer choices as a guide, let us subtract 74 from each part of this inequality. We have that $65 - 74 = -9$ and $83 - 74 = 9$. Therefore, we have $-9 < x - 74 < 9$. This is equivalent to $|x - 74| < 9$, choice **G**.

9.
* Since $k \ne 0$, k^2 must be positive. It follows that $-k^2$ is negative. But $|x| + |y|$ can *never* be negative. So the answer is 0, choice **A**.

10.
* The first equation is equivalent to $-3a + 9 = 6$ or $-3a + 9 = -6$. These two equations have solutions $a = 1$ and $a = 5$, respectively. Similarly, the second equation is equivalent to $-2b + 10 = 20$ or $-2b + 10 = -20$. These equations have solutions $b = -5$ and $b = 15$, respectively. Finally, we get the greatest value of ab by multiplying the greatest value of a with the greatest value of b. So $ab = (5)(15) = 75$, choice **J**.

11.

* The first sentence is precisely the statement of II. Letting $s = 1000$ and $t = 0$ gives a counterexample for both I and III. The answer is choice **B**.

12.

* **Solution by starting with choice H:** Let's start with choice H. We have $f(1) = 1^2 - 5 = -4$, $|f(-1)| = |(-1)^2 - 5| = |1 - 5| = |-4| = 4$. Since $-4 < 4$, the inequality in choice H is true.

Let's try choice J next. Now $f(0) = 0^2 - 5 = -5$, $|f(0)| = |-5| = 5$. Since $f(0)$ is different from $|f(0)|$, the equation in choice J is false. Therefore, the answer is choice **J**.

Remark: The other three computations are similar. You may want to do them for extra practice.

Download additional solutions for free here:

www.satprepget800.com/28LesAdv

LESSON 11
GEOMETRY

Reminder: Before beginning this lesson remember to redo the problems from Lessons 3 and 7 that you have marked off. Do not "unmark" a question unless you get it correct.

Similarity

Two polygons P and Q are **similar**, written $P \sim Q$, if their angles are congruent. Note that similar polygons **do not** have to be the same size. On the ACT, questions about similarity often involve triangles, but questions about the similarity of other polygons have also appeared. Note that to show that two triangles are similar we need only show that two pairs of angles are congruent. We get the third pair for free because all triangles have angle measures summing to 180 degrees.

Example:

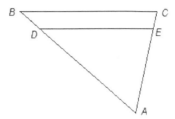

In the figure above, assume that $\overline{BC}$ is parallel to $\overline{DE}$. It then follows that angles ADE and ABC are congruent (corresponding angles). Since triangles ADE and ABC share angle A, the two triangles are similar.

Note that **corresponding sides of similar polygons are in proportion**. So for example, in the figure above $\frac{AD}{AB} = \frac{DE}{BC}$.

Now consider the following figure.

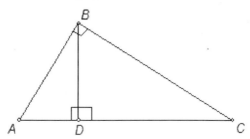

We have a right triangle with an **altitude** drawn from the right angle to the hypotenuse. In this figure triangles BDC, ADB and ABC are similar to each other. When solving a problem involving this figure I strongly recommend redrawing all 3 triangles next to each other so that congruent angles match up. The 3 figures will look like this.

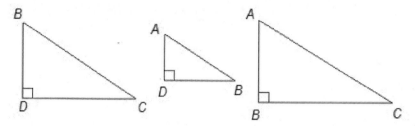

As an example, let's find h in the following figure.

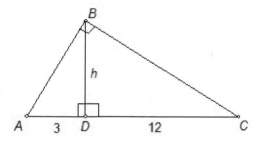

Solution: We redraw the three triangles next to each other so that congruent angles match up.

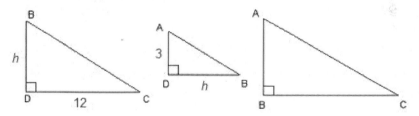

We now set up a ratio, cross multiply, and divide: $\frac{h}{12} = \frac{3}{h}$. So $h^2 = 36$, and therefore $h = 6$.

Remark: Clearly we didn't need to redraw the third triangle, but I suggest drawing all three until you get the hang of this.

The Measure of an Exterior Angle of a Triangle is the Sum of the Measures of the Two Opposite Interior Angles of the Triangle

LEVEL 2: GEOMETRY

1. In $\triangle ABD$ below, if $y = 39$, what is the value of z ?

A. 42
B. 44
C. 46
D. 48
E. 50

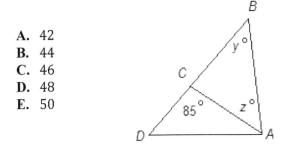

* $85 = 39 + z$, and therefore $z = 85 - 39 = 46$, choice **C**.

Alternate method: Angles ACD and ACB form a **linear pair** and are therefore **supplementary**. It follows that angle ACB measures $180 - 85 = 95$ degrees. Since the angle measures of a triangle add up to 180 degrees, it follows that $z = 180 - 39 - 95 = 46$, choice **C**.

Parallel Lines Cut by a Transversal

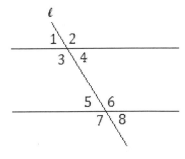

The figure above shows two parallel lines cut by the transversal ℓ.

Angles 1, 4, 5, and 8 all have the same measure. Also, angles 2, 3, 6, and 7 all have the same measure. Any two angles that do not have the same measure are supplementary, that is their measures add to $180°$.

138

LEVEL 2: GEOMETRY

2. In the figure below, line ℓ is parallel to line k. Transversals m and n intersect at point P on ℓ and intersect k at points R and Q, respectively. Point Y is on k, the measure of $\angle PRY$ is 140°, and the measure of $\angle QPR$ is 100°. How many of the angles formed by rays ℓ, k, m, and n have measure 40° ?

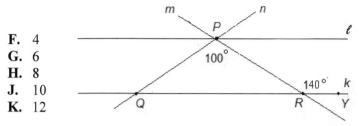

F. 4
G. 6
H. 8
J. 10
K. 12

* $\angle QRP$ is supplementary with $\angle PRY$. So $m\angle QRP$ is $180 - 140 = 40°$. We can then use vertical angles to get the remaining angles in the lower right hand corner.

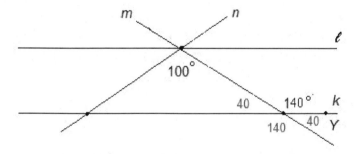

We now use the fact that the sum of the angle measures in a triangle is 180° to get that the measure of the third angle of the triangle is $180 - 100 - 40 = 40°$. We then once again use supplementary and vertical angles to get the remaining angles in the lower left hand corner.

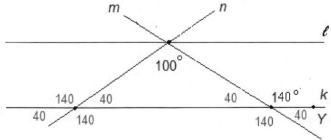

139

Now notice the following alternate interior angles.

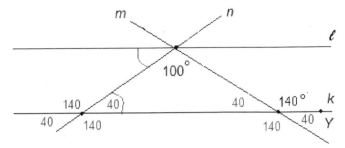

Since $\ell \parallel k$, the alternate interior angles are congruent. So the angle marked above has a measure of 40°. We use supplementary and vertical angles to find the remaining angle measures.

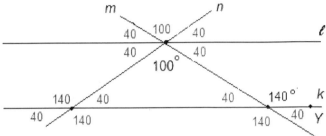

Finally, we see that there are eight angles with measure 40°, choice **H**.

Quadrilaterals

A **quadrilateral** is a two-dimensional geometric figure with four sides and four angles. The sum of the degree measures of all four angles of a quadrilateral is 360.

A **rectangle** is a quadrilateral in which each angle is a right angle. That is, each angle has a measure of 90 degrees.

The **perimeter** of a rectangle is $P = 2l + 2w$, and the area of a rectangle is $A = lw$.

A **square** is a rectangle with four equal sides.

The area of a square is $A = s^2$.

Example:

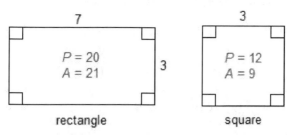

Example: Find the perimeter of a square with area 49.

Solution: The length of a side of the square is $s = \sqrt{49} = 7$. So the perimeter is $P = 4(7) = 28$.

Example: Find the area of a rectangle with perimeter of 100 and length 20.

Solution: We have

$$P = 2l + 2w$$
$$100 = 2(20) + 2w$$
$$100 = 40 + 2w$$
$$60 = 2w$$
$$30 = w$$

Sp $A = lw = (20)(30) = \mathbf{600}$.

Example: Find the area of a rectangle with perimeter 100.

Solution: This cannot be determined! In the last example we saw that A can be 600. If $l = 10$, then $w = \frac{100-2(10)}{2} = \frac{100-20}{2} = \frac{80}{2} = 40$, and therefore $A = (10)(40) = 400$.

A **parallelogram** is a quadrilateral whose opposite sides are parallel.

Facts about parallelograms:
(1) opposite sides are congruent
(2) opposite angles are congruent
(3) adjacent angles are supplementary
(4) the diagonals bisect each other

Note that rectangles are parallelograms, and therefore squares are also parallelograms.

The **area** of a parallelogram is $A = bh$.

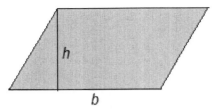

A **rhombus** is a parallelogram with four equal sides.

Facts about rhombuses:
(1) the diagonals are perpendicular
(2) the diagonals bisect the angles

Note that squares are rhombuses.

A **trapezoid** is a quadrilateral with two parallel sides (and two nonparallel sides).

The two parallel sides are called **bases**, and the nonparallel sides are called **legs**.

A trapezoid is **isosceles** if the nonparallel sides are congruent.

Note that isosceles trapezoids have two pairs of congruent angles, and noncongruent angles are supplementary.

isosceles trapezoid   nonisosceles trapezoid

The **area** of a trapezoid is $A = \frac{(b_1 + b_2)}{2} h$.

In other words, to compute the area of a trapezoid we take the average of the two bases and multiply by the height.

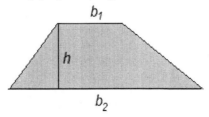

142

Angles of Regular Polygons

A **regular** polygon is a polygon with all sides equal in length, and all angles equal in measure.

The total number of degrees in the interior of an n-sided polygon is

$$(n - 2) \cdot 180$$

For example, a six-sided polygon (or hexagon) has

$$(6 - 2) \cdot 180 = 4 \cdot 180 = 720 \text{ degrees}$$

in its interior. Therefore, each angle of a **regular** hexagon has

$$\frac{720}{6} = 120 \text{ degrees.}$$

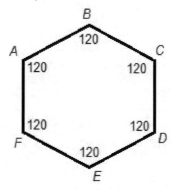

For those of us that do not like to memorize formulas, there is a quick visual way to determine the total number of degrees in the interior of an n-sided polygon. Simply split the polygon up into triangles and quadrilaterals by drawing nonintersecting line segments between vertices. Then add 180 degrees for each triangle and 360 degrees for each quadrilateral. For example, here is one way to do it for a hexagon.

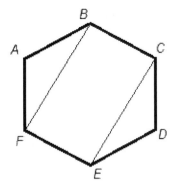

Since the hexagon has been split up into 2 triangles and 1 quadrilateral, the hexagon has $2(180) + 360 = \mathbf{720}$ degrees. This is the same number we got from the formula.

To avoid potential errors, let me give a picture that would be incorrect.

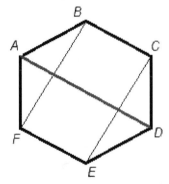

The above figure **cannot** be used to compute the number of interior angles in the hexagon because segment $\overline{AD}$ is "crossing through" segment $\overline{BF}$.

Now let's draw a segment from the center of a regular hexagon to each vertex of the hexagon.

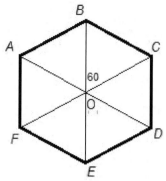

We see that the central angles formed must add up to 360 degrees. Therefore, each central angle measures 60 degrees as shown in the figure above.

In general, the number of degrees in a central angle of a regular n-sided polygon is $\frac{360}{n}$.

It is worth looking at a regular hexagon in a bit more detail.

Each of the segments just drawn in the previous figure is a radius of the circumscribed circle of this hexagon, and therefore they are all congruent. This means that each triangle is isosceles, and so the measure of each of the other two angles of any of these triangles is $\frac{180-60}{2} = 60$. Therefore, each of these triangles is equilateral. This fact is worth committing to memory.

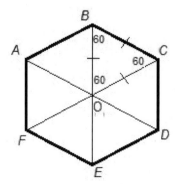

Now try to solve each of the following problems. The answers to these problems, followed by full solutions are at the end of this lesson. **Do not** look at the answers until you have attempted these problems yourself. Please remember to mark off any problems you get wrong.

LEVEL 2: GEOMETRY

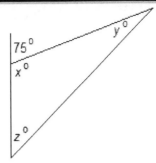

3.   In the figure above, one side of a triangle is extended. Which of the following is true?

    A. $y = 75$
    B. $z = 75$
    C. $z - y = 75$
    D. $y + z = 75$
    E. $x = y + z$

LEVEL 3: GEOMETRY

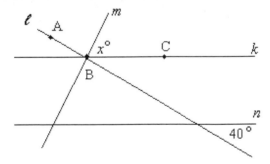

4.   In the figure above, line k is parallel to line n. If line m bisects angle ABC, what is the value of x ?

    F. 40
    G. 50
    H. 60
    J. 70
    K. 80

5. A rectangle has a perimeter of 16 meters and an area of 15 square meters. What is the longest of the side lengths, in meters, of the rectangle?

    A. 3
    B. 5
    C. 10
    D. 15
    E. 16

6. In parallelogram $PQRS$, which of the following must be true about the measures of $\angle PQR$ and $\angle QRS$?

    F. each are 90°
    G. each are less than 90°
    H. each are greater than 90°
    J. they add up to 90°
    K. they add up to 180°

LEVEL 4: GEOMETRY

7. In the figure below, the center of the circle is O and $\overline{PQ}$ is tangent to the circle at Q. What is the area of the shaded region to the nearest tenth?

    A. 2.7
    B. 2.9
    C. 3.1
    D. 3.3
    E. 3.5

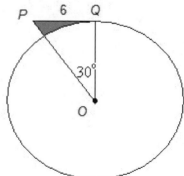

8. The consecutive vertices of a certain isosceles trapezoid are P, Q, R, and S where $\overline{PQ} \parallel \overline{SR}$. Which of the following are NOT congruent?

    F. $\angle P$ and $\angle Q$
    G. $\angle R$ and $\angle S$
    H. $\overline{PS}$ and $\overline{QR}$
    J. $\overline{PQ}$ and $\overline{SR}$
    K. $\overline{PR}$ and $\overline{QS}$

LEVEL 5: GEOMETRY

9. In the triangle below, $DC = 3$ and $BC = 6$. What is the value of AC ?

    A. 3
    B. 6
    C. 9
    D. 12
    E. 15

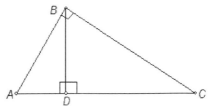

10. In the figure below, $ABCDEF$ is a regular hexagon and $CD = 6$. What is the perimeter of rectangle $BCEF$ to the nearest tenth?

    F. 1.7
    G. 3.5
    H. 24.0
    J. 28.6
    K. 32.8

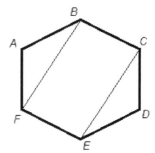

11. In the figure below, what is $xw + xz + yw + yz$ in terms of k?

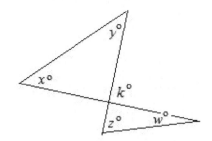

A. $\dfrac{k^2}{4}$

B. $\dfrac{k}{2}$

C. k

D. k^2

E. $4k^2$

12. In the figure below, $\overline{QS}$ is the shorter diagonal of rhombus $PQRS$ and T is on $\overleftrightarrow{PS}$. The measure of angle PQS is $x°$. What is the measure of RST, in terms of x ?

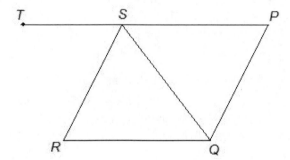

F. $x°$

G. $2x°$

H. $\dfrac{1}{2}x°$

J. $90° - x°$

K. $180° - 2x°$

Answers

1. C	5. B	9. D
2. H	6. K	10. K
3. D	7. B	11. D
4. J	8. J	12. K

Full Solutions

4.

* Let's isolate one of the transversals.

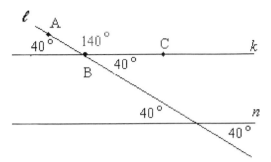

Note that the transversal ℓ creates 8 angles, four of which have measure 40 degrees. The other four are 140 degrees (only one is labeled in the picture). Any two non-congruent angles are supplementary, ie. they add up to 180 degrees. Finally, we note that x is half of 140 because line m bisects angle ABC. Thus, $x = 70$, choice **J**.

5.

* **Solution by plugging in answer choices:** Since $3 \cdot 5 = 15$, choice B seems like a reasonable guess. So let's guess that the longest side of the rectangle is 5. Then the shorter side of the rectangle is 3. It follows that the perimeter of the rectangle is 2(3) + 2(5) = 16. Since this is correct, the answer is choice **B**.

Note: Here is a picture of the rectangle.

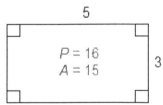

6.

* Let's draw a picture.

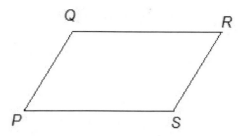

Now note that $\angle PQR$ and $\angle QRS$ are adjacent, and therefore supplementary (see Fact (3) above). So the answer is choice **K**.

Notes: (1) If you have forgotten that adjacent angles of a parallelogram are supplementary, you can also solve this problem by process of elimination as follows.

Note that the measure of angle PQR is greater than 90 degrees, and the measure of angle QRS is less than 90 degrees. So we can eliminate choices F, G, and H.

Since the measure of angle PQR by itself is greater than 90 degrees, we can eliminate choice J. Therefore, the answer is choice **K**.

(2) If you have trouble eliminating choices from the general picture above, try choosing specific angle measures. Here is an example:

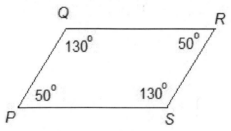

Observe that we had to choose angle measures that sum to 360 (since $PQRS$ is a quadrilateral). We also had to make sure that opposite angles were congruent (since $PQRS$ is a parallelogram).

7.

* A tangent line to a circle is perpendicular to the radius so that the triangle is a 30, 60, 90 right triangle. Since the side opposite 30 is 6, the side opposite 60 is $6\sqrt{3}$. In a right triangle we can think of the two legs as the base and the height. So the area of the triangle is

$$A = \tfrac{1}{2}bh = \tfrac{1}{2}(6) \cdot 6\sqrt{3} = 18\sqrt{3}.$$

We already found that the radius of the circle is $6\sqrt{3}$. Thus, the area of the circle is

$$A = \pi r^2 = \pi\left(6\sqrt{3}\right)^2 = \pi \cdot 36 \cdot 3 = 108\pi.$$

The sector shown is $\frac{1}{12}$ of the entire circle. So the area of the sector is

$$A = \left(\frac{1}{12}\right) \cdot 108\pi = 9\pi.$$

The area of the shaded region is the area of the triangle minus the area of the sector.

$$A = 18\sqrt{3} - 9\pi \approx 2.90258065$$

Rounding to the nearest tenth gives us 2.9, choice **B**.

Remarks: (1) We know that the sector is $\frac{1}{12}$ of the circle because there are 360 degrees in a circle and $\frac{30}{360} = \frac{1}{12}$.

(2) We can more formally find the area of the sector by using the following ratio:

	Sector	Circle
Angle	30	360
Area	x	108π

$$\frac{30}{x} = \frac{360}{108\pi}$$
$$3240\pi = 360x$$
$$x = \frac{3240\pi}{360} = 9\pi$$

See Lesson 19 for more details.

8.
Solution: Let's draw a picture

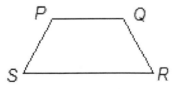

From the picture we can see that $\overline{PQ}$ and $\overline{SR}$ are not congruent. So the answer is choice **J**.

Note: The symbol ∥ means "is parallel to."

9.

Solution: We redraw the three triangles next to each other so that congruent angles match up.

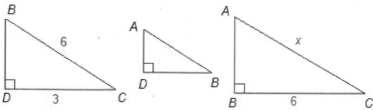

We now set up a ratio, cross multiply, and divide: $\frac{6}{3} = \frac{x}{6}$. So $36 = 3x$, and therefore $x = 12$, choice **D**.

10.

* Since the hexagon is regular, $BC = EF = CD = 6$. Now let's add a bit to the picture.

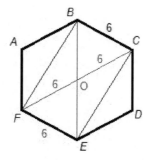

Again, note that the hexagon is regular. So each angle of triangle BOC is 60 degrees. Thus, triangle BOC is equilateral. Therefore, we have $OF = OC = BC = 6$. Since $EF = 6$ and $FC = 12$, triangle CEF is a 30, 60, 90 triangle. It follows that $CE = 6\sqrt{3}$. Since $BCEF$ is a rectangle, $BF = 6\sqrt{3}$ as well. Therefore, the perimeter of the rectangle is $6 + 6 + 6\sqrt{3} + 6\sqrt{3} = 12 + 12\sqrt{3} \approx 32.78$. To the nearest tenth the answer is 32.8, choice **K**.

11.

* First note that

$$xw + xz + yw + yz = x(w + z) + y(w + z) = (x + y)(w + z).$$

Now, $k = x + y$, $k = w + z$, and so $(x + y)(w + z) = k \cdot k = k^2$. So the answer is choice **D**.

153

Remark: Note that the angle labeled k is an exterior angle of both triangles.

Solution by picking numbers: Let's choose values for x, y and z, say $x = 40$, $y = 50$, and $z = 30$. Each unlabeled interior angle has measure $180 - 40 - 50 = 90$, and so $w = 180 - 90 - 30 = 60$. Now,

$xw + xz + yw + yz = (40)(60) + (40)(30) + (50)(60) + (50)(30) = \mathbf{8100}$

Since the angle labeled with k is supplementary with the unlabeled angle, $k = 180 - 90 = 90$. So let's plug $k = 90$ into each answer choice.

    A. 2025
    B. 45
    C. 90
    D. 8100
    E. 32,400

Since A, B, C, and E came out incorrect, the answer is choice **D**.

    12.
* The diagonals of a rhombus are perpendicular. So we get the following picture.

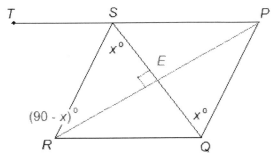

Note that RS and PQ are parallel lines cut by the transversal SQ and $\angle RSQ$ and $\angle PQS$ are **alternate interior angles**. It follows that the measure of angle RSQ is also $x°$.

Since triangle SER is a right triangle, it follows that the measure of angle SRP is $(90 - x)°$.

Since $PQRS$ is a rhombus, $SR = PS$ so that $\angle SPR$ has the same measure as $\angle SRP$. So the measure of $\angle SPR$ is $(90 - x)°$.

Now $\angle RST$ is an exterior angle to triangle PRS. Since **the measure of an exterior angle of a triangle is the sum of the measures of the two opposite interior angles of the triangle**, we have

$$m\angle RST = 90 - x + 90 - x = (180 - 2x)°$$

This is choice **K**.

OPTIONAL MATERIAL

CHALLENGE QUESTION

1. Suppose that quadrilateral $PQRS$ has four congruent sides and satisfies $PQ = PR$. What is the value of $\frac{QS}{PR}$?

Solution

1.

* Note that the quadrilateral is a rhombus. Let's draw a picture.

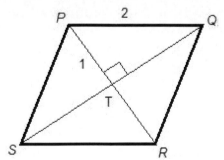

Now, let's choose a value for PQ, say $PQ = 2$. Since $PQ = PR$, $PR = 2$ as well. In a rhombus, the diagonals bisect each other, and are perpendicular to each other. It follows that $PT = 1$ and angle PTQ is a right angle. So triangle PTQ is a 30, 60, 90 triangle, and $QT = \sqrt{3}$. Thus, $QS = 2\sqrt{3}$, and it follows that $\frac{QS}{PR} = \frac{2\sqrt{3}}{2} = \boldsymbol{\sqrt{3}}$.

Note: If we let $PT = x$, then $PQ = 2x$, and by a similar argument to the solution above $PR = 2x$ and $QS = 2x\sqrt{3}$. So $\frac{QS}{PR} = \frac{2x\sqrt{3}}{2x} = \sqrt{3}$, as before.

155

LESSON 12
COUNTING

Reminder: Before beginning this lesson remember to redo the problems from Lessons 4 and 8 that you have marked off. Do not "unmark" a question unless you get it correct.

Writing a List

Sometimes the easiest way to count the number of possibilities is to simply list them all. When doing this it is important that we have a systematic way of forming our list. This will reduce the likelihood of missing something, or listing something twice.

Try to answer the following question by writing a list. **Do not** check the solution until you have attempted this question yourself.

LEVEL 5: COUNTING

1. How many integers between 3000 and 4000 have digits that are all different and that increase from left to right?

    A. 16
    B. 17
    C. 18
    D. 19
    E. 20

* **Solution:** Let's form a list:

3456	3567
7	8
8	9
9	78
67	9
8	89
9	678
78	9
9	89
89	789

156

There are 20 integers in this list, choice **E**.

Remarks: (1) Notice that we wrote down only the necessary information when forming our list. For example, the second entry was just written "7" instead of "3457." This will save a substantial amount of time.

(2) A clear and definite pattern was used in forming this list. In this case the list was written in increasing order. This will minimize the risk of duplicating or leaving out entries.

Counting Principle

The **counting principle** says that if one event is followed by a second independent event, the number of possibilities is multiplied.

More generally, if $E_1, E_2, ..., E_n$ are n independent events with $m_1, m_2, ..., m_n$ possibilities, respectively, then event E_1 followed by event E_2, followed by event $E_3, ...,$ followed by event E_n has $m_1 \cdot m_2 \cdots m_n$ possibilities.

Try to answer the following question by using the counting principle. **Do not** check the solution until you have attempted this question yourself.

LEVEL 3: COUNTING

2. How many integers between 9 and 300 have the tens digit equal to 2, 3, or 4 and the units digit (ones digit) equal to 5 or 6?

   F.   5
   G.   6
   H.   8
   J.   18
   K.   23

Solution

* There are 2 possibilities for the ones digit (5 or 6). There are 3 possibilities for the tens digit (2, 3, or 4). There are 3 possibilities for the hundreds digit (0, 1, or 2).

The counting principle says that we multiply the possibilities to get $(2)(3)(3) = 18$, choice **J**.

Before we go on try to also solve this problem by writing a list.

Solution

Let's try to list the numbers in **increasing order**.

$$25 \quad 26 \quad 35 \quad 36 \quad 45 \quad 46$$
$$125 \quad 126 \quad 135 \quad 136 \quad 145 \quad 146$$
$$225 \quad 226 \quad 235 \quad 236 \quad 245 \quad 246$$

And that's it. We see that the answer is 18, choice **J**.

Permutations and Combinations

The **factorial** of a positive integer n, written $n!$, is the product of all positive integers less than or equal to n.

$$n! = 1 \cdot 2 \cdot 3 \cdots n$$

0! is defined to be 1, so that $n!$ is defined for all nonnegative integers n.

A **permutation** is just an arrangement of elements from a set. The number of permutations of n things taken r at a time is $_nP_r = \frac{n!}{(n-r)!}$. For example, the number of permutations of {1, 2, 3} taken 2 at a time is $_3P_2 = \frac{3!}{1!} = 6$. These permutations are 12, 21, 13, 31, 23, and 32.

Note that on the ACT you **do not** need to know the permutation formula. You can do this computation very quickly on your graphing calculator. To compute $_3P_2$, type 3 into your calculator, then in the **Math** menu scroll over to **Prb** and select **nPr** (or press **2**). Then type 2 and press **Enter**. You will get an answer of 6.

A **combination** is just a subset containing a specific number of the elements of a particular set. The number of combinations of n things taken r at a time is $_nC_r = \frac{n!}{r!(n-r)!}$. For example, the number of combinations of $\{1, 2, 3\}$ taken 2 at a time is $_3C_2 = \frac{3!}{2!1!} = 3$. These combinations are 12, 13, and 23.

Note that on the ACT you **do not** need to know the combination formula. You can do this computation very quickly on your graphing calculator. To compute $_3C_2$, type 3 into your calculator, then in the **Math** menu scroll over to **Prb** and select **nCr** (or press **3**). Then type 2 and press **Enter**. You will get an answer of 3.

Note that 12 and 21 are different permutations, but the same combination.

Example: Compute the number of permutations and combinations of elements from {a, b, c, d} taken (a) 2 at a time, and (b) 4 at a time.

$$_4P_2 = \frac{4!}{2!} = 12, \ _4C_2 = \frac{4!}{2!2!} = 6, \ _4P_4 = \frac{4!}{0!} = 24, \ _4C_4 = \frac{4!}{4!0!} = 1$$

Notes: (1) The permutations taken 2 at a time are $ab, ba, ac, ca, ad, da, bc, cb, bd, db, cd,$ and dc.

(2) The combinations taken 2 at a time are $ab, ac, ad, bc, bd,$ and cd.

Now see if you can list all 24 permutations of $\{a, b, c, d\}$ taken 4 at a time. Note that all 24 of these permutations represent the same combination.

Example: How many committees of 4 people can be formed from a group of 9?

The order in which we choose the 4 people does not matter. Therefore, this is the combination $_9C_4 = 126$.

LEVEL 1: COUNTING

3. A menu lists 7 meals and 5 drinks. How many different meal-drink combinations are possible from this menu?

    A. 35
    B. 32
    C. 24
    D. 13
    E. 12

LEVEL 2: COUNTING

4. Five different books are to be stacked in a pile. In how many different orders can the books be placed on the stack?

    F.   5
    G.   9
    H.   15
    J.   120
    K. 3125

159

LEVEL 3: COUNTING

5. A chemist is testing 9 different liquids. For each test, the chemist chooses 4 of the liquids and mixes them together. What is the least number of tests that must be done so that every possible combination of liquids is tested?

   A. 36
   B. 126
   C. 2736
   D. 5472
   E. 6561

6. Nine different books are to be stacked in a pile. One book is chosen for the bottom of the pile and another book is chosen for the top of the pile. In how many different orders can the remaining books be placed on the stack?

   F. 7
   G. 42
   H. 5040
   J. 40,320
   K. 393,120

LEVEL 4: COUNTING

7. Any 2 points determine a line. If there are 18 points in a plane, no 3 of which lie on the same line, how many lines are determined by pairs of these 18 points?

   A. 35
   B. 36
   C. 153
   D. 306
   E. 4896

8. Segments $\overline{AC}, \overline{AD}, \overline{BE}$, and $\overline{EC}$ intersect at the labeled points as shown in the figure below. Define two points as "dependent" if they lie on the same segment in the figure. Of the labeled points in the figure, how many pairs of dependent points are there?

    F. None
    G. Three
    H. Six
    J. Nine
    K. Twelve

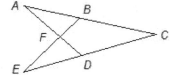

9. A wall is to be painted one color with a stripe of a different color running through the middle. If 9 different colors are available, how many color combinations are possible?

    A. 81
    B. 72
    C. 36
    D. 18
    E. 17

LEVEL 5: COUNTING

10. Regular pentagons have 5 diagonals as shown below. How many diagonals does a regular octagon have? (An octagon is a polygon with 8 sides)

    F. 40
    G. 30
    H. 20
    J. 16
    K. 8

11. If seven cards, each of a different color are placed in a row so that the green one is placed at an end, how many different arrangements are possible?

    A.   7
    B.   42
    C.   720
    D. 1440
    E. 9030

12. How many positive integers less than 4,000 are multiples of 5 and are equal to 13 times an even integer?

    F. 15
    G. 30
    H. 40
    J. 50
    K. 60

Answers

1. E	5. B	9. B
2. J	6. H	10. H
3. A	7. C	11. D
4. J	8. K	12. G

Full Solutions

5.

* Solution using combinations: We are counting the number of ways to choose 4 of the 9 liquids. This is $_9C_4 = 126$, choice **B**.

6.

* There are seven books left to stack. Therefore, we see that there are $7! = (7)(6)(5)(4)(3)(2)(1) = 5040$ ways to stack these books, choice **H**.

Calculator remark: You can compute 7! in your calculator as follows. After typing 7, simply press MATH, scroll to PRB and then select ! (or press 4).

162

7.

* Solution using combinations: We need to count the number of ways to choose 2 points from 18. This is the combination $_{18}C_2 = 153$, choice **C**.

8.

* Solution using strategy 21: Let's list the dependent pairs of points.

$$A,F \quad F,D \quad A,D \quad E,F \quad F,B \quad E,B$$
$$A,B \quad B,C \quad A,C \quad E,D \quad D,C \quad E,C$$

So there are twelve pairs of dependent points, choice **K**.

Note: Notice that our list follows a definite pattern. Here we took one long segment at a time, and listed first the two pairs of points adjoining the two shorter segments, and then the pair adjoining the long segment.

* Solution using combinations: We can count the pairs without actually making a list. There are 4 line segments, each with 3 points. So each segment has $_3C_2 = 3$ pairs of dependent points. So there are $4 \cdot 3 = 12$ pairs of dependent points all together, choice **K**.

9.

* Solution using the counting principle: There are 9 ways to choose a color for the wall. Once this color is chosen there are now 8 ways to choose a color for the stripe. Therefore, there are $(9)(8) = 72$ possibilities, choice **B**.

Solution using permutations: There are $_9P_2 = 72$ ways to choose 2 colors from 9, and place them in a specific order, choice **B**.

Important note: Don't let the word "combinations" in the problem itself trick you. This is **not** a combination in the mathematical sense. If you paint the wall red and the stripe blue, then this is a **different** choice from painting the wall blue and the stripe red.

10.

* Solution using combinations: The number of diagonals of a regular octagon is $_8C_2 - 8 = 28 - 8 = 20$, choice **H**.

Notes: $_8C_2$ is the number of ways to choose 2 vertices from 8. Each such choice gives us either a diagonal OR a side of the octagon. Since we want ONLY the diagonals, we subtract off the number of sides, which is 8.

Alternate solution: If we focus on just one vertex of an octagon, we see that there are 5 diagonals that include that vertex.

Since there are 8 vertices, it seems that we should multiply $8 \cdot 5 = 40$ to get the answer. But note that we counted each diagonal twice (once for each vertex), and so we need to divide this answer by 2 to get 20, choice **H**.

  11.
* Solution using the counting principle: There are 2 ways to place the green card. Once the green card is placed, there are 6 ways to place the next card, 5 ways to place the card after that, then 4, then 3, then 2, and finally 1 way to place the last card. By the counting principle there are $(2)(6)(5)(4)(3)(2)(1) = 1440$ different arrangements, choice **D**.

  12.
* Note that 13 times an even integer is just a multiple of $(13)(2) = 26$. So we are looking for positive integers less than 4000 that are multiples of both 5 and 26. Since 5 and 26 have no prime factors in common, we are just looking for multiples of $(5)(26) = 130$ that are less than 4000. The answer is just the integer part of $\frac{4000}{130} \approx 30.7692$. So the answer is 30, choice **G**.

OPTIONAL MATERIAL

CHALLENGE QUESTIONS

1. Let j and k be positive integers with $j \leq k$. In how many ways can k be written as a sum of j positive integers?

2. How many arrangements of the word EFFLORESCENCE have consecutive C's and F's but no consecutive E's?

Solutions

1.

Let's begin with some simple examples. Let's try $j = 2$, $k = 3$. Then we have $3 = 1 + 2 = 2 + 1$. So there are 2 possibilities.

Now let's try $j = 3$, $k = 5$. We have

$$5 = 1 + 1 + 3 = 1 + 3 + 1 = 3 + 1 + 1 = 1 + 2 + 2 = 2 + 1 + 2 = 2 + 2 + 1.$$

Let's think about what we did here. Think of 5 as $1 + 1 + 1 + 1 + 1$, and notice that there are 4 plus signs. We can think of adding two adjacent ones as "choosing" a plus sign. For example, if we choose the first plus sign we get $2 + 1 + 1 + 1$. It's not enough to choose just 1 plus sign. We need to choose 2 of them (in this example). If we choose the last two plus signs we get $1 + 1 + 3$. If we choose the first and last plus sign we get $2 + 1 + 2$, and so on. In other words, we are counting the number of ways to choose 2 of the plus signs from the 4 plus signs. Also, note that the number of plus signs is 1 less than 5, and the number we need to choose is 1 less than 3.

For general j and k with $j \leq k$, we have $k - 1$ plus signs, and we need to choose $j - 1$ of them. So the answer is $_{k-1}C_{j-1}$.

2.

First place the E's. We need to place seven other "letters":

CC, FF, L, O, R, S, and N.

To make things simpler let's imagine these are 7 different scrabble tiles. For now, turn all of them face down. Let's call them "non-E" tiles.

Place a non-E tile face down between the first and the second E, one non-E tile face down between the second and the third E and finally another non-E tile face down between the third and the fourth E. Now the E's are separated.

Place the remaining 4 non-E tiles wherever you want in the 5 regions determined by the E tiles. There are $_8C_4$ ways to do this. At this point you have a 13-letter word consisting of E tiles and non-E tiles.

Finally, turn the non-E tiles face up. Since they are all different there are 7! possible arrangements.

So the final answer is $1 \cdot 1 \cdot {_8C_4} \cdot 7 = \mathbf{352,800}$.

** Thanks to Dan Ismailescu for providing this solution!

LESSON 13
NUMBER THEORY

Reminder: Before beginning this lesson remember to redo the problems from Lessons 1, 5 and 9 that you have marked off. Do not "unmark" a question unless you get it correct.

Arithmetic Sequences

An **arithmetic sequence** is a sequence of numbers such that the difference d between consecutive terms is constant. The number d is called the **common difference** of the arithmetic sequence.

Here is a simple example of an arithmetic sequence: $1, 3, 5, 7, 9, 11, \ldots$ In this example, the common difference is $d = 2$.

Arithmetic sequence formula: $a_n = a_1 + (n-1)d$

In the above formula, a_n is the nth term of the sequence. For example, a_1 is the first term of the sequence.

Example: In the arithmetic sequence $1, 3, 5, 7, 9, 11, \ldots$ note that $a_1 = 1$ and $d = 2$. Therefore, $a_n = 1 + (n-1)(2) = 1 + (2n - 2) = 2n - 1$.

Linear equations and arithmetic sequences: Questions about arithmetic sequences can easily be thought of as questions about lines and linear equations. We can identify terms of the sequence with points on a line where the x-coordinate is the term number and the y-coordinate is the term itself.

In the example above, since the first term of the sequence is 1, we can identify this term with the point $(1, 1)$. Since the second term of the sequence is 3, we can identify this with the point $(2, 3)$. Note that the common difference d is just the slope of the line that passes through these two points, i.e., $d = \dfrac{3-1}{2-1} = 2$.

If we were to write an equation of the line passing through $(1, 1)$ with slope 2 in point-slope form, we get $y - 1 = 2(x - 1)$ (see Lesson 3 if you need to review this). Distributing the 2 and adding 1 to each side of the equation gives $y = 2x - 1$. Compare this to the expression $a_n = 2n - 1$ that we arrived at earlier. They are the same except for the names of the unknowns!

166

Try to solve the following problem in two ways.

(1) Using the arithmetic sequence formula
(2) Using geometry

LEVEL 4: NUMBER THEORY

1. Each term of a certain sequence is greater than the term before it. The difference between any two consecutive terms in the sequence is always the same number. If the fifth and ninth terms of the sequence are 33 and 97, respectively, what is the twelfth term?

   A. 129
   B. 145
   C. 161
   D. 177
   E. 193

Solutions

(1) Substituting 5 in for n and 33 in for a_n into the arithmetic sequence formula gives us $33 = a_1 + 4d$.

Similarly, substituting 9 in for n and 97 in for a_n into the arithmetic sequence formula gives us $97 = a_1 + 8d$.

So we solve the following system of equations to find d.

$$
\begin{aligned}
97 &= a_1 + 8d \\
\underline{33} &= \underline{a_1 + 4d} \\
64 &= 4d
\end{aligned}
$$

The last equation comes from subtraction. We now divide each side of this last equation by 4 to get $d = 16$.

Finally, we add 16 to 97 three times to get $97 + 16(3) = 145$, choice **B**.

Remarks: (1) We used the elimination method to find d here. This method (as well as others) was described in Lesson 2.

(2) Once we have that $d = 16$, we can substitute this into either of the original equations to find a_1. For example, we have $33 = a_1 + 4(16)$, so that $a_1 = 33 - 64 = -31$. The nth term of the sequence is then

$$a_n = -31 + (n-1)(16) = -31 + 16n - 16 = 16n - 47$$

In particular, $a_{12} = 16(12) - 47 = 145$.

* (2) We identify the two given terms with the points $(5, 33)$ and $(9, 97)$. The common difference is then $d = \frac{97-33}{9-5} = \frac{64}{4} = 16$. As in the previous solution, the twelfth term is $97 + 16(3) = 145$, choice **B**.

Remark: If we want to write the equation of the line in point-slope form we get $y - 33 = 16(x - 5)$. We can then find the twelfth term by plugging in a 12 for x: $y - 33 = 16(12 - 5) = 16(7) = 112$. Thus, $y = 112 + 33 = 145$.

If we were to use the point $(9, 97)$ instead of $(5, 33)$ we would get the same answer.

Fence-Post Formula

The number of integers from a to b, inclusive, is $b - a + 1$.

For example, let's count the number of integers from 5 to 12, inclusive. They are $5, 6, 7, 8, 9, 10, 11, 12$, and we see that there are 8 of them. Now $12 - 5 = 7$ which is not the correct amount, but $12 - 5 + 1 = 8$ which is the correct amount.

If you ever happen to forget this little formula test it out on a small list of numbers as I just did. But it's nice to have this one committed to memory so that it is there for you when you need it.

Remark: If you put up a fence that is 10 feet long, and put up fence-posts every foot, then there are $10 - 0 + 1 = 11$ fence-posts.

Try to answer the following question using the fence-post formula. **Do not** check the solution until you have attempted this question yourself.

LEVEL 5: NUMBER THEORY

2. How many numbers between 72 and 356 can be expressed as $5x + 3$, where x is an integer?

　　F. 55
　　G. 56
　　H. 57
　　J. 58
　　K. 59

Solution

* Let's keep guessing x-values until we find the smallest and largest values of x satisfying $72 < 5x + 3 < 356$. Since $5(13) + 3 = 68$ and $5(14) + 3 = 73$ we see that 14 is the smallest value of x satisfying the inequality. Since $5(70) + 3 = 353$ and $5(71) + 3 = 358$ we see that 70 is the largest value of x satisfying the inequality. Therefore, it follows that the answer is $70 - 14 + 1 = 57$, choice **H**.

Remarks: (1) We used the fence-post formula together with the strategy of Taking a Guess from Lesson 1 here.

(2) We could have also found the two extreme x-values algebraically as follows.

$$72 < 5x + 3 < 356$$
$$69 < 5x < 353$$
$$\frac{69}{5} < x < \frac{353}{5}$$
$$13.8 < x < 70.6$$
$$14 \leq x \leq 70$$

We get the last inequality because x must be an integer. Notice that this last inequality is **not** strict (It is $\leq$ instead of $<$).

Differences of Large Sums

The quickest way to subtract two large sums is to follow these steps:

    (1) Write out each sum formally.
    (2) Figure out how to line them up properly.
    (3) Subtract term by term.
    (4) Finish the computation.

Try to answer the following question using this strategy. **Do not** check the solution until you have attempted this question yourself.

LEVEL 5: NUMBER THEORY

3. If x denotes the sum of the integers from 10 to 70 inclusive, and y denotes the sum of the integers from 80 to 140 inclusive, what is the value of $y - x$?

    A.   70
    B.   130
    C.   700
    D. 1400
    E. 4270

Solution

* We write out each sum formally and line them up with y above x.

$$80 + 81 + 82 + \cdots + 140$$
$$10 + 11 + 12 + \cdots + 70$$

Now subtract term by term.

$$80 + 81 + 82 + \cdots + 140$$
$$\underline{10 + 11 + 12 + \cdots + 70}$$
$$70 + 70 + 70 + \cdots + 70$$

Now notice that we're adding 70 to itself $70 - 10 + 1 = 61$ times (by the fence-post formula). This is the same as multiplying 70 by 61. So we get $(70)(61) = 4270$, choice **E**.

Remark: Although it is possible to get the answer by performing these long computations in your calculator, this is not recommended. Most students do not get the correct answer this way due to computational error. Also, a lot of time is wasted.

You can also use the sum feature on your graphing calculator to solve this problem as follows.

Calculator Solution

Press the **2nd** button followed by the **List** button (same as **Stat** button).
Go to **Math** and select **5: sum(** or press **5**.
Press **2nd** followed by **List** again.
Go to **Ops** and select **5: seq(** or press **5**.
Enter **x, x, 10, 70))**.

170

The display should look like this:

sum(seq(x, x, 10, 70))

Press **Enter** and you should get the answer **2440**.

Next enter **sum(seq(x, x, 80, 140))** and you should get the answer **6710**. Finally, $y - x = 6710 - 2440 = 4270$, choice **E**.

Time-Saving Remark: After entering **sum(seq(x, x, 10, 70))** and getting an answer of 2440, you can press the **2nd** button followed by the **ENTER** button to bring **sum(seq(x, x, 10, 70))** back up in your calculator. Then move the cursor back, change the 10 to an 80 and the 70 to 140 and press **ENTER** again.

Also, you do not need to type the closing parentheses. For example, it is okay to enter **sum(seq(x, x, 10, 70** instead of **sum(seq(x, x, 10, 70))**.

Arithmetic Series

The sum of the terms of a sequence is called a **series**. A series is **arithmetic** if any two consecutive terms have the same difference. There is a simple formula for the sum of an arithmetic series:

$A_n = n \cdot m$ where n is the number of terms and m is the average (arithmetic mean) of the first and last term.

Arithmetic Series Solution to Question 3

The sum of the integers from 10 to 70 inclusive is $61(\frac{10 + 70}{2}) = 2440$, and the sum from 80 to 140 inclusive is $61(\frac{80 + 140}{2}) = 6710$. It follows that $y - x = 6710 - 2440 = 4270$, choice **E**.

Remark: We used the fence-post formula to get that $n = 61$.

See the optional material at the end of this lesson for a derivation of the arithmetic series formula.

Geometric Sequences

A **geometric sequence** is a sequence of numbers such that the quotient r between consecutive terms is constant. The number r is called the **common ratio** of the geometric sequence.

Here is a simple example of a geometric sequence: $1, 2, 4, 8, 16, 32, \ldots$

In this example the common ratio is $r = 2$.

Geometric sequence formula: $g_n = g_1 \cdot r^{n-1}$

In the above formula, g_n is the nth term of the sequence. For example, g_1 is the first term of the sequence.

Example: In the geometric sequence $1, 2, 4, 8, 16, 32, \ldots$ note that $g_1 = 1$ and $r = 2$. Therefore, $g_n = 1 \cdot 2^{n-1} = 2^{n-1}$.

Finding the common ratio using nonconsecutive terms: If we know two consecutive terms of a geometric sequence, we can find the common ratio simply by dividing the second known term by the first known term. What if we know 2 terms of a geometric sequence, but they are not consecutive? In this case we can still find the common ratio quickly as follows. Suppose g_n and g_m are the nth and mth term of a geometric sequence with $m > n$. Then the common ratio of the geometric sequence is

$$r = \sqrt[m-n]{\frac{g_m}{g_n}} = \left(\frac{g_m}{g_n}\right)^{\frac{1}{m-n}}$$

The above formula looks a lot more complicated than it is. In words it says, "divide the second known term by the first known term, and then take a root." Which root do we take? Well we take the distance between the two terms, and that's the root we use! Let's take the sequence from our example: $1, 2, 4, 8, 16, 32, \ldots$

Note that the second term of this sequence is 2 and the fifth term of this sequence is 16. Let's find the common ratio of the sequence using the second and fifth terms.

Step 1: Divide the fifth term by the second term: $16 \div 2 = 8$.
Step 2: Find the distance between the two terms: $5 - 2 = 3$.
Step 3: Take the appropriate root (in this case the cube root): $\sqrt[3]{8} = 2$.

So the common ratio is 2, as we already knew.

Note that if we plug the numbers into the formula above directly we get

$$r = \sqrt[5-2]{\frac{16}{2}} = \sqrt[3]{8} = 2$$

172

Geometric Series

A series is **geometric** if any two consecutive terms have the same ratio. The sum G of an infinite geometric series with first term g and common ratio r with $-1 < r < 1$ is

$$G = \frac{g}{1-r}$$

For example, $1 + \frac{1}{2} + \frac{1}{4} + \frac{1}{8} + \cdots = \frac{1}{1-\frac{1}{2}} = 1 \div \frac{1}{2} = 1 \cdot \frac{2}{1} = 2.$

Now try to solve each of the following problems. The answers to these problems, followed by full solutions are at the end of this lesson. **Do not** look at the answers until you have attempted these problems yourself. Please remember to mark off any problems you get wrong.

LEVEL 1: NUMBER THEORY

4. The first term is 2 in the geometric sequence $2, -4, 8, -16, \cdots$. What is the EIGHTH term of the geometric sequence?

    F. -512
    G. -256
    H. 128
    J. 256
    K. 512

LEVEL 4: NUMBER THEORY

5. What is the third term of the geometric sequence whose second term is $-\frac{1}{9}$ and whose fifth term is $\frac{1}{243}$?

    A. $-\frac{1}{3}$
    B. $-\frac{1}{27}$
    C. $-\frac{1}{81}$
    D. $\frac{1}{27}$
    E. $\frac{1}{3}$

173

LEVEL 5: NUMBER THEORY

6. A 700-foot-long fence is constructed. Fence-posts are placed at each end and also placed every 10 feet along the fence. How many fence-posts are there in all in the 700-foot stretch?

    F. 68
    G. 69
    H. 70
    J. 71
    K. 72

7. If x denotes the sum of the integers from 1 to 40 inclusive, and y denotes the sum of the integers from 41 to 80 inclusive, what is the value of $y - x$?

    A.   40
    B.   80
    C. 120
    D. 1600
    E. 3200

$$\frac{51}{(2)(3)}, \frac{51}{(3)(4)}, \frac{51}{(4)(5)}, \frac{51}{(5)(6)}$$

8. The first four terms of a sequence are given above. The nth term of the sequence is $\frac{51}{(n+1)(n+2)}$, which is equal to $\frac{51}{n+1} - \frac{51}{n+2}$. What is the sum of the first 100 terms of this sequence?

    F. $\frac{51}{2}$
    G. 25
    H. $\frac{2499}{50}$
    J. $\frac{1224}{50}$
    K. $\frac{1}{50}$

174

9. In a certain sequence, each term after the second is the product of the two preceding terms. If the sixth term is 32 and the seventh term is 512, what is the second term of this sequence?

    A. $\frac{1}{8}$
    B. $\frac{1}{4}$
    C. 2
    D. 8
    E. 16

10. The sum of the positive odd integers less than 200 is subtracted from the sum of the positive even integers less than or equal to 200. What is the resulting difference?

    F. 25
    G. 50
    H. 100
    J. 200
    K. 400

$$3, 9, 27, \ldots$$

11. The first term of the sequence above is 3, and each term after the first is three times the preceding term. Which of the following expressions represents the nth term of the sequence?

    A. $3n$
    B. $(n-1)^3$
    C. n^3
    D. 3^{n-1}
    E. 3^n

175

12. 125 blank cards are lined up in one long row. In the upper left hand corner of each card a number is written beginning with 1 on the first card, 2 on the second card, and so on until 125 is written in the upper left hand corner of the last card in the row. Now another number is written in the lower right hand corner of each card, this time beginning with 125 on the first card, 124 on the second card, and so on until 1 is written in the lower right hand corner of the last card. Which of the following is a pair of numbers written on the same card?

    F. 71 and 57
    G. 70 and 56
    H. 69 and 55
    J. 68 and 54
    K. 67 and 53

Answers

1. B	5. D	9. B
2. H	6. J	10. H
3. E	7. D	11. E
4. G	8. G	12. G

Note: The full solutions for question 7 has been omitted because its solution is very similar to the solution for question 3.

Full Solutions

5.

* The common ratio of the geometric sequence is

$$r = \sqrt[m-n]{\frac{g_m}{g_n}} = \sqrt[5-2]{\frac{\left(\frac{1}{243}\right)}{\left(-\frac{1}{9}\right)}} = \sqrt[3]{\left(\frac{1}{243}\right)(-9)} = \sqrt[3]{\left(-\frac{1}{27}\right)} = -\frac{1}{3}$$

Since the second term is $-\frac{1}{9}$, the third term is $\left(-\frac{1}{9}\right)\left(-\frac{1}{3}\right) = \frac{1}{27}$, choice **D**.

6.

* **Solution using the fence-post formula:** Since $\frac{700}{10} = 70$, we can identify the posts with the integers from 0 to 70, inclusive. By the fence-post formula, the number of fence-posts is $70 - 0 + 1 = 71$, choice **J**.

176

8.

* The second form of the sequence is much nicer to work with. We get the first term by substituting in a 1 for n. So the 1st term of the sequence is $\frac{51}{2} - \frac{51}{3}$. Similarly, the 2nd term of the sequence is $\frac{51}{3} - \frac{51}{4}$. Continuing in this fashion we get that the 100th term of the sequence is $\frac{51}{101} - \frac{51}{102}$. When we add all these up we get the following.

$$\left(\frac{51}{2} - \frac{51}{3}\right) + \left(\frac{51}{3} - \frac{51}{4}\right) + \left(\frac{51}{4} - \frac{51}{5}\right) + \cdots + \left(\frac{51}{101} - \frac{51}{102}\right).$$

This is called a **telescoping sum**. These sums are nice because a lot of cancellation takes place. Notice that everything goes away except for $\frac{51}{2} - \frac{51}{102}$. Type this into your calculator to get 25, choice **G**.

9.

* The fifth term is $\frac{512}{32} = 16$. The fourth term is $\frac{32}{16} = 2$. The third term is $\frac{16}{2} = 8$. The second term is $\frac{2}{8} = \frac{1}{4}$, choice **B**.

10.

We write out each sum formally, line them up, and subtract term by term.

$$2 + 4 + 6 + \cdots + 200$$
$$1 + 3 + 5 + \cdots + 199$$
$$1 + 1 + 1 + \cdots + \quad 1$$

Now notice that we're adding 1 to itself 100 times. So the answer is 100, choice **H**.

Note: It is easiest to see that we are adding 100 ones by looking at the sum of the positive even integers less than or equal to 200. There are $\frac{200}{2} = 100$ terms in this sum.

* **Quick computation:** Once you get a little practice with this type of problem you can simply compute $100 \cdot 1 = 100$, choice **H**.

Solution using the sum feature on your graphing calculator: Press the 2nd button followed by the **List** button (same as **Stat** button).
Go to **Math** and select **5: sum(** or press **5**.
Press 2nd followed by **List** again.
Go to **Ops** and select **5: seq(** or press **5**.
Enter **x, x, 1, 199, 2))**.

The display should look like this: **sum(seq(x, x, 1, 199, 2))**.
Press **Enter** and you should get the answer **10, 000**.
Next enter **sum(seq(x, x, 2, 200, 2))** and you should get the answer **10, 100**. Finally, $10,100 - 10,000 = 100$, choice **H**.

Note: In the expression **sum(seq(x, x, 2, 200, 2))** the last 2 indicates the **step size**. Here we are adding every other number.

See the solution to problem 3 for a time-saving remark, and a third solution using the Arithmetic Series formula.

11.
* **Solution by picking numbers:** Let's choose a value for n, say $n = 2$. We see that the 2nd term of the sequence is **9**. **Put a nice big circle around this number.** Now substitute $n = 2$ into each answer choice.

A. 6
B. 1
C. 8
D. 3
E. 9

Since A, B, C and D are incorrect we can eliminate them. Therefore, the answer is choice **E**.

* **Quick solution:** We can rewrite the sequence as $3^1, 3^2, 3^3,...$

Note that the 1st term is 3^1, the 2nd term is 3^2, the 3rd term is 3^3, etc. Thus, the nth term is is 3^n, choice **E**.

12.
* Note that the sum of the numbers on the first card is $1 + 125 = 126$, the sum of the numbers on the second card is $2 + 124 = 126$, etc. So we are looking for two numbers that add to 126. Since $70 + 56 = 126$, the answer is choice **G**.

OPTIONAL MATERIAL

CHALLENGE QUESTION

1. Find the sum of the integers from 24 to 276 inclusive.

178

2. Show that the sum of an arithmetic series is $A_n = n \cdot m$ where n is the number of terms and m is the average (arithmetic mean) of the first and last term.

Solutions

1.

* We formally write out this sum forward and backward, and then add.

$$24 + 25 + \cdots + 275 + 276$$
$$\underline{276 + 275 + \cdots + 25 + 24}$$
$$300 + 300 + \cdots + 300 + 300$$

By the fence-post formula we are adding 300 to itself $276 - 24 + 1 = 253$ times. This gives $300(253) = 75,900$. Since we added the sum twice we now divide by 2 to get **37,950**.

2.

Let a be the first term of the series and let d be the common difference.

$$\begin{array}{llllll}
A_n = & a & + & (a+d) & + & (a+2d) & +\ldots+ & (a+(n-1)d) \\
A_n = & (a+(n-1)d) & + & (a+(n-2)d) & + & (a+(n-3)d) & +\ldots+ & a \\
\hline
2A_n = & (2a+(n-1)d) & + & (2a+(n-1)d) & + & (2a+(n-1)d) & +\ldots+ & (2a+(n-1)d)
\end{array}$$

$$2A_n = n(2a + (n-1)d) = n(a + a + (n-1)d) = n(a + a_n).$$
$$A_n = n\left(\frac{a+a_n}{2}\right) = n \cdot m.$$

Remarks: Recall that $a_n = a + (n-1)d$ where a is the first term of the arithmetic sequence, d is the common difference, and a_n is the nth term of the arithmetic sequence. In the first equation we are formally writing out the sum of the first n terms of the arithmetic sequence. Note that to get from one term to the next we simply add the common difference d. We form the second equation by reversing the order in which the terms were written in the first equation. Note that we add the equations term by term. Each term gives the same sum of $2a + (n-1)d$. Since this expression is repeated n times, the sum is equal to $n(2a + (n-1)d)$. We then use the arithmetic sequence formula to replace $a + (n-1)d$ by a_n. Finally, recall that $m = \frac{a+a_n}{2}$, the average of the first and last term.

179

LESSON 14
ALGEBRA AND FUNCTIONS

Reminder: Before beginning this lesson remember to redo the problems from Lessons 2, 6 and 10 that you have marked off. Do not "unmark" a question unless you get it correct.

Laws of Exponents

Law	Example
$x^0 = 1$	$3^0 = 1$
$x^1 = x$	$9^1 = 9$
$x^a x^b = x^{a+b}$	$x^3 x^5 = x^8$
$x^a / x^b = x^{a-b}$	$x^{11}/x^4 = x^7$
$(x^a)^b = x^{ab}$	$(x^5)^3 = x^{15}$
$(xy)^a = x^a y^a$	$(xy)^4 = x^4 y^4$
$(x/y)^a = x^a / y^a$	$(x/y)^6 = x^6 / y^6$
$x^{-1} = 1/x$	$3^{-1} = 1/3$
$x^{-a} = 1/x^a$	$9^{-2} = 1/81$
$x^{1/n} = \sqrt[n]{x}$	$x^{1/3} = \sqrt[3]{x}$
$x^{m/n} = \sqrt[n]{x^m} = \left(\sqrt[n]{x}\right)^m$	$x^{9/2} = \sqrt{x^9} = \left(\sqrt{x}\right)^9$

Now let's practice. Simplify the following expressions using the basic laws of exponents. Get rid of all negative and fractional exponents.

1. $5^2 \cdot 5^3$

2. $\dfrac{5^3}{5^2}$

3. $\dfrac{x^5 \cdot x^3}{x^8}$

4. $(2^3)^4$

5. $\dfrac{(xy)^7 (yz)^2}{y^9}$

6. $\left(\dfrac{2}{3}\right)^3 \left(\dfrac{9}{4}\right)^2$

7. $\dfrac{x^4 + x^2}{x^2}$

8. $\dfrac{(x^{10} + x^9 + x^8)(y^5 + y^4)}{y^4 (x^2 + x + 1)}$

9. 7^{-1}

10. $\dfrac{5^2}{5^5}$

11. $\dfrac{x^{-5} \cdot x^{-3}}{x^{-4}}$

12. $5^{\frac{1}{2}}$

13. $5^{-\frac{1}{2}}$

14. $7^{-\frac{11}{3}}$

15. $\dfrac{x^{-\frac{5}{2}} \cdot x^{-1}}{x^{-\frac{4}{3}}}$

180

Answers

1. $5^5 = 3125$

2. $5^1 = 5$

3. $\dfrac{x^8}{x^8} = 1$

4. $2^{12} = 4096$

5. $\dfrac{x^7 y^7 y^2 z^2}{y^9} = \dfrac{x^7 y^9 z^2}{y^9} = x^7 z^2$

6. $\dfrac{2^3}{3^3} \cdot \dfrac{9^2}{4^2} = \dfrac{2^3}{3^3} \cdot \dfrac{(3^2)^2}{(2^2)^2} = \dfrac{2^3}{3^3} \cdot \dfrac{3^4}{2^4} = \dfrac{3^1}{2^1} = \dfrac{3}{2}$

7. $\dfrac{x^2(x^2+1)}{x^2} = x^2 + 1$

8. $\dfrac{x^8(x^2+x+1)y^4(y+1)}{y^4(x^2+x+1)} = x^8(y+1)$

9. $\dfrac{1}{7}$

10. $5^{-3} = \dfrac{1}{5^3} = \dfrac{1}{125}$

11. $\dfrac{x^{-8}}{x^{-4}} = x^{-4} = \dfrac{1}{x^4}$

12. $\sqrt{5}$

13. $\dfrac{1}{5^{\frac{1}{2}}} = \dfrac{1}{\sqrt{5}}$

14. $\dfrac{1}{7^{\frac{11}{3}}} = \dfrac{1}{\sqrt[3]{7^{11}}}$

15. $\dfrac{x^{-\frac{7}{2}}}{x^{-\frac{4}{3}}} = x^{-\frac{13}{6}} = \dfrac{1}{x^{\frac{13}{6}}} = \dfrac{1}{\sqrt[6]{x^{13}}}$

Logarithms

The word **"logarithm"** just means "exponent." For example, in the exponential equation $9 = 3^2$, the logarithm is 2. The number 3 is called the **base**. We say "2 is the logarithm of 9 when we use a base of 3," and abbreviate this as $2 = \log_3 9$. More generally, the following two equations are equivalent: $y = a^x$ and $x = \log_a y$

Laws of Logarithms

Law	Example
$\log_b 1 = 0$	$\log_2 1 = 0$
$\log_b b = 1$	$\log_6 6 = 1$
$\log_b x + \log_b y = \log_b(xy)$	$\log_5 7 + \log_5 2 = \log_5 14$
$\log_b x - \log_b y = \log_b(\frac{x}{y})$	$\log_3 21 - \log_3 7 = \log_3 3 = 1$
$\log_b x^n = n\log_b x$	$\log_8 3^5 = 5\log_8 3$

Now let's practice. Simplify the following expressions using the basic laws of logarithms. Assume all unknowns are positive.

1. $\log_2 8$

2. $\log_4 2$

3. $\log_5 \dfrac{1}{25}$

4. $\log_b \dfrac{b^2}{b^7}$

5. $\log 10^3$

6. $\log_4 2 + \log_4 8$

7. $\log_{xy} x^2 + \log_{xy} y^2$

8. $\dfrac{1}{b}\log_a a^b$

9. $\log_5 x - \log_5 \dfrac{x}{\sqrt{5}}$

Answers

1. 3 (because $2^3 = 8$)
2. $\frac{1}{2}$ (because $4^{\frac{1}{2}} = \sqrt{4} = 2$)
3. -2 (because $5^{-2} = \frac{1}{25}$)
4. $\log_b b^{2-7} = \log_b b^{-5} = -5$
5. $3 \log 10 = 3$ (**Note:** $\log x = \log_{10} x$)
6. $\log_4(2 \cdot 8) = \log_4 16 = 2$
7. $\log_{xy}(x^2 y^2) = \log_{xy}(xy)^2 = 2 \log_{xy} xy = 2$
8. $\log_a\left(a^b\right)^{\frac{1}{b}} = \log_a a^{b \cdot \frac{1}{b}} = \log_a a = 1$
9. $\log_5\left(x \div \frac{x}{\sqrt{5}}\right) = \log_5\left(x \cdot \frac{\sqrt{5}}{x}\right) = \log_5 \sqrt{5} = \log_5 5^{\frac{1}{2}} = \frac{1}{2}\log_5 5 = \frac{1}{2}$

Now try to solve each of the following problems. The answers to these problems, followed by full solutions are at the end of this lesson. **Do not** look at the answers until you have attempted these problems yourself. Please remember to mark off any problems you get wrong.

LEVEL 1: ALGEBRA

1. $7y^{11} \cdot 4y^{11}$ is equivalent to:

   A. $11y^{22}$
   B. $11y^{121}$
   C. $28y^{11}$
   D. $28y^{22}$
   E. $28y^{121}$

LEVEL 3: ALGEBRA

2. If $7^x = 6$, then $7^{3x} =$

   F. 2
   G. 9
   H. 18
   J. 36
   K. 216

3. Which of the following expressions is equivalent to $\frac{(2y)^3}{y^7}$?

    A. $\frac{2}{y^4}$

    B. $\frac{6}{y^4}$

    C. $\frac{8}{y^4}$

    D. $2y^{10}$

    E. $6y^{10}$

LEVEL 4: ALGEBRA AND FUNCTIONS

4. For all $x > 0$, which of the following expressions is equivalent to $\log\left((6x)^{\frac{1}{3}}\right)$?

    F. $\log 2x$

    G. $\log 2 + \log\frac{x}{3}$

    H. $\log 6 + \frac{1}{3}\log x$

    J. $\frac{1}{3}\log 6 + \frac{1}{3}\log x$

    K. $\frac{1}{3}(\log 6)(\log x)$

$$\sqrt[3]{x^{15}} = x^5$$

5. What are the real number values of x that make the above equation true?

    A. $x < 0$

    B. $x > 0$

    C. $x \le 0$

    D. $x \ge 0$

    E. All real numbers

6. If k and r are positive rational numbers such that $k^{5r} = 4$, then $k^{15r} = ?$

    F. 8

    G. 12

    H. 16

    J. 60

    K. 64

7. For what real value of z is $\dfrac{5^7 5^z}{(5^7)^6} = \dfrac{1}{125}$ true?

    A. 6
    B. 7
    C. 25
    D. 32
    E. 35

8. Let a and b be nonzero real numbers such that $3^{a+2} = 9b$. Which of the following is an expression for 3^{a+5} in terms of b ?

    F. $\dfrac{1}{54b^3}$
    G. $\dfrac{1}{27b}$
    H. b^5
    J. $3^2 b^3$
    K. $3^5 b$

9. For how many rational numbers q is the equation $7^{5q+2} = 49^{q-3}$ true?

    A. 0
    B. 1
    C. 2
    D. 3
    E. An infinite number

10. For all positive real numbers r, which of the following expressions is equivalent to $\dfrac{\left(\dfrac{x^{32}}{x^8}\right)}{\left(\dfrac{1}{x^3}\right)}$?

    F. $\sqrt[3]{x^4}$
    G. x^{12}
    H. x^{21}
    J. x^{24}
    K. x^{27}

184

LEVEL 5: ALGEBRA

11. Whenever x and y are positive numbers such that $\frac{1}{\sqrt{5}^x} = 25^y$, what is the value of $\frac{y}{x}$?

      A. $-\frac{1}{4}$

      B. -2

      C. -4

      D. 1

      E. 4

12. For what real value of x, if any, is $\log_{(x+5)}(x^2 + 5) = 2$?

      F. -3

      G. -2

      H. -1

      J. 0

      K. There is no such value of x.

Answers

1. D	5. E	9. B
2. K	6. K	10. K
3. C	7. D	11. A
4. J	8. K	12. G

Full Solutions

2.

* **Algebraic solution:** $7^{3x} = (7x)^3 = 63 = 216$, choice **K**.

Solution by estimating: When $x = 1$, $7^x = 7^1 = 7$ which is close to 6. So the answer should be close to $7^{3x} = 7^{3\cdot1} = 7^3 = 343$. Therefore, the most likely answer is 216, choice **K**.

Note: We can use our calculator to get a better estimate for x by taking guesses that are a little less than 1. By trial and error, we see that $7^{0.92} \approx 5.99$. We then have $7^{3x} \approx 215$. So clearly the answer is 216, choice **K**.

3.

* $\frac{(2y)^3}{y^7} = \frac{2^3 \cdot y^3}{y^7} = \frac{2^3}{y^{7-3}} = \frac{8}{y^4}$, choice **C**.

4.

* $\log\left((6x)^{\frac{1}{3}}\right) = \frac{1}{3}\log(6x) = \frac{1}{3}[\log 6 + \log x] = \frac{1}{3}\log 6 + \frac{1}{3}\log x$. This is choice **J**.

5.

* $\sqrt[3]{x^{15}} = x^{\frac{15}{3}} = x^5$. It follows that the given equation is true for all real x, choice **E**.

Note: We can also solve this problem by picking numbers. If we try a positive value, a negative value, and zero for x, we will see that they all make the given equation true. Thus, the answer must be **E**.

6.

* **Solution using laws of exponents:** $k^{15r} = k^{5r \cdot 3} = (k^{5r})^3 = 4^3 = 64$, choice **K**.

Solution using logarithms (not recommended): Taking the logarithm base k of each side of the first equation gives $\log_k k^{5r} = \log_k 4$, or equivalently, $5r = \log_k 4$. So $r = \frac{1}{5}\log_k 4$.

Now, $k^{15r} = k^{15 \cdot \frac{1}{5}\log_k 4} = k^{3\log_k 4} = k^{\log_k 4^3} = 4^3 = 64$, choice **K**.

7.

* $\frac{5^7 5^z}{(5^7)^6} = \frac{5^{7+z}}{5^{7 \cdot 6}} = \frac{5^{7+z}}{5^{42}} = 5^{7+z-42} = 5^{z-35}$ and $\frac{1}{125} = \frac{1}{5^3} = 5^{-3}$. So we have $5^{z-35} = 5^{-3}$, and therefore, $z - 35 = -3$. So $z = -3 + 35 = 32$, choice **D**.

8.

* $3^{a+5} = 3^{a+2+3} = 3^{a+2} \cdot 3^3 = 9b \cdot 3^3 = 3^2 b \cdot 3^3 = 3^{2+3} b = 3^5 b$.

This is choice **K**.

Note: This problem can also be solved by picking numbers. I leave this solution to the reader.

9.

* $49^{q-3} = (7^2)^{q-3} = 7^{2q-6}$. So $5q + 2 = 2q - 6$, and therefore we have $3q = -8$. So $q = -\frac{8}{3}$ is the only solution to the given equation. Since $-\frac{8}{3}$ is a rational number, the answer is 1, choice **B**.

10.

* **Algebraic solution:**

$$\frac{\left(\frac{x^{32}}{x^8}\right)}{\left(\frac{1}{x^3}\right)} = \left(\frac{x^{32}}{x^8}\right)\left(\frac{x^3}{1}\right) = \frac{x^{32}x^3}{x^8} = x^{32+3-8} = x^{27}$$

This is choice **K**.

Note: This problem can also be solved by picking numbers. I leave this solution to the reader.

11.

Solution by picking numbers: If we let $x = -4$ and $y = 1$, then the equation reduces to $25 = 25$ which is true, and $\frac{y}{x} = \frac{1}{-4} = -\frac{1}{4}$, choice **A**.

Note: We can choose any values for x and y that make the equation true. We will get the same answer.

* **Algebraic solution:** $\frac{1}{\sqrt{5}^x} = \frac{1}{5^{\frac{x}{2}}} = 5^{-\frac{x}{2}}$ and $25^y = (5^2)^y = 5^{2y}$. So we have $5^{-\frac{x}{2}} = 5^{2y}$, and therefore, $-\frac{x}{2} = 2y$. We multiply each side of this last equation by 2 to get $-x = 4y$.

Finally, we **cross divide** to get $\frac{y}{x} = -\frac{1}{4}$, choice **A**.

12.

* **Solution by starting with choice H:** Let's start with choice H and guess that $x = -1$. Then $\log_{(x+5)}(x^2 + 5) = \log_4 6 \neq 2$. So we can eliminate choice H.

Let's try G next, and guess that $x = -2$. In this case, we have $\log_{(x+5)}(x^2 + 5) = \log_3 9 = 2$. This is correct, and so the answer is **G**.

Algebraic solution: $\log_{(x+5)}(x^2 + 5) = 2$ is equivalent to the equation $x^2 + 5 = (x + 5)^2 = x^2 + 10x + 25$. Cancelling x^2 from each side yields $5 = 10x + 25$. So $10x = 5 - 25 = -20$, and so $x = -\frac{20}{10} = -2$, choice **G**.

187

Note: After solving an equation involving logarithms, it is important that you check all potential solutions back into the original equation. In this case, the check that -2 is an actual solution (as opposed to an **extraneous** solution) was performed in the first solution above.

OPTIONAL MATERIAL

CHALLENGE QUESTION

1. Let the function h be defined by $h(x) = x^3 + 12$. If c is a positive number such that $h(c^2) = h(3d)$ and $d = \sqrt{c}$, what is the value of $c^{\frac{3}{2}}$?

Solution

1.

*

$h(c^2) = (c^2)^3 + 12 = c^6 + 12$ and $h(3d) = (3d)^3 + 12 = 27d^3 + 12$.

So we have $c^6 + 12 = 27d^3 + 12$, and so $\dfrac{c^6}{d^3} = 27$. Substituting $c^{\frac{1}{2}}$ for d, we have $\dfrac{c^6}{c^{\frac{3}{2}}} = 27$. Now $\dfrac{c^6}{c^{\frac{3}{2}}} = c^{6-\frac{3}{2}} = c^{\frac{9}{2}}$. So $c^{\frac{9}{2}} = 27$. Now let's raise each side of this equation to the $\dfrac{1}{3}$ power. So $\left(c^{\frac{9}{2}}\right)^{\frac{1}{3}} = 27^{\frac{1}{3}}$, and finally, $c^{\frac{3}{2}} = 3$.

Download additional solutions for free here:

www.satprepget800.com/28LesAdv

LESSON 15
GEOMETRY

Reminder: Before beginning this lesson remember to redo the problems from Lessons 3, 7 and 11 that you have marked off. Do not "unmark" a question unless you get it correct.

Move the Sides of a Figure Around

Try to answer the following question using this strategy. **Do not** check the solution until you have attempted this question yourself.

LEVEL 4: GEOMETRY

1. Let P be the perimeter of the figure below in meters, and let A be the area of the figure below in square meters. What is the value of $P + A$?

    A. 25
    B. 30
    C. 35
    D. 40
    E. 45

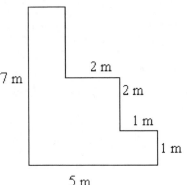

Solution

* Recall that to compute the **perimeter** of the figure we need to add up the lengths of all 8 line segments in the figure. We "move" the two smaller horizontal segments up and the two smaller vertical segments to the right as shown below.

189

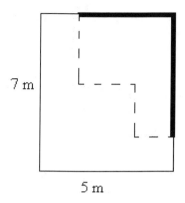

5 m

Note that the "bold" length is equal to the "dashed" length. Thus, the perimeter is

$$P = (2)(7) + (2)(5) = 14 + 10 = \textbf{24 m}.$$

To compute the **area** of the figure we break the figure up into 3 rectangles and compute the length and width of each rectangle.

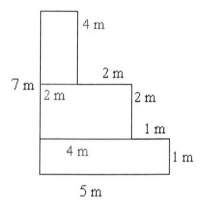

5 m

The length and width of the bottom rectangle are 5 and 1 making the area $5 \cdot 1 = 5\ m^2$. The length of the middle rectangle is $5 - 1 = 4$, and the width is given as 2. So the area is $4 \cdot 2 = 8\ m^2$. The length of the top rectangle is $4 - 2 = 2$, and the width of that rectangle is $7 - 1 - 2 = 4$ Thus, the area is $2 \cdot 4 = 8\ m^2$. We then get the total area by adding up the areas of the three rectangles: $A = 5 + 8 + 8 = \textbf{21 m}^2$.

Finally, $P + A = 24 + 21 = 45$, choice **E**.

Remark: Notice that if we have the full length of a line segment, and one partial length of the same line segment, then we get the other partial length by subtracting the two given lengths.

Areas of Shaded Regions

Finding the area of a shaded region often involves subtracting two areas.

Try to answer the following question using this strategy. **Do not** check the solution until you have attempted this question yourself.

LEVEL 4: GEOMETRY

2. In the figure below, AB is a diameter of the circle with center O and $ABCD$ is a square. What is the area of the shaded region if the radius of the circle is 5?

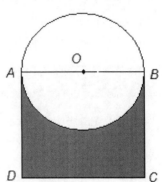

   F. $25(4 - \frac{\pi}{2})$

   G. $25(2 - \frac{\pi}{2})$

   H. $\pi(4 - \pi)$

   J. $\pi(2 - \pi)$

   K. $\pi(1 - \pi)$

Solution

* A side of the square has length $s = 2r = 2 \cdot 5 = 10$. The area of the square is then $s^2 = 10^2 = 100$.

The area of the circle is $\pi r^2 = \pi(5)^2 = 25\pi$. The area of the semicircle is then $\frac{25\pi}{2}$. The area of the shaded region is

$$\text{Area of Square} - \text{Area of Semicircle}$$
$$100 - \frac{25\pi}{2}$$
$$25(4 - \frac{\pi}{2})$$

Thus, the answer is choice **F**.

191

Note: As an alternative to factoring in the last step we can do the computation $100 - \frac{25\pi}{2}$ in the calculator to get **60.73009183**. We then do the same with the answer choices until we get one that matches up. We would then see that choice F gives the same answer. Of course, this would be more time consuming, but it is better to be safe if you are not good at factoring, or you simply do not see that you need to factor.

Fitting Geometric Objects Inside Another Object

To see how many two-dimensional objects fit inside another two-dimensional object we divide areas. To see how many three-dimensional objects fit inside another three-dimensional object we divide volumes.

Try to answer the following question using this strategy. **Do not** check the solution until you have attempted this question yourself.

LEVEL 4: GEOMETRY

3. Rectangular bricks measuring $\frac{1}{2}$ meter by $\frac{1}{3}$ meter are sold in boxes containing 8 bricks each. What is the least number of boxes of bricks needed to cover a rectangular area that has dimensions 9 meters by 11 meters?

    A.   3
    B.   17
    C.   75
    D.   132
    E.   4752

Solution

* The area of a face of one rectangular brick is $(\frac{1}{2})(\frac{1}{3}) = \frac{1}{6}$. The area of the rectangular region we want to cover is $9 \cdot 11 = 99$. We can see how many bricks we need to cover this area by dividing the two areas.

$$99 \div (\tfrac{1}{6}) = 99 \cdot 6 = 594.$$

Now, $\frac{594}{8} = 74.25$. So the number of boxes needed is 75, choice **C**.

Remark: A common error would be to round 74.25 to 74. This is incorrect because 74 boxes will not contain enough bricks to cover the entire area. Indeed, $8(74) = 592 < 594$.

Surface Area of a Rectangular Solid

The **surface area of a rectangular solid** is just the sum of the areas of all 6 faces. The formula is

$$A = 2lw + 2lh + 2wh$$

where l, w and h are the length, width and height of the rectangular solid, respectively.

In particular, the **surface area of a cube** is

$$A = 6s^2$$

where s is the length of a side of the cube.

Try to answer the following question about the surface area of a cube. **Do not** check the solution until you have attempted this question yourself.

LEVEL 4: GEOMETRY

4. In the figure below, segment $\overline{AB}$ joins two vertices of the cube. If the length of $\overline{AB}$ is $3\sqrt{2}$, what is the surface area of the cube?

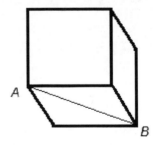

    F. 27
    G. 54
    H. 56
    J. 72
    K. 81

Solution

* The area of one of the faces is $s^2 = 9$ (see below for several methods of computing this). Thus, the surface area is $A = 6s^2 = 6 \cdot 9 = 54$, choice **G**.

193

Methods for computing the area of a face:

(1) Since all sides of a square have equal length, an isosceles right triangle is formed. An isosceles right triangle is the same as a 45, 45, 90 triangle. So we can get the length of a side of the triangle just by looking at the formula for a 45, 45, 90 right triangle. Here s is 3. The area of the square is then $3 \cdot 3 = 9$.

(2) If we let s be the length of a side of the square, then by the Pythagorean Theorem

$$s^2 + s^2 = \left(3\sqrt{2}\right)^2$$
$$2s^2 = 18$$
$$s^2 = 9$$

(3) The area of a square is $A = \dfrac{d^2}{2}$ where d is the length of the diagonal of the square. Therefore, in this problem

$$A = \frac{d^2}{2} = \frac{\left(3\sqrt{2}\right)^2}{2} = \frac{18}{2} = 9.$$

You're doing great! Let's just practice a bit more. Try to solve each of the following problems. The answers to these problems, followed by full solutions are at the end of this lesson. **Do not** look at the answers until you have attempted these problems yourself. Please remember to mark off any problems you get wrong.

LEVEL 3: GEOMETRY

5. How many spherical snowballs with a radius of 4 centimeters can be made with the amount of snow in a spherical snowball of radius 8 centimeters? (the volume V of a sphere with radius r is given by $\frac{4}{3}\pi r^3$.)

   A. 4
   B. 8
   C. 4π
   D. 8π
   E. 12

194

6. How many figures of the size and shape below are needed to completely cover a rectangle measuring 80 inches by 30 inches?

F. 37
G. 330
H. 700
J. 740
K. 800

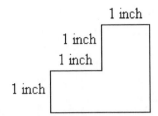

LEVEL 4: GEOMETRY

7. Cube X has surface area A. The edges of cube Y are 4 times as long as the edges of cube X. What is the surface area of cube Y in terms of A?

A. $2A$
B. $4A$
C. $8A$
D. $16A$
E. $64A$

8. If a 2-centimeter cube were cut in half in all three directions, then in square centimeters, the total surface area of the separated smaller cubes would be how much greater than the surface area of the original 2-centimeter cube?

F. 0
G. 12
H. 24
J. 36
K. 48

195

LEVEL 5: GEOMETRY

9. For any cube, if the volume is V cubic centimeters and the surface area is S square centimeters, then S is directly proportional to V^n for $n =$

    A. $\dfrac{1}{2}$

    B. $\dfrac{2}{3}$

    C. $\dfrac{3}{2}$

    D. 2

    E. 3

10. $\overline{AB}$, $\overline{BC}$, and $\overline{AC}$ are diameters of the three circles shown below. If $BC = 4$ and $AB = 5BC$, what is the area of the shaded region?

    F. 48π
    G. 24π
    H. 12π
    J. 6π
    K. 3π

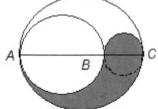

11. How many solid wood cubes, each with a total surface area of 294 square centimeters, can be cut from a solid wood cube with a total surface area of 2,646 square centimeters if no wood is lost in the cutting?

    A. 3
    B. 9
    C. 27
    D. 81
    E. 243

196

12. In the figure below, $AB = 4$, $BC = 24$, and $AD = 26$. What is the length of line segment $\overline{CD}$?

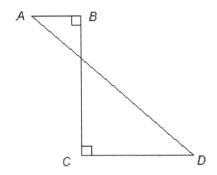

F. 3
G. 4
H. 5
J. 6
K. 7

Answers

1. E	5. B	9. B
2. F	6. K	10. G
3. C	7. D	11. C
4. G	8. H	12. J

Full Solutions

5.

* Solution by dividing volumes:

$$\frac{\frac{4}{3}\pi \cdot 8^3}{\frac{4}{3}\pi \cdot 4^3} = \frac{8^3}{4^3} = \frac{512}{64} = 8, \text{ choice } \textbf{B}.$$

6.

* Solution by dividing areas: The area of the given figure is 3 inches^2 and the area of the rectangle is $80 \cdot 30 = 400$ inches^2. We can see how many of the given figures cover the rectangle by dividing the two areas.

$$\frac{2400}{3} = 800, \text{ choice } \textbf{K}.$$

Note: We can get the area of the given figure by splitting it into 3 squares each with area 1 inch^2 as shown to the right. Then

$$1 + 1 + 1 = 3.$$

1 inch

1 inch

1 inch

1 inch

7.

Solution by picking numbers: Let's choose a value for the length of an edge of cube X, say $s = 1$. It follows that the surface area of X is $A = 6s^2 = 6(1)^2 = 6$. The length of an edge of cube Y is $4(1) = 4$, and so the surface area of Y is $6(4)^2 = 6 \cdot 16 = \mathbf{96}$. Now we plug in $A = 6$ into each answer choice and eliminate any choice that does not come out to 96.

    A. 12
    B. 24
    C. 48
    D. 96
    E. 384

Since A, B, C, and E all came out incorrect we can eliminate them. Therefore, the answer is choice **D**.

* Algebraic solution: Let s be the length of an edge of cube X. Then we have $A = 6s^2$. Since an edge of cube Y is 4 times the length of an edge of cube X, the length of an edge of cube Y is $4s$, so that the surface area of cube Y is $6(4s)^2 = 6 \cdot 16s^2 = 16(6s^2) = 16A$, choice **D**.

8.
* The surface area of the 2-centimeter cube is $6(2)^2 = 6(4) = 24$. The surface area of each 1-centimeter cube is $6(1)^2 = 6(1) = 6$. Now, there are 8 of these smaller cubes so that the total surface area of the smaller cubes is $8(6) = 48$. So the answer is $48 - 24 = 24$, choice **H**.

9.
Solution by picking numbers: Let's choose a value for the length of a side of the cube, say $s = 1$. Then $S = 6(1)^2 = 6$ and $V = 1^3 = 1$.

Now let's try $s = 2$. Then we have $S = 6(2)^2 = 6(4) = 24$ and $V = 2^3 = 8$. We need

$$\frac{6}{1^n} = \frac{24}{8^n}$$

Cross multiplying gives us $6 \cdot 8^n = 24 \cdot 1^n = 24$, or equivalently $8^n = 4$. To solve this equation let's write $8 = 2^3$ and $4 = 2^2$. So we have $(2^3)^n = 2^2$, or equivalently $2^{3n} = 2^2$. Since the bases are the same we can set the exponents equal to each other. So $3n = 2$, and $n = \frac{2}{3}$, choice **B**.

* **Algebraic solution:** If s is the length of a side of the cube, then we have $S = 6s^2$ and $V = s^3$. Solving the second equation for s, we have $s = V^{\frac{1}{3}}$. Therefore, $S = 6\left(V^{\frac{1}{3}}\right)^2 = 6V^{\frac{2}{3}}$. So S is directly proportional to $V^{\frac{2}{3}}$ (with constant of proportionality 6). So $n = \frac{2}{3}$, choice **B**.

10.

* We first find the radius of each of the three circles. The diameter of the small circle is 4, and so its radius is 2. The diameter of the medium-sized circle is $5 \cdot 4 = 20$, and so its radius is 10. The diameter of the largest circle is $20 + 4 = 24$, and so its radius is 12. We can now find the area of the shaded region as follows.

$$A = \tfrac{1}{2}(\text{Area of big circle}) - \tfrac{1}{2}(\text{Area of medium circle}) + \tfrac{1}{2}(\text{Area of small circle})$$
$$= \frac{1}{2}(\pi \cdot 12^2) - \frac{1}{2}(\pi \cdot 10^2) + \frac{1}{2}(\pi \cdot 2^2)$$
$$= \frac{1}{2}(\pi \cdot 144) - \frac{1}{2}(\pi \cdot 100) + \frac{1}{2}(\pi \cdot 4)$$
$$= \frac{1}{2} \cdot 48\pi$$
$$= 24\pi$$

Thus, the answer is choice **G**.

11.

* **Solution by dividing volumes:** We first find the length of a side of each cube.

$$6s^2 = 294 \quad \text{and} \quad 6s^2 = 2646$$
$$s^2 = 49 \qquad\qquad s^2 = 441$$
$$s = 7 \qquad\qquad\quad s = 21$$

Thus, the volume of each cube is $7^3 = 343$ and $21^3 = 9261$, respectively. We can see how many smaller cubes can be cut from the larger cube by dividing the two volumes: $\frac{9261}{343} = 27$, choice **C**.

12.

* **Solution by moving the sides of the figure around:** The problem becomes much simpler if we "move" $\overline{BC}$ to the left and $\overline{AB}$ to the bottom as shown below.

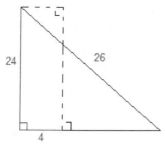

We now have a single right triangle and we can either use the Pythagorean Theorem, or better yet notice that $26 = (13)(2)$ and $24 = (12)(2)$. Thus, the other leg of the triangle is $(5)(2) = 10$. So we see that $\overline{CD}$ must have length $10 - 4 = \mathbf{6}$.

Remark: If we didn't notice that this was a multiple of a $5 - 12 - 13$ triangle, then we would use the Pythagorean Theorem as follows.

$$(x + 4)^2 + 24^2 = 26^2$$
$$(x + 4)^2 + 576 = 676$$
$$(x + 4)^2 = 100$$
$$x + 4 = 10$$
$$x = \mathbf{6}$$

This is choice **J**.

Download additional solutions for free here:

www.satprepget800.com/28LesAdv

LESSON 16
PROBABILITY

Reminder: Before beginning this lesson remember to redo the problems from Lessons 4, 8 and 12 that you have marked off. Do not "unmark" a question unless you get it correct.

Simple Probability Principle

To compute a simple probability where all outcomes are equally likely, divide the number of "successes" by the total number of outcomes.

Try to answer the following question using the simple probability principle. **Do not** check the solution until you have attempted this question yourself.

LEVEL 4: PROBABILITY

1. If one of the positive factors of 60 is to be chosen at random, what is the probability that the chosen factor will NOT be a multiple of 15?

    A. $\frac{1}{4}$
    B. $\frac{1}{3}$
    C. $\frac{7}{12}$
    D. $\frac{3}{4}$
    E. $\frac{5}{6}$

Solution

* Let's begin by listing all the positive factors of 60.

$$1, 2, 3, 4, 5, 6, 10, 12, 15, 20, 30, 60$$

The total number of factors is 12. Of these, 9 are **not** multiples of 15. By the simple probability principle, the probability is $\frac{9}{12} = \frac{3}{4}$, choice **D**.

Note: Since factors come in pairs, it is not too difficult to ensure that we have listed them all. The factor pairs in this example are 1 and 60, 2 and 30, 3 and 20, 4 and 15, 5 and 12, and 6 and 10.

Now try to solve each of the following problems. The answers to these problems, followed by full solutions are at the end of this lesson. **Do not** look at the answers until you have attempted these problems yourself. Please remember to mark off any problems you get wrong.

LEVEL 1: PROBABILITY

2. In a jar there are exactly 72 marbles, each of which is yellow, purple, or blue. The probability of randomly selecting a yellow marble from the jar is $\frac{5}{9}$ and the probability of randomly selecting a purple marble from the jar is $\frac{3}{9}$. How many marbles in the jar are blue?

    F. 8
    G. 24
    H. 32
    J. 40
    K. 64

LEVEL 2: PROBABILITY

3. Of the marbles in a jar, 21 are red. Joseph randomly takes one marble out of the jar. If the probability is $\frac{7}{15}$ that the marble he chooses is red, how many marbles are in the jar?

    A. 32
    B. 45
    C. 47
    D. 53
    E. 55

LEVEL 3: PROBABILITY

4. Shown below, a circular board with a spinner has 3 regions (white, black, and grey) whose areas are in the ratio of $1:3:4$, repectively. The spinner is spun and it lands in one of the three regions at random. What is the probability that the region it lands in is NOT the black region?

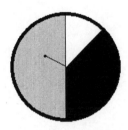

F. $\dfrac{1}{8}$

G. $\dfrac{3}{8}$

H. $\dfrac{1}{2}$

J. $\dfrac{5}{8}$

K. $\dfrac{7}{8}$

LEVEL 4: PROBABILITY

5. Jennifer has 7 shirts and 7 pairs of shoes, and each shirt matches a different pair of shoes. If she chooses one of these shirts and one pair of shoes at random, what is the probability that they will <u>not</u> match?

A. $\dfrac{1}{7}$

B. $\dfrac{5}{7}$

C. $\dfrac{6}{7}$

D. $\dfrac{1}{49}$

E. $\dfrac{48}{49}$

203

6. A jar contains a number of gems of which 75 are blue, 19 are red, and the remainder are white. If the probability of picking a white gem from this jar at random is $\frac{1}{3}$, how many white gems are in the jar?

    F.   6
    G. 25
    H. 32
    J.   47
    K. 63

7. The x- and y-coordinates of point A are each to be chosen at random from the set of integers -2 through 10. What is the probability that A will be in quadrant III?

    A. $\frac{4}{13}$
    B. $\frac{5}{13}$
    C. $\frac{4}{169}$
    D. $\frac{7}{169}$
    E. $\frac{20}{169}$

8. A set of numbers consists of the even integers that are greater than 50 and less than 100. What is the probability that a number picked at random from the set will be divisible by 8 ?

    F. $\frac{1}{4}$
    G. $\frac{1}{3}$
    H. $\frac{7}{12}$
    J. $\frac{3}{8}$
    K. $\frac{3}{4}$

204

9. Exactly 5 musicians try out to play 5 different instruments for a particular performance. If each musician can play each of the 5 instruments, and each musician is assigned an instrument, what is the probability that Gary will play the piano?

A. $\dfrac{1}{5}$

B. $\dfrac{3}{5}$

C. $\dfrac{1}{25}$

D. $\dfrac{2}{25}$

E. $\dfrac{4}{25}$

LEVEL 5: PROBABILITY

10. Suppose that x will be randomly selected from the set $\{-\dfrac{3}{2}, -1, -\dfrac{1}{2}, 0, \dfrac{5}{2}\}$ and that y will be randomly selected from the set $\{-\dfrac{3}{4}, -\dfrac{1}{4}, 2, \dfrac{11}{4}\}$. What is the probability that $\dfrac{x}{y} < 0$?

F. $\dfrac{1}{100}$

G. $\dfrac{1}{20}$

H. $\dfrac{3}{20}$

J. $\dfrac{1}{3}$

K. $\dfrac{2}{5}$

205

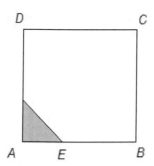

11. In the figure above, $ABCD$ is a square, the triangle is isosceles, $EB = 10 - 2c$, and $AD = 10$. A point in square $ABCD$ is to be chosen at random. If the probability that the point will be in the shaded triangle is $\frac{2}{25}$, what is the value of c?

   A. 1
   B. 2
   C. 3
   D. 4
   E. 5

12. A jar contains 1 black marble, 3 white marbles, and 4 yellow marbles. A marble is drawn at random and returned to the jar, then a second marble is drawn at random. What is the probability that the first marble is yellow and the second marble is black?

   F. $\frac{1}{16}$
   G. $\frac{1}{5}$
   H. $\frac{1}{4}$
   J. $\frac{3}{4}$
   K. $\frac{5}{6}$

Answers

1. D	5. C	9. A
2. F	6. J	10. K
3. B	7. C	11. B
4. J	8. F	12. F

206

Full Solutions

4.

Algebraic solution: If we let the area of the white region be x, then the area of the black region is $3x$, and the area of the grey region is $4x$.

The total is then $x + 3x + 4x = 8x$ and the "successes" is $x + 4x = 5x$.

By the simple probability principle, the desired probability is $\frac{5x}{8x} = \frac{5}{8}$, choice **J**.

* Quick solution: $\frac{1+4}{1+3+4} = \frac{5}{8}$, choice **J**.

5.

* By the counting principle there are $(7)(7) = 49$ shirt/shoe combinations. 7 of these combinations are matching. Therefore, there are $49 - 7 = 42$ nonmatching combinations. So the probability the shirt and shoes will not match is $\frac{42}{49} = \frac{6}{7}$, choice **C**.

6.

* Quick solution: There are $75 + 19 = 94$ gems that are not white. Also we have that $1 - \frac{1}{3} = \frac{2}{3}$ of the gems are not white. It follows that $\frac{2}{3}$ of the total number of gems is 94. So $\frac{1}{3}$ of the total number of gems is $\frac{94}{2} = 47$, choice **J**.

Algebraic solution: Let x be the total number of gems. Then we have $\frac{2}{3}x = 75 + 19 = 94$. So $x = 94(\frac{3}{2}) = 141$. The number of white gems is then $(\frac{1}{3})(141) = 47$, choice **J**.

Remark: Instead of solving for x, and then multiplying by $\frac{1}{3}$, we can solve for $\frac{x}{3}$ right away. Once we have $\frac{2}{3}x = 94$, simply divide each side of this equation by 2 to get $\frac{1}{3}x = 47$.

7.

* There are 13 integers from -2 through 10 (see note below). By the counting principle, there are $13 \cdot 13 = 169$ points in total. For a point to be in quadrant III both coordinates must be negative. There are 4 possibilities: $(-1, -1)$, $(-1, -2)$, $(-2, -1)$, $(-2, -2)$. So the desired probability is $\frac{4}{169}$, choice **C**.

207

Note: There are several ways to count the integers from -2 through 10.

(1) List them: $-2, -1, 0, 1, 2, 3, 4, 5, 6, 7, 8, 9, 10$.

(2) Note that there are 10 integers from 1 through 10, 2 integers from -2 to -1, and add one more for 0.

(3) Use the **fence-post formula** to get $10 - (-2) + 1 = 13$ (see Lesson 13).

8.

* The number of even integers greater than 50 and less than 100 is 24, and the number of these integers that is divisible by 8 is 6. So the desired probability is $\frac{6}{24} = \frac{1}{4}$, choice **F**.

Notes: (1) We can simply list the even integers greater than 50 and less than 100:

$$52, 54, \mathbf{56}, 58, 60$$
$$62, \mathbf{64}, 66, 68, 70$$
$$\mathbf{72}, 74, 76, 78, \mathbf{80}$$
$$82, 84, 86, \mathbf{88}, 90$$
$$92, 94, \mathbf{96}, 98$$

Observe that there are $5 \cdot 4 + 4 = 20 + 4 = 24$ integers in the list.

(2) In the list in note (1), the bold numbers are the integers from the list that are divisible by 8. Observe that there are 6 of them.

(3) We get the answer to the question by using notes (1) and (2), and the simple probability principle.

9.

* The number of possible assignments is $_5P_5 = 5! = 120$. The number of assignments which have Gary playing the piano is $_4P_4 = 4! = 24$. So the probability that Gary will play the piano is $\frac{24}{120} = \frac{1}{5}$, choice **A**.

10.

* There are 5 possible values for x and 4 possible values for y. By the counting principle, there are $5 \cdot 4 = 20$ possibilities for xy (possibly with some repetition).

In order for $\frac{x}{y} < 0$ to be true, x and y need to be opposite in sign. The number of ways for this to happen (possibly with repetition) is

$$3 \cdot 2 + 1 \cdot 2 = 6 + 2 = 8$$

So the desired probability is $\frac{8}{20} = \frac{2}{5}$, choice **K**.

Notes: (1) In this question when we mention the possibilities for xy, we are ignoring the fact that there could be repeated values. For example, we have $(0)\left(-\frac{3}{4}\right) = 0$ and $(0)\left(-\frac{1}{4}\right) = 0$. Technically these two computations give a single value for xy. Nonetheless, to compute the desired probability we need to think of these as distinct possibilities.

(2) There are 3 negative values for x and 2 positive values for y. This gives us $3 \cdot 2 = 6$ negative values for xy.

There is 1 positive value for x and 2 negative values for y. This gives us $1 \cdot 2 = 2$ more negative values for xy.

So altogether there are $6 + 2 = 8$ possibilities that lead to a negative value for xy.

11.
* $AE = 10 - (10 - 2c) = 10 - 10 + 2c = 2c$. So the area of the triangle is

$$\left(\tfrac{1}{2}\right)(2c)(2c) = 2c^2.$$

The area of the square is $10 \cdot 10 = 100$. Thus, the probability of choosing a point in the triangle is $\frac{2c^2}{100} = \frac{c^2}{50}$. We are given that this is equal to $\frac{2}{25}$. We cross multiply and divide to get $25c^2 = 100$. So $c^2 = 4$, and thus, $c = 2$, choice **B**.

12.
* There are a total of $1 + 3 + 4 = 8$ marbles in the jar. By the counting principle, the number of ways to draw a marble, replace it, and draw a second marble is $8 \cdot 8 = 64$.

The number of ways that the first marble is yellow and the second marble is black is (again by the counting principle) $4 \cdot 1 = 4$.

By the simple probability principle, the desired probability is $\frac{4}{64} = \frac{1}{16}$, choice **F**.

OPTIONAL MATERIAL

CHALLENGE QUESTION

1. If 2 real numbers are randomly chosen from a line segment of length 10, what is the probability that the distance between them is at least 7?

Solution

We may assume that the two real numbers, a and b, are chosen to be between 0 and 10. Consider the following picture.

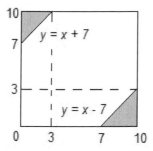

Note that we are trying to compute the probability that $|a - b| \geq 7$. This is equivalent to the two inequalities $a - b \leq -7$ and $a - b \geq 7$. Solving each of these inequalities for b gives $b \geq a + 7$ and $b \leq a - 7$. These inequalities correspond to the two shaded triangles in the figure above. The area of the shaded region is $2(\frac{1}{2})(3)(3) = 9$ and the area of the whole square is $10^2 = 100$. Therefore, the probability we are looking for is $\frac{9}{100}$ or $.09$.

Download additional solutions for free here:

www.satprepget800.com/28LesAdv

LESSON 17
NUMBER THEORY

Reminder: Before beginning this lesson remember to redo the problems from Lessons 1, 5, 9 and 13 that you have marked off. Do not "unmark" a question unless you get it correct.

Xiggi's Formula

The following simple formula can be used to find an average speed when two individual speeds for the same distance are known.

$$\text{Average Speed} = \frac{2(\text{Speed 1})(\text{Speed 2})}{\text{Speed 1} + \text{Speed 2}}$$

*Xiggi's formula is more widely known as the Harmonic Mean formula.

Try to answer the following question using Xiggi's formula. **Do not** check the solution until you have attempted this question yourself.

LEVEL 5: NUMBER THEORY

1. An elephant traveled 7 miles at an average rate of 4 miles per hour and then traveled the next 7 miles at an average rate of 1 mile per hour. What was the average speed, in miles per hour, of the elephant for the 14 miles?

   A. 1
   B. 1.6
   C. 2.5
   D. 4.375
   E. 5.6

Solution

* We simply apply Xiggi's formula:

Average Speed = $\frac{2(4)(1)}{4+1}$ = 1.6, choice **B**.

"distance = rate · time charts"

When trying to solve difficult problems involving distance, rate, and time, it helps to set up a little chart, and use the formula when necessary.

Let's answer the last question using a chart.

Solution

Let's put the given information into the following chart.

	Distance	Rate	Time
1st part of trip	7	4	$\frac{7}{4}$
2nd part of trip	7	1	$\frac{7}{1} = 7$
total	14		8.75

Note that we computed the times by using "distance = rate · time" in the form "time = $\frac{distance}{rate}$." Finally, we use the formula in the form

$$\text{rate} = \frac{distance}{time} = \frac{14}{8.75} = 1.6, \text{ choice } \textbf{B}.$$

Note: To get the total distance we add the two distances, and to get the total time we add the two times. Be careful – this doesn't work for rates!

Percent = "Out of 100"

Since the word percent means "out of 100," use the number 100 for totals in percent problems. This is just a specific example of the strategy of "picking numbers" from Lesson 1.

Try to answer the following question using the number 100. **Do not** check the solution until you have attempted this question yourself.

www.ACTPrepGet36.com

LEVEL 5: NUMBER THEORY

2. If Ted's weight increased by 36 percent and Jessica's weight decreased by 22 percent during a certain year, the ratio of Ted's weight to Jessica's weight at the end of the year was how many times the ratio at the beginning of the year?

F. $\frac{39}{68}$

G. $\frac{11}{18}$

H. $\frac{68}{61}$

J. $\frac{18}{11}$

K. $\frac{68}{39}$

Solution

* Solution by picking numbers: Since this is a percent problem, let's choose 100 pounds for both Ted's weight and Jessica's weight at the beginning of the year. Ted's weight at the end of the year was then $100 + 36 = 136$ pounds and Jessica's weight at the end of the year was $100 - 22 = 78$ pounds. We then have that the ratio of Ted's weight to Jessica's weight at the beginning of the year was $\frac{100}{100} = 1$, and the ratio of Ted's weight to Jessica's weight at the end of the year was $\frac{136}{78} = \frac{68}{39}$. So the answer is **K**.

Note: The computations are only this simple because we chose both numbers to be 100. Let's choose different numbers so that you can see how the computations become more difficult. Let's choose 150 pounds for Ted's weight at the beginning of the year and 75 pounds for Jessica's weight at the beginning of the year. 36% of 150 is $150(0.36) = 54$. So we have that Ted's weight was $150 + 54 = 204$ at the end of the year. Also, 22% of 75 is $75(0.22) = 16.5$ pounds. It follows that Jessica's weight at the end of the year was $75 - 16.5 = 58.5$ pounds. The ratio of Ted's weight to Jessica's weight at the beginning of the year was $\frac{150}{75} = 2$, and the ratio of Ted's to Jessica's weight at the end of the year was $\frac{204}{58.5}$. Finally, we have to solve the equation $2x = \frac{204}{58.5}$ to get

213

$$x = \frac{204}{58.5 \cdot 2} = \frac{204}{117} = \frac{68}{39}, \text{ choice } \textbf{K}.$$

Try to also solve this problem algebraically (without plugging in any numbers).

Solution

Let Ted's and Jessica's weights at the beginning of the year be x and y, respectively. Then at the end of the year their weights are $1.36x$ and $0.78y$. The ratio of Ted's weight to Jessica's weight at the beginning of the year was $\frac{x}{y}$, and the ratio of Ted's weight to Jessica's weight at the end of the year was $\frac{1.36x}{0.78y} = \frac{68}{39} \cdot \frac{x}{y}$ which is $\frac{68}{39}$ times the ratio at the beginning of the year. The answer is therefore **K**.

Now try to solve each of the following problems. The answers to these problems, followed by full solutions are at the end of this lesson. **Do not** look at the answers until you have attempted these problems yourself. Please remember to mark off any problems you get wrong.

LEVEL 1: NUMBER THEORY

3. If Edna drove s miles in t hours, which of the following represents her average speed, in miles per hour?

    A. $\frac{s}{t}$

    B. $\frac{t}{s}$

    C. $\frac{1}{st}$

    D. st

    E. $s^2 t$

LEVEL 2: NUMBER THEORY

4. Running at a constant speed, an antelope traveled 150 miles in 6 hours. At this rate, how many miles did the antelope travel in 5 hours?

    F. 80
    G. 100
    H. 112
    J. 125
    K. 180

LEVEL 3: NUMBER THEORY

5. The ratio of the number of elephants to the number of zebras in a zoo is 3 to 5. What percent of the animals in the zoo are zebras?

    A. 12.5%
    B. 37.5%
    C. 60%
    D. 62.5%
    E. 70%

6. What percent of 60 is 12?

    F. 10
    G. 12
    H. 15
    J. 18
    K. 20

LEVEL 4: NUMBER THEORY

7. For nonzero numbers $a, b,$ and c, if c is three times b and b is $\frac{1}{5}$ of a, what is the ratio of a^2 to c^2 ?

    A. 9 to 25
    B. 25 to 9
    C. 5 to 9
    D. 5 to 3
    E. 3 to 5

8. If the ratio of two positive integers is 7 to 6, which of the following statements about these integers CANNOT be true?

    F. Their sum is an even integer.
    G. Their sum is an odd integer.
    H. Their product is divisible by 11.
    J. Their product is an even integer.
    K. Their product is an odd integer.

9. If $x > 0$, then 4 percent of 7 percent of $5x$ equals what percent of x ?

    A. 0.14
    B. 1.4
    C. 14
    D. 28
    E. 140

10. Joseph drove from home to work at an average speed of 30 miles per hour and returned home along the same route at an average speed of 45 miles per hour. If his total driving time for the trip was 3 hours, how many <u>minutes</u> did it take Joseph to drive from work to home?

    F. 135
    G. 72
    H. 60
    J. 50
    K. 30

LEVEL 5: NUMBER THEORY

11. There are m bricks that need to be stacked. After n of them have been stacked, then in terms of m and n, what percent of the bricks have not yet been stacked?

    A. $\dfrac{m}{100(m-n)}\%$

    B. $\dfrac{100(m-n)}{m}\%$

    C. $\dfrac{100m}{n}\%$

    D. $\dfrac{100n}{m}\%$

    E. $\dfrac{m}{100n}\%$

12. Jason ran a race of 1600 meters in two laps of equal distance. His average speeds for the first and second laps were 11 meters per second and 7 meters per second, respectively. To the nearest tenth, what was his average speed for the entire race, in meters per second?

    F. 8.0
    G. 8.6
    H. 9.0
    J. 9.6
    K. 10.0

Answers

1. B	5. D	9. B
2. K	6. K	10. G
3. A	7. B	11. B
4. J	8. K	12. G

Full Solutions

5.

We can represent the number of elephants in the zoo by $3x$ and the number of zebras in the zoo by $5x$ for some number x. Then the total number of animals in the zoo is $8x$ which we set equal to 100. Now $8x = 100$ implies that $x = \frac{100}{8} = 12.5$. Since we want the percent of the animals in the park that are zebras, we need to find $5x$. We have $5x = 5(12.5) = 62.5\%$, choice **D**.

Important note: After you find x make sure you look at what the question is asking for. A common error is to give an answer of 12.5%. But the number of zebras is **not** equal to x. It is equal to $5x$.

* Alternate solution: We set up a ratio of the amount of zebras in the zoo to the total number of animals in the zoo.

$$\begin{array}{ccc} \text{zebras} & 5 & x \\ \text{animals} & 8 & 100 \end{array}$$

$$\frac{5}{8} = \frac{x}{100}$$
$$8x = 500$$
$$x = \frac{500}{8} = 62.5, \text{ choice } \mathbf{D}.$$

6.

* The word "what" indicates an unknown, let's call it x. The word percent means "out of 100" or "divided by 100." The word "of" indicates multiplication, and the word "is" indicates an equal sign. So we translate the given sentence into an algebraic equation as follows.

$$\frac{x}{100} \cdot 60 = 12$$

So $x = \frac{12 \cdot 100}{60} = 20$, choice **K**.

7.

* **Solution by picking a number:** Let's choose a value for a, say $a = 5$. Then $b = 1$, $c = 3$, and therefore the ratio of a^2 to c^2 is 25 to 9, choice **B**.

Algebraic solution: $b = \frac{1}{5}a$, and so $c = 3b = 3\left(\frac{1}{5}\right)a = \frac{3a}{5}$. It follows that $\frac{a^2}{c^2} = \frac{a^2}{\left(\frac{3a}{5}\right)^2} = \frac{a^2 \cdot 25}{9a^2} = \frac{25}{9}$. Therefore, the ratio of a^2 to c^2 is 25 to 9, choice **B**.

8.

Solution by picking numbers: Let's choose two positive integers that are in the ratio of 7 to 6, say 7 and 6. Then we have $7 + 6 = 13$ and $(7)(6) = 42$. Since 13 is odd, we can eliminate choice G. Since 42 is even we can eliminate choice J. The answer is therefore F, G, or K.

We will now choose two new numbers that are in the same ratio. A simple way to do this is to multiply our original numbers by an integer, say 2. So our new numbers are 14 and 12. Then we have $14 + 12 = 26$ and $(14)(12) = 168$. Since 26 is even we can eliminate choice F. So we're down to either H or K.

Looking at choice H seems to indicate that perhaps we should multiply our original numbers by 11. So our new numbers are $(7)(11) = 77$ and $(6)(11) = 66$. The product of these numbers is $(77)(66) = 5082$. This is divisible by 11. We can therefore eliminate choice H, and the answer is choice **K**.

Notes: (1) Choice K is correct because we eliminated the other 4 choices. The reality of the situation is that we have not actually answered this question. Using the previous method there is no reason to believe that there is no choice of integers that will produce an odd product. In this sense the more advanced method below is more enlightening.

(2) To see that 5082 is divisible by 11 we can simply divide 5082 by 11 in our calculator. The result is 462. Since this is an integer, 5082 is divisible by 11. In fact, $5082 = (11)(462)$.

* Advanced Method: If the ratio of two positive integers is 7 to 6, then the integers can be written as $7x$ and $6x$ for some number x. It then follows that the sum is $7x + 6x = 13x$, and the product is $(7x)(6x) = 42x^2 = 2(21x^2)$. Since the product has a factor of 2 it is always even. Thus, the product can never be odd, and the answer is choice **K**.

Remarks: (1) If x is an odd integer, then $13x$ is the product of two odd integers. Therefore, the sum will be odd. If x is an even integer, then $13x$ is the product of an odd integer and an even integer. Therefore, the sum will be even.

(2) If x is any multiple of 11, then $42x^2$ will be divisible by 11.

(3) Note that in order for $7x$ and $6x$ to both be integers, x must also be an integer because 7 and 6 have no common factors (contrast this with $2x$ and $4x$, where x can be any multiple of $\frac{1}{2}$). This shows that when we substitute an acceptable value for x in the expression $2(21x^2)$ we will not inadvertently cancel the 2.

9.
Solution by picking a number: Since this is a percent problem let's choose $x = 100$. Then 7 percent of $5x$ is 7 percent of 500 which is $(0.07)(500) = 35$. 4 percent of 7 percent of $5x$ is 4 percent of 35 which is $(0.04)(35) = 1.4$. Since we began with $x = 100$, the answer is 1.4, choice **B**.

* Direct solution: 4 percent of 7 percent of $5x$ is $(0.04)(.07)(5x) = 0.014x$ which is 1.4 percent of x. So the answer is **B**.

10.

Solution by starting with choice H: If it took Joseph 60 minutes (or 1 hour) to get from work to home, then the distance from work to home is $d = 45$ miles. This is the same as the distance from home to work. Therefore, the total time for Joseph to get from home to work would be $t = \frac{d}{r} = \frac{45}{30} = 1.5$ hours. But that means that the total trip took only 2.5 hours. So we can eliminate choices H, J, and K. Since Joseph is traveling faster from work to home, it should take him less than half the time to get home. So the answer is less than 1.5 hours = 90 minutes. This eliminates choice F, and therefore the answer is choice **G**.

* Solution by estimation: 3 hours is the same as 180 minutes. If Joseph was travelling at the same rate for the whole trip, it would take him exactly half this time to get from work to home, 90 minutes. Since Joseph is travelling a little faster on the way from work to home, the answer will be a little less than 90, most likely 72, choice **G**.

An algebraic solution: We use the simple formula distance = rate · time. Let's put the given information into the following chart.

	Distance	Rate	Time
home to work	d	30	$d/30$
work to home	d	45	$d/45$
total			3

Note that although we don't know either distance, we do know that they are the same, so we can call them both "d."

Also, since distance = rate · time, we have that time = distance/rate. We use this to get the first two entries in column three. The total time is given in the question. So we have

$$\frac{d}{30} + \frac{d}{45} = 3$$
$$45d + 30d = 3 \cdot 30 \cdot 45$$
$$75d = 3 \cdot 30 \cdot 45$$
$$d = \frac{3 \cdot 30 \cdot 45}{75}$$

We want the time it takes Joseph to drive from work to home, that is we want $\frac{d}{45}$.

220

This is equal to $\frac{d}{45} = \frac{3\cdot30}{75}$ in hours. To convert to minutes, we multiply by 60: $\frac{d}{45} = \frac{3\cdot30\cdot60}{75} = 72$ minutes, choice **G**.

Solution using Xiggi's formula:

$$\text{Average Speed} = \frac{2(30)(45)}{30 + 45} = 36$$

$$\text{So Total Round Trip Distance} = r \cdot t = 36 \cdot 3 = 108$$

$$\text{Distance from Work to Home} = \frac{108}{2} = 54$$

$$\text{Time from Work to Home} = \frac{\text{distance}}{\text{rate}} = \frac{54}{45} = 1.2.$$

Finally, multiply by 60 to convert to minutes: $1.2 \cdot 60 = 72$, choice **G**.

Remark: This example shows that Xiggi's formula does not always immediately give a solution. It depends on what is being asked.

11.

Solution by picking numbers: Since this is a percent problem we choose 100 for the total number of bricks. So $m = 100$. For n, let's choose 25, so that 25 bricks have been stacked, and $100 - 25 = 75$ have not been stacked. Since we started with 100 as our total, **75% of the bricks have not been stacked. Remember to put a big, dark circle around 75%.** We make the substitutions m = 100 and n = 25 into each answer choice.

 A. $100/7500 \approx 0.0133\%$
 B. $7500/100 = 75\%$
 C. $10,000/25 = 400\%$
 D. $2500/100 = 25\%$
 E. $25/10,000 = 0.0025\%$

We now compare each of these percents to the percent that we put a nice big, dark circle around. Since A, C, D, and E are incorrect we can eliminate them. Therefore, the answer is choice **B**.

Important note: B is **not** the correct answer simply because it is equal to 75%. It is correct because all 4 of the other choices are **not** 75%. **You absolutely must check all five choices!**

221

* **Algebraic solution:** The total number of bricks is m. Since n bricks have been stacked, it follows that $m - n$ have not been stacked. To get the **fraction** of bricks that have not been stacked we divide the **number** that have not been stacked by the total. This is $\frac{m-n}{m}$. To change this to a **percent** we multiply by 100, to get $\frac{100(m-n)}{m}$ %., choice **B**.

Note: The last step in the algebraic solution is equivalent to the usual ratio computation where we are changing the denominator to 100.

bricks not stacked	$m - n$	x
total bricks	m	100

$$\frac{m-n}{m} = \frac{x}{100}$$
$$100(m - n) = mx$$
$$\frac{100(m - n)}{m} = x$$

12.
* **Solution using Xiggi's formula:**

Average Speed $= \frac{2(11)(7)}{11+7} = \frac{154}{18} \approx 8.555555$. To the nearest tenth, this is 8.6, choice **G**.

Solution using a chart:

	Distance	Rate	Time
lap 1	800	11	$\frac{800}{11} \approx 72.727$
lap 2	800	7	$\frac{800}{7} \approx 114.286$
total	1600	x	187.01

$$x = \text{average rate} = \frac{\text{distance}}{\text{time}} \approx \frac{1600}{187.01} \approx 8.5555$$

To the nearest tenth, this is 8.6, choice **G**.

OPTIONAL MATERIAL

CHALLENGE QUESTION

1. Use the formula $d = rt$ to derive Xiggi's formula.

Solution

* Recall that Xiggi's formula is used when we are given two rates for the **same** distance. So let d be the common distance, and r_1 and r_2 the two rates. Let's use a chart.

Distance	Rate	Time
d	r_1	$\dfrac{d}{r_1}$
d	r_2	$\dfrac{d}{r_2}$
$2d$		$\dfrac{d}{r_1} + \dfrac{d}{r_2}$

Note that we get the first two entries in the last column by using the formula $d = rt$, and we get the last row by addition (observe that this cannot be done in the middle column). We now apply the formula $d = rt$ to the middle column to get $2d = r(\frac{d}{r_1} + \frac{d}{r_2})$. Multiply each side of this equation by $r_1 r_2$ to get $2dr_1 r_2 = r(dr_2 + dr_1) = rd(r_1 + r_2)$. Finally, we divide each side of this equation by $d(r_1 + r_2)$ to get $r = \frac{2r_1 r_2}{r_1 + r_2}$.

Download additional solutions for free here:

www.satprepget800.com/28LesAdv

LESSON 18
FUNCTIONS AND GRAPHS

Reminder: Before beginning this lesson remember to redo the problems from Lessons 2, 6, 10 and 14 that you have marked off. Do not "unmark" a question unless you get it correct.

Graphs of Functions

If f is a function, then

$f(a) = b$ is equivalent to "the point (a, b) lies on the graph of f."

Example 1:

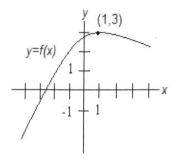

In the figure above we see that the point $(1, 3)$ lies on the graph of the function f. Therefore $f(1) = 3$.

Try to answer the following question using this fact. **Do not** check the solution until you have attempted this question yourself.

LEVEL 4: FUNCTIONS

1. In the xy-plane, the graph of the function h, with equation $h(x) = ax^2 - 16$, passes through the point $(-2,4)$. What is the value of a?

    A. -2
    B.   4
    C.   5
    D.   20
    E.   24

Solution

* **Solution:** Since the graph of h passes through the point $(-2, 4)$, $h(-2) = 4$. But by direct computation

$$h(-2) = a(-2)^2 - 16 = 4a - 16.$$

So $4a - 16 = 4$. Therefore, $4a = 20$, and so $a = 5$, choice **C**.

Function Facts

Fact 1: The **y-intercept** of the graph of a function $y = f(x)$ is the point on the graph where $x = 0$ (if it exists). There can be at most one y-intercept for the graph of a function. A y-intercept has the form $(0, b)$ for some real number b. Equivalently, $f(0) = b$.

Fact 2: An **x-intercept** of the graph of a function is a point on the graph where $y = 0$. There can be more than one x-intercept for the graph of a function or none at all. An x-intercept has the form $(a, 0)$ for some real number a. Equivalently, $f(a) = 0$.

Example 2: In the figure to the right we see that the graph of f has y-intercept $(0, 2)$ and x-intercepts $(-3, 0)$, $(2, 0)$, and $(4, 0)$.

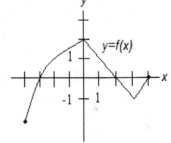

The numbers -3, 2, and 4 are also called **zeros**, **roots**, or **solutions** of the function.

Fact 3: If the graph of $f(x)$ is above the x-axis, then $f(x) > 0$. If the graph of f is below the x-axis, then $f(x) < 0$. If the graph of f is higher than the graph of g, then $f(x) > g(x)$

Example 3: In the figure for example 2 above, observe that $f(x) < 0$ for $-4 \leq x < -3$ and $2 < x < 4$. Also $f(x) > 0$ for $-3 < x < 2$.

Fact 4: As x gets very large, $\frac{1}{x}$ gets very small.

Example 4: Let $f(x) = \frac{3x^2 + \frac{1}{x}}{x^2}$. Then for large x, $f(x) \approx \frac{3x^2}{x^2} = 3$. So, for example $f(10^{100}) \approx 3$.

Even and Odd Functions

A function f with the property that $f(-x) = f(x)$ for all x is called an **even** function. For example, $f(x) = |x|$ is an even function because

$$f(-x) = |-x| = |x| = f(x).$$

A function f with the property that $f(-x) = -f(x)$ for all x is called an **odd** function. For example, $g(x) = \frac{1}{x}$ is odd because

$$g(-x) = \frac{1}{-x} = -\frac{1}{x} = -g(x).$$

A **polynomial function** is a function for which each **term** has the form ax^n where a is a real number and n is a positive integer.

Polynomial functions with only even powers of x are even functions. Keep in mind that a constant c is the same as cx^0, and so c is an even power of x. Here are some examples of polynomial functions that are even.

$$f(x) = x^2 \qquad g(x) = 4 \qquad h(x) = 3x^8 - 2x^6 + 9$$

Polynomial functions with only odd powers of x are odd functions. Keep in mind that x is the same as x^1, and so x is an odd power of x. Here are some examples of polynomial functions that are odd.

$$f(x) = x^3 \qquad g(x) = x \qquad h(x) = 3x^{11} - 2x^5 + 9x$$

A quick graphical analysis of even and odd functions: The graph of an even function is **symmetrical with respect to the y-axis**. This means that the y-axis acts like a "mirror," and the graph "reflects" across this mirror.

The graph of an odd function is **symmetrical with respect to the origin**. This means that if you rotate the graph 180 degrees (or equivalently, turn it upside down) it will look the same as it did right side up.

So another way to determine if $f(-x) = f(x)$ is to graph f in your graphing calculator, and see if the y-axis acts like a mirror. Another way to determine if $f(-x) = -f(x)$ is to graph f in your graphing calculator, and see if it looks the same upside down. This technique will work for **all** functions (not just polynomials).

Try to answer the following question about even functions. **Do not** check the solution until you have attempted this question yourself.

LEVEL 5: FUNCTIONS

2. For which of the following functions is it true that $f(-x) = f(x)$ for all values of x?

    F. $f(x) = x^2 + 5$
    G. $f(x) = x^2 + 5x$
    H. $f(x) = x^3 + 5x$
    J. $f(x) = x^3 + 5$
    K. $f(x) = x + 5$

Solutions

Solution by picking numbers: Let's choose a value for x, say $x = 2$. We compute $f(-2)$ and $f(2)$ for each answer choice.

	$f(-2)$	$f(2)$
F.	9	9
G.	-6	14
H.	-18	18
J.	-3	13
K.	3	7

Since choices G, H, J, and K do not match up, we can eliminate them. The answer is therefore choice **F**.

Important note: F is **not** the correct answer simply because both computations gave the same answer. It is correct because all 4 of the other choices did **not** work. **You absolutely must check all five choices!**

* Quick solution: We are looking for an even function. Each answer choice is a polynomial. Therefore, the answer is the one with only even powers of x. This is choice **F** (remember that $5 = 5x^0$).

Graphical solution: Begin putting each of the four answer choices into your graphing calculator (starting with choice H), and choose the one that is symmetrical with respect to the y-axis. This is choice **F**.

Basic Transformations

Let $y = f(x)$, and $k > 0$. We can move the graph of f around by applying the following basic transformations.

227

$y = f(x) + k$ shift up k units $y = f(x) - k$ shift down k units

$y = f(x - k)$ shift right k units $y = f(x + k)$ shift left k units

$y = -f(x)$ reflect in x-axis $y = f(-x)$ reflect in y-axis.

Example: Let $f(x) = x^2$. If you move the graph of f right 3 units and down 2 units, you get the graph of the function g. What is the definition of g?

We have $g(x) = (x - 3)^2 - 2$. Here is a picture.

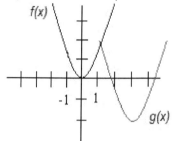

Standard Form for an Equation of a Circle

The standard form for the equation of a circle with center (h, k) and radius r is

$$(x - h)^2 + (y - k)^2 = r^2.$$

Example: Find the center and radius of the circle with equation $(x - 1)^2 + (y + 2)^2 = 3$

We have $h = 1$ and $k = -2$. So the center of the circle is $(1, -2)$. The radius is $r = \sqrt{3}$.

Remark: Note that in this example $(y + 2) = (y - (-2))$. This is why $k = -2$ instead of 2.

General Form for an Equation of a Circle

The general form for the equation of a circle is

$$x^2 + y^2 + ax + by + c = 0.$$

This form for the equation is not very useful since we cannot easily determine the center or radius of the circle. We will want to apply the method of completing the square (Lesson 6) twice in order to change the equation into standard form. Let's use an example to illustrate this procedure.

LEVEL 4: FUNCTIONS AND GRAPHS

3.   In the standard (x, y) coordinate plane, what are the coordinates of the center of the circle whose equation is

$$x^2 - 8x + y^2 + 10y + 15 = 0 \ ?$$

A. $(4, 5)$
B. $(4, -5)$
C. $(-4, 0)$
D. $(-4, 5)$
E. $(-5, -4)$

* Solution by completing the square:

$$x^2 - 8x = x^2 - 8x + 16 - 16 = (x - 4)^2 - 16.$$

$$y^2 + 10y = y^2 + 10y + 25 - 25 = (y + 5)^2 - 25.$$

So $x^2 - 8x + y^2 + 10y + 15 = (x - 4)^2 - 16 + (y + 5)^2 - 25 + 15$
$$= (x - 4)^2 + (y + 5)^2 - 26.$$

So the center of the circle is $(4, -5)$, choice **B**.

Notes: (1) To complete the square in the expression $x^2 - 8x$, we first take half of -8 to get -4. We then square this result to get 16. Note that $x^2 - 8x + 16 = (x - 4)(x - 4) = (x - 4)^2$.

But be aware that it is not really okay to add 16 here – this changes the expression. So we have to undo the damage we just did. We undo this damage by subtracting 16.

(2) To complete the square in the expression $y^2 + 10y$, we first take half of 10 to get 5. We then square this result to get 25. Note that we have $y^2 + 10y + 25 = (y + 5)(y + 5) = (y + 5)^2$.

But be aware that it is not really okay to add 25 here – this changes the expression. So we have to undo the damage we just did. We undo this damage by subtracting 25.

(3) Note that we never finished writing the equation of the circle. We didn't need to since the question asked only to find the center of the circle.

For completeness let's write the equation of the circle in standard form. We have

$$(x - 4)^2 + (y + 5)^2 - 26 = 0,$$

or equivalently

$$(x - 4)^2 + (y + 5)^2 = 26$$

So we have an equation of a circle with center $(4, -5)$ and radius $\sqrt{26}$.

Standard Form for an Equation of an Ellipse

The standard form for an equation of an ellipse is

$$\frac{(x - h)^2}{a^2} + \frac{(y - k)^2}{b^2} = 1$$

The **center** of this ellipse is (h, k). a is the horizontal distance from the center of the ellipse to a vertex of the ellipse, and b is the vertical distance from the center of the ellipse to a vertex of the ellipse. The lengths of the two **axes** of the ellipse are $2a$ and $2b$. The larger of these two numbers is the **major axis** and the smaller of these two numbers is the **minor axis**.

If the ellipse is centered at $(0, 0)$ (the origin), then the equation simplifies to

$$\frac{x^2}{a^2} + \frac{y^2}{b^2} = 1$$

Example: Graphed in the standard (x, y) coordinate plane below is an ellipse. Write an equation for the ellipse, find the major and minor axes, and find the distance from P to Q.

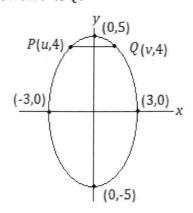

230

We have $a = 3$ and $b = 5$, and so an equation of the ellipse is

$$\frac{x^2}{9} + \frac{y^2}{25} = 1$$

The major axis is $2 \cdot 5 = \mathbf{10}$ and the minor axis is $2 \cdot 3 = \mathbf{6}$.

We can find u and v by replacing y by 4 in the equation:

$$\frac{x^2}{9} + \frac{4^2}{25} = 1 \Rightarrow \frac{x^2}{9} = 1 - \frac{16}{25} = \frac{25}{25} - \frac{16}{25} = \frac{9}{25} \Rightarrow x^2 = \frac{81}{25} \Rightarrow x = \pm\frac{9}{5}$$

So $u = -\frac{9}{5}$, $v = \frac{9}{5}$, and so the distance from P to Q is $\frac{18}{5} = \mathbf{3.6}$.

Now try to solve each of the following problems. The answers to these problems, followed by full solutions are at the end of this lesson. **Do not look at the answers until you have attempted these problems yourself.** Please remember to mark off any problems you get wrong.

LEVEL 4: FUNCTIONS

4. If $r^2s > 10^{200}$, then the value of $\frac{rs + \frac{1}{r}}{7rs}$ is closest to which of the following?

    F. 0.1
    G. 0.15
    H. 0.2
    J. 0.25
    K. 0.3

5. The figure below shows the graph of the function g in the xy-plane. Which of the following are true?

    I. $g(b) = 0$
    II. $g(a) + g(b) + g(0) = 0$
    III. $g(a) > g(b)$

    A. None
    B. I only
    C. II only
    D. I and II only
    E. I, II, and III

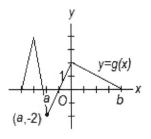

$y = g(x)$

$(a,-2)$

231

6. In the xy-plane below, the graph of the function f is a parabola, and the graph of the function g is a line. The graphs of f and g intersect at $(-2, 1)$ and $(2, -2)$. For which of the following values of x is $f(x) - g(x) < 0$?

    F. -3
    G. -1
    H. 0
    J. 1
    K. 2

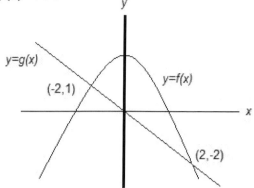

7. The figure below shows the graph of the function h and line segment $\overline{AB}$, which has a y-intercept of $(0, b)$. For how many values of x between j and k does $h(x) = b$?

    A. Zero
    B. One
    C. Two
    D. Three
    E. Four

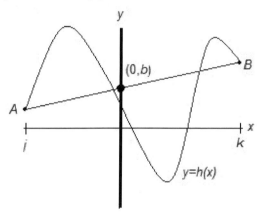

232

8. A portion of the graph of the function g is shown in the xy-plane below. What is the x-intercept of the graph of the function h defined by $h(x) = g(x - 1)$?

F. $(1, 0)$
G. $(2, 0)$
H. $(3, 0)$
J. $(4, 0)$
K. $(6, 0)$

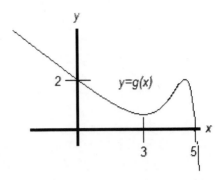

9. The figure below shows the graph of the function f on the interval $a < x < e$. Which of the following expressions represents the difference between the maximum and minimum values of $f(x)$ on this interval?

A. $f(b - e)$
B. $f(b - c)$
C. $f(a) - f(e)$
D. $f(b) - f(c)$
E. $f(b) - f(e)$

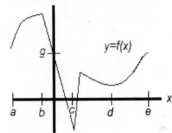

233

LEVEL 5: FUNCTIONS

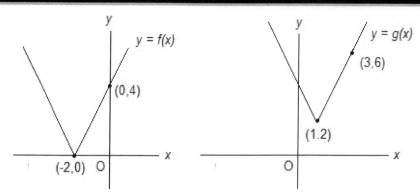

10. The figures above show the graphs of the functions f and g. The function f is defined by $f(x) = 2|x + 2|$ and the function g is defined by $g(x) = f(x + h) + k$, where h and k are constants. What is the value of hk?

    F. −6
    G. −3
    H. −2
    J.   3
    K.   6

11. A circle in the standard (x, y) coordinate plane is tangent to the x-axis at 3 and tangent to the y-axis at −3. Which of the following is an equation of the circle?

    A. $x^2 + y^2 = 3$
    B. $x^2 - y^2 = 9$
    C. $(x - 3)^2 + (y + 3)^2 = 3$
    D. $(x - 3)^2 + (y + 3)^2 = 9$
    E. $(x + 3)^2 + (y - 3)^2 = 9$

12. How long is the minor axis of the ellipse whose equation is $\frac{(x-3)^2}{25} + \frac{(y+2)^2}{49} = 1$?

    F.   5
    G.   7
    H. 10
    J. 14
    K. 25

234

Answers

1. C	5. D	9. D
2. F	6. F	10. F
3. B	7. D	11. D
4. G	8. K	12. H

Full Solutions

4.

Solution by picking numbers: Let's let $s = 1$. Then r must be very large. We cannot make r as large as the problem would like (our calculators will give an error), but we can still plug in a large value for r, say $r = 100,000$. So we get $\frac{(100,000)(1)+\frac{1}{100,000}}{7(100,000)(1)} \approx 0.14286$. The closest number in the answer choices to this value is 0.15, choice **G**.

Algebraic solution: Let's simplify the complex fraction by multiplying the numerator and denominator by r. Then the expression becomes $\frac{r\left(rs+\frac{1}{r}\right)}{r(7rs)} = \frac{(r^2s+1)}{7r^2s} = \frac{r^2s}{7r^2s} + \frac{1}{7r^2s} = \frac{1}{7} + \frac{1}{7r^2s}$. Since r^{2s} is very large, $\frac{1}{r^2s}$ is very small, and $\frac{1}{7r^2s}$ is even smaller. So $\frac{1}{7} + 0 = \frac{1}{7} \approx 0.14286$ is a very close approximation to the answer. The closest number in the answer choices to this value is 0.15, choice **G**.

* A combination of the two methods: We can begin by plugging in a 1 for s. It follows that r^2 is extremely large. Although r is much smaller than r^2 it is still extremely large so that $\frac{1}{r}$ is extremely small. So we can approximate the value of the expression by setting $\frac{1}{r} = 0$. So, after setting $s = 1$ and $\frac{1}{r} = 0$ we get $\frac{r}{7r} = \frac{1}{7} \approx 0.14286$. The closest number in the answer choices to this value is 0.15, choice **G**.

5.

* Note that $(a, -2)$, $(0, 2)$, and $(b, 0)$ are on the graph. Equivalently, we have $g(a) = -2$, $g(0) = 2$, and $g(b) = 0$.

Since $g(b) = 0$, I is true. Also $g(a) + g(b) + g(0) = -2 + 0 + 2 = 0$. So II is true. Since $-2 < 0$, we see that III is false. Thus, the answer is choice **D**.

6.

Solution by starting with choice H: Let's add some information to the picture.

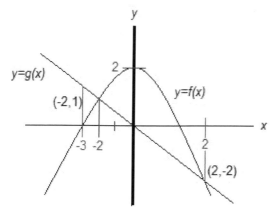

Now let's start with choice H. Since the point $(0, 2)$ is on the graph of f, we have that $f(0) = 2$. Since the point $(0, 0)$ is on the graph of g, we have $g(0) = 0$. So $f(0) - g(0) = 2 - 0 = 2 > 0$. So we can eliminate choice H.

A moment's thought should lead you to suspect that choice F might be the answer (if you do not see this it is okay – just keep trying answer choices until you get there). Since the point $(-3, 0)$ is on the graph of f, we have $f(-3) = 0$. It looks like $(-3, 1.5)$ is on the graph of g, so that $g(-3) = 1.5$. So $f(-3) - g(-3) = 0 - 1.5 = -1.5 < 0$. Thus, the answer is choice **F**.

* **Geometric solution:** $f(x) - g(x) < 0$ is equivalent to $f(x) < g(x)$. Graphically this means that $f(x)$ is lower than $g(x)$. This happens at $x = -3$, choice **F**.

Remark: If $-2 < x < 2$, then the graph of f is higher than the graph of g. This means that $f(x) > g(x)$, or equivalently $f(x) - g(x) > 0$. If $x < -2$ or $x > 2$, then the graph of f is lower than the graph of g. This means $f(x) < g(x)$, or equivalently $f(x) - g(x) < 0$.

7.

* Let's draw a horizontal line through the point $(0, b)$.

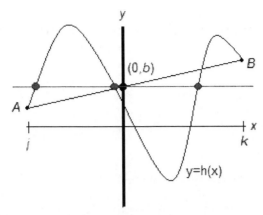

Now, notice that this line hits the graph of h Three times., choice **D**.

8.

Geometric solution: Since the point $(5, 0)$ is on the graph, $g(5) = 0$. It follows that $h(6) = g(6 - 1) = g(5) = 0$. So the point $(6,0)$ is on the graph of h, choice **K**.

Remark: Formally, we can solve the equation $x - 1 = 5$ to get $x = 6$.

* Solution using a basic transformation: If we replace x by $x - 1$ in the function g, then the graph of g is shifted to the right 1 unit. So the "new" x-intercept is at $(6 ,0)$, choice **K,**.

9.

* Let's just point out the maximum and minimum values of $f(x)$ in the figure.

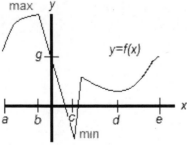

Simply note that the maximum is $f(b)$ and the minimum is $f(c)$. Thus, the difference between the maximum and minimum is $f(b) - f(c)$, choice **D**.

237

Note: The maximum and minimum values of a function f are always the y-coordinates of the points. Equivalently, they have the form $f(x)$. We say that the maximum or minimum **occurs** at x.

10.

* Notice that to get the graph of g we shift the graph of f 3 units to the right, and 2 units up. Therefore $g(x) = f(x-3) + 2$. So $h = -3$ and $k = 2$. Therefore, $hk = (-3)(2) = -6$, choice **F**.

11.

Solution by drawing a picture: Let's draw the circle:

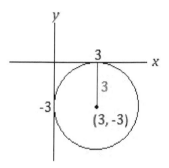

Now simply observe that the circle has center $(3, -3)$ and radius 3. So the equation of the circle is $(x-3)^2 + (y+3)^2 = 9$, choice **D**.

12.

* The length of the minor axis is $2a = 2 \cdot 5 = 10$, choice **H**.

Notes: (1) In the given equation, we have $a^2 = 25$, so that $a = 5$, and the length of the minor axis is $2a = 2 \cdot 5 = 10$.

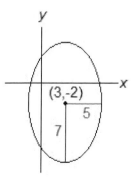

(2) A picture of this ellipse is shown to the right. The line segment labelled with length 5 is half of the minor axis.

OPTIONAL MATERIAL

CHALLENGE QUESTION

1. The graphs of $y = bx^2$ and $y = k - bx^2$ intersect at points A and B. If the length of $\overline{AB}$ is equal to d, what is the value of $\frac{bd^2}{k}$?

Solution

* Let's begin by drawing a picture.

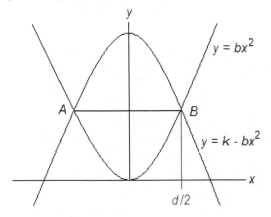

First note that the x-coordinate of point B is $\frac{d}{2}$. Since the two graphs intersect at B, we have $b\left(\frac{d}{2}\right)^2 = k - b\left(\frac{d}{2}\right)^2$. So $2b\left(\frac{d}{2}\right)^2 = k$. Thus, $\frac{2bd^2}{2^2} = k$, so $bd^2 = 2k$, and therefore $\frac{bd^2}{k} = 2$.

Download additional solutions for free here:

www.satprepget800.com/28LesAdv

239

LESSON 19
GEOMETRY

Reminder: Before beginning this lesson remember to redo the problems from Lessons 3, 7, 11 and 15 that you have marked off. Do not "unmark" a question unless you get it correct.

Advanced Relationships in Circles

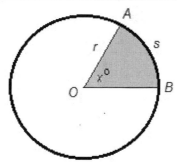

Consider the circle in the figure above. Notice that $\overline{OA}$ and $\overline{OB}$ are both radii of the circle. Therefore $OA = OB = r$. If we know the radius r, then we can find the diameter d of the circle, the circumference C of the circle, and the area A of the circle. Indeed, $d = 2r$, $C = 2\pi r$, and $A = \pi r^2$. In fact, if we know any one of the four quantities we can find the other three. For example, if we know that the area of a circle is $A = 9\pi$, then it follows that $r = 3$, $d = 6$, and $C = 6\pi$.

Now, suppose that in addition to the radius r, we know the angle x. We can then use the following ratio to find the length s of arc AB.

$$\frac{x}{360} = \frac{s}{C}$$

For example, if we are given that $r = 5$ and $x = 45$, then we have

$$\frac{45}{360} = \frac{s}{10\pi}$$

So $360s = 450\pi$, and therefore $s = \frac{450\pi}{360} = \frac{5\pi}{4}$.

240

In this particular example we can use a little shortcut. Just note that a 45-degree angle gives $\frac{1}{8}$ of the total degree measure of the circle, and therefore the arc length is $\frac{1}{8}$ of the circumference. So $s = \frac{10\pi}{8} = \frac{5\pi}{4}$.

We can also use the following ratio to find the area a of sector AOB.

$$\frac{x}{360} = \frac{a}{A}$$

For example, if again we are given that $r = 5$ and $x = 45$, then we have

$$\frac{45}{360} = \frac{a}{25\pi}$$

So $360a = 1125\pi$, and therefore $a = \frac{1125\pi}{360} = \frac{25\pi}{8}$.

Again, we can take a shortcut in this example and just divide the area of the circle by 8 to get $a = \frac{25\pi}{8}$.

A very difficult problem might give you the angle x and the area of sector AOB and ask you to find the length of arc AB, or vice versa.

Example: Suppose that A and B are points on a circle with center O, the measure of angle AOB is 35 degrees and minor arc AB has length π. What is the area of sector AOB?

We begin by setting up a ratio to find the circumference of the circle.

$$\frac{35}{360} = \frac{\pi}{C}$$

We cross multiply to get $35C = 360\pi$. So $C = \frac{360\pi}{35} = \frac{72\pi}{7}$.

Next we find the radius of the circle using the formula $C = 2\pi r$. So we have $2\pi r = \frac{72\pi}{7}$, and so $r = \frac{36}{7}$.

Now, the area of the circle is $\pi \left(\frac{36}{7}\right)^2 = \frac{1296\pi}{49}$.

Finally, we set up another ratio to find the area a of the sector.

$$\frac{35}{360} = \frac{a}{\left(\frac{1296\pi}{49}\right)}$$

We cross multiply to get $\frac{6480\pi}{7} = 360a$. Therefore, $a = \frac{6480\pi}{7 \cdot 360} = \frac{18\pi}{7}$.

241

Now try to solve each of the following problems. The answers to these problems, followed by full solutions are at the end of this lesson. **Do not** look at the answers until you have attempted these problems yourself. Please remember to mark off any problems you get wrong.

LEVEL 2: GEOMETRY

1. In the xy-plane, the point $(0, 2)$ is the center of a circle that has radius 2. Which of the following is NOT a point on the circle?

    A. $(0, 4)$
    B. $(-2, 4)$
    C. $(2, 2)$
    D. $(-2, 2)$
    E. $(0, 0)$

LEVEL 3: GEOMETRY

2. What is the total area of the shaded region below to the nearest integer?

    F. 96
    G. 102
    H. 110
    J. 120
    K. 128

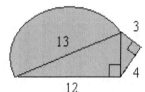

LEVEL 4: GEOMETRY

3. In the figure below, the diameters of the four semicircles are equal and lie on line segment $\overline{PQ}$. If the length of line segment $\overline{PQ}$ is $\frac{96}{\pi}$, what is the length of the curve from P to Q?

    A. 96π
    B. 48π
    C. 96
    D. 48
    E. 24

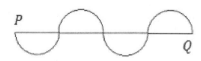

4. In the figure below, each of the points $A, B, C,$ and D is the center of a circle of diameter 6. Each of the four large circles is tangent to two of the other large circles, the small circle, and two sides of the square. What is the length of segment $\overline{BD}$?

F. $6\sqrt{3}$
G. $6\sqrt{2}$
H. $3\sqrt{2}$
J. 9
K. 6

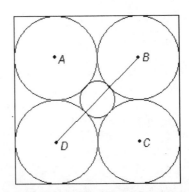

LEVEL 5: GEOMETRY

5. In the figure below, the circle has center O and radius 8. What is the length of arc PRQ?

A. 12π
B. $24\sqrt{2}$
C. 6π
D. $12\sqrt{2}$
E. $3\pi\sqrt{2}$

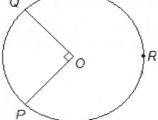

6. When the area of a certain circle is divided by 4π, the result is the cube of an integer. Which of the following could be the circumference of the circle?

F. 2π
G. 8π
H. 16π
J. 32π
K. 64π

243

7. If the diameter of a circle is doubled, by what percent is the area of the circle increased?

    A. 300%
    B. 200%
    C. 30%
    D. 20%
    E. 3%

8. In the figure below, O is the center of the circle, the two triangles have legs of lengths a, b, c, and d, as shown, $a^2 + b^2 + c^2 + d^2 = 15$, and the area of the circle is $k\pi$. What is the value of k?

    F. 7
    G. $\dfrac{15}{2}$
    H. 8
    J. $\dfrac{17}{2}$
    K. 15

9. In the figure below, arcs ABC and ADC each measure 270 degrees and each of these arcs is part of a circle of radius 8 inches. What is the area of the shaded region to the nearest inch?

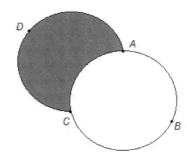

    A. 37
    B. 165
    C. 233
    D. 238
    E. 366

10. In the figure below, each of the four large circles is tangent to two of the other large circles, the small circle, and two sides of the square. If the radius of each of the large circles is 4, what is the <u>diameter</u> of the small circle?

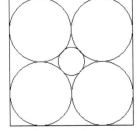

    F. $\sqrt{2}$ (approximately 1.414)
    G. 1
    H. $8\sqrt{2} - 8$ (approximately 3.314)
    J. $4\sqrt{2} - 4$ (approximately 1.657)
    K. $\sqrt{2} - 1$ (approximately 0.414)

11. In the figure below, AB is the arc of a circle with center O. If the length of arc AB is 4π, what is the area of region OAB to the nearest tenth?

    A. 89.2
    B. 89.5
    C. 89.8
    D. 90.2
    E. 90.5

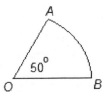

12. In the diagram below, chord $\overline{RS}$ is parallel to diameter $\overline{PQ}$. The length of $\overline{RS}$ is 10 centimeters and the length of $\overline{PQ}$ is 12 centimeters. What is the distance, in centimeters, of O, the center of the circle, to T, the midpoint of $\overline{RS}$?

    F. $\sqrt{11}$
    G. $\sqrt{13}$
    H. $2\sqrt{11}$
    J. 11
    K. 13

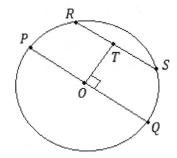

Answers

1. B	5. A	9. B
2. G	6. J	10. H
3. D	7. A	11. E
4. G	8. G	12. F

Full Solutions

2.

* Note that the side not labeled in the picture has length 5. To see this, you can use the Pythagorean triples $3 - 4 - 5$, or $5 - 12 - 13$. If you do not remember these triples you can use the Pythagorean Theorem:

$$c^2 = 3^2 + 4^2 = 9 + 16 = 25. \text{ So } c = 5.$$

or

$$13^2 = 12^2 + b^2. \text{ So } 169 = 144 + b^2, \text{ and } b^2 = 25. \text{ Thus, } b = 5.$$

Recall that the area of a triangle is $A = \frac{1}{2}bh$. The area of the smaller triangle is $(\frac{1}{2})3 \cdot 4 = 6$. The area of the larger triangle is $(\frac{1}{2})12 \cdot 5 = 30$.

Recall also that the area of a circle is πr^2. Thus, the area of the given semicircle is $\left(\frac{1}{2}\right)\pi\left(\frac{13}{2}\right)^2 = \left(\frac{169}{8}\right)\pi \approx 66.36614481 = 66$ to the nearest integer. Therefore, the total area to the nearest integer is

$$6 + 30 + 66 = 102.$$

This is choice **G**.

3.

* The diameter of each semicircle is $\frac{96}{\pi} \div 4 = \frac{24}{\pi}$. So the circumference of each semicircle is $\frac{1}{2}(\pi)(\frac{24}{\pi}) = 12$. Since we are adding up the lengths of four such semicircles, the answer is $(4)(12) = 48$, choice **D**.

Remark: Since a semicircle is half of a circle, the circumference of a semicircle with radius r is $C = \pi r$ (or $C = \frac{\pi d}{2}$).

4.

* We form a right triangle and observe that segments BC and CD each have length 6.

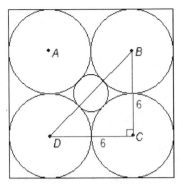

Note that a 45, 45, 90 triangle is formed (or use the Pythagorean Theorem) to get that $BD = 6\sqrt{2}$, choice **G**.

5.

Solution using a ratio: Note that there are 270 degrees in arc PRQ and the circumference of the circle is $C = 2\pi r = 16\pi$. So we solve for s in the following ratio.

$$\frac{270}{360} = \frac{s}{16\pi}$$

Cross multiplying gives $360s = 4320\pi$, and so $s = \frac{4320\pi}{360} = 12\pi$, choice **A**.

* **Quick solution:** Note that arc PQR is $\frac{3}{4}$ of the circumference of the circle and therefore PQR has length $s = (\frac{3}{4})(16\pi) = 12\pi$, choice **A**.

6.

* **Solution by starting with choice H:** Let's begin with choice H and suppose that the circumference is $C = 2\pi r = 16\pi$. Then $r = 8$ and $A = 64\pi$. When we divide 64π by 4π we get 16 which is **not** the cube of an integer.

Let's try choice J next. Then $C = 2\pi r = 32\pi$, so that $r = 16$ and $A = 256\pi$. When we divide 256π by 4π we get 64. Since $64 = 4^3$, the answer is choice **J**.

7.

Solution by picking numbers: Let's start with $d = 2$. Then $r = 1$ and $A = \pi$. Now let's double the diameter to $d = 4$. Then we have $r = 2$ and $A = 4\pi$. We now use the percent change formula.

$$Percent\ Change = \frac{Change}{Original} \times 100$$

The **original** value is π and the **change** is $4\pi - \pi = 3\pi$. So the area of the circle is increased by $\left(\frac{3\pi}{\pi}\right) \cdot 100 = 300\%$, choice **A**.

* Algebraic solution: Note that if the diameter is doubled, then so is the radius. So, if the area of the original circle is πr^2, then the area of the new circle is $\pi(2r)^2 = 4\pi r^2$. Thus, the **change** is $4\pi r^2 - \pi r^2 = 3\pi r^2$. Therefore, the area of the circle is increased by $\left(\frac{3\pi r^2}{\pi r^2}\right) \cdot 100 = 300\%$, choice **A**.

8.
* Notice that the hypotenuse of each triangle is a radius of the circle. By the Pythagorean Theorem, $a^2 + b^2 = r^2$ and $c^2 + d^2 = r^2$. So,

$$a^2 + b^2 + c^2 + d^2 = 2r^2.$$

Since the left hand side of the above equation is also equal to 15, we have that $2r^2 = 15$, and therefore $r^2 = \frac{15}{2}$.

Since the area of a circle is $A = \pi r^2$, we see that $k = \frac{15}{2}$, choice **G**.

9.
* Let's draw some pictures.

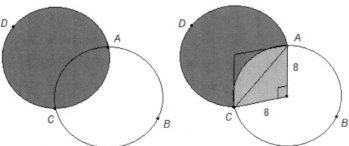

First note that the area we are looking for is the area of the whole circle (the shaded region in the figure on the left) minus the smaller shaded area in the figure on the left. The area of the whole circle is $\pi r^2 = 64\pi$.

We can find half of that smaller area by taking the light grey area on the left minus the light gray triangle on the left in the rightmost figure.

The light grey area is the area of a sector of the circle that is $\frac{1}{4}$ the area of the whole circle. So it is 16π. The area of the triangle is $(\frac{1}{2})(8)(8) = 32$. So half the area we are looking for is $16\pi - 32$.

Final area: $A = 64\pi - 2(16\pi - 32) = 64\pi - 32\pi + 64 = 32\pi + 64$

To the nearest inch, this is 165, choice **B**.

10.

* We draw an isosceles right triangle.

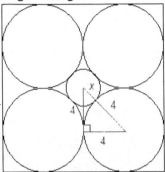

Note that each length labeled with a 4 is equal to the radius of one of the larger circles (the radius is half the diameter). The length labeled x is the radius of the smaller circle. An isosceles right triangle is the same as a 45, 45, 90 right triangle. By looking at the formula for a 45, 45, 90 triangle we see that $x + 4 = 4\sqrt{2}$ and so $x = 4\sqrt{2} - 4$. The diameter is then $2x = 2(4\sqrt{2} - 4) = 8\sqrt{2} - 8$, choice **H**.

Remark: We can also use the Pythagorean Theorem to find x. We have $(x + 4)^2 = 4^2 + 4^2 = 16 + 16 = 32$. So $x + 4 = \sqrt{32} = 4\sqrt{2}$ and so $x = 4\sqrt{2} - 4$, choice H.

Also, if you are uncomfortable simplifying square roots, you can simply perform the computations in your calculator and compare with the numbers next to "approximately" in the answer choices.

11.

* We first find the circumference of the circle using the ratio $\frac{50}{360} = \frac{4\pi}{c}$.

Cross multiplying gives $50C = 1440\pi$, so $C = \frac{1440\pi}{50} = \frac{144\pi}{5}$. Since $C = 2\pi r$, we have $2\pi r = \frac{144\pi}{5}$, so $r = \frac{72}{5}$. The area of the circle is $A = \pi r^2 = \frac{5184\pi}{25}$. Now we find the area of the sector using the ratio $\frac{50}{360} = \frac{a}{(5184\pi)/25}$.

Cross multiplying gives us $360a = 10{,}368\pi$. So $a = \frac{10{,}368\pi}{360} \approx 90.478$. To the nearest tenth this is 90.5, choice **E**.

12.
* Let's add some information to the diagram.

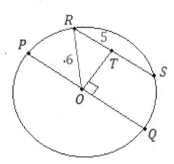

Since $RS = 12$ and T is the midpoint of $\overline{RS}$, it follows that $RT = 5$. Similarly, $OP = 6$. Since $\overline{OR}$ is a radius of the circle, it has the same length as the radius $\overline{OP}$, and so we have $OR = OP = 6$. By the Pythagorean Theorem, $OT^2 + 5^2 = 6^2$, and so $OT^2 = 36 - 25 = 11$. Therefore, $OT = \sqrt{11}$, choice **F**.

OPTIONAL MATERIAL

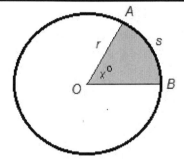

If we solve for s and a in the ratios $\frac{x}{360} = \frac{s}{C}$ and $\frac{x}{360} = \frac{a}{A}$, we get

$$s = \frac{\pi r x}{180} \qquad \text{and} \qquad a = \frac{\pi r^2 x}{360}$$

If you like you can memorize these formulas. I prefer to just set up the ratios.

LESSON 20
STATISTICS

Reminder: Before beginning this lesson remember to redo the problems from Lessons 4, 8, 12 and 16 that you have marked off. Do not "unmark" a question unless you get it correct.

Change Averages to Sums

A problem involving averages often becomes much easier when we first convert the averages to sums. We can easily change an average to a sum using the following simple formula.

Sum = Average · Number

Many problems with averages involve one or more conversions to sums, followed by a subtraction.

Try to answer the following question using this strategy. **Do not** check the solution until you have attempted this question yourself.

LEVEL 3: STATISTICS

1. The average of x, y, z, and w is 15 and the average of z and w is 11. What is the average of x and y?

    A. 11
    B. 13
    C. 15
    D. 17
    E. 19

Solution

* The Sum of x, y, z, and w is $15 \cdot 4 = 60$. The Sum of z and w is $11 \cdot 2 = 22$. Thus, the Sum of x and y is $60 - 22 = 38$. Finally, the Average of x and y is $\frac{38}{2} = 19$, choice **E**.

Notes: (1) We used the formula "**Sum = Average · Number**" twice here. (2) More formally we have the following.

251

$$x + y + z + w = 60$$
$$\underline{z + w = 22}$$
$$x + y \qquad\quad = 38$$

Thus, $\frac{x+y}{2} = \frac{38}{2} = 19$.

Before we go on, try to solve this problem in two other ways.

(1) By "Picking Numbers"
(2) Algebraically (the way you would do it in school)

Solutions

(1) Let's let $z = w = 11$ and $x = y = 19$. Note that the average of x, y, z, and w is 15 and the average of z and w is 11. Now just observe that the average of x and y is 19, choice **E**.

Remarks: (1) If all numbers in a list are all equal, then the average of these numbers is that number as well.

(2) When choosing numbers to form a certain average, just "balance" these numbers around the average. In this example we chose z and w to be $15 - 4 = 11$. Since 11 is 4 less than the average, we chose x and y to be 4 greater than the average.

(2) We are given that $\frac{x+y+z+w}{4} = 15$ and $\frac{z+w}{2} = 11$. We multiply each side of the first equation by 4 and each side of the second equation by 2 to eliminate the denominators. Then we subtract the second equation from the first.

$$x + y + z + w = 60$$
$$\underline{z + w = 22}$$
$$x + y \qquad\quad = 38$$

Finally, the average of x and y is $\frac{x+y}{2} = \frac{38}{2} = 19$, choice **E**.

Important note: You should avoid this method on the actual ACT. It is too time consuming.

The Median of a Set of Consecutive Integers

If x is the least integer in a list of $n + 1$ consecutive integers, then the median of the set is $x + \frac{n}{2}$.

Example: Compute the median of 5, 6, 7,..., 127.

By the fence-post formula there are $127 - 5 + 1 = 123$ integers in this list. Therefore, the median is $5 + \frac{122}{2} = \mathbf{66}$.

Remarks: (1) See Lesson 13 for a review of the fence-post formula.

(2) Note that if the number of integers in the list is odd, the median will be an integer. If the number of integers in the list is even, the median will not be an integer.

(3) If the number of integers in the list is even, then there are two middle numbers, and the median is the average of these two numbers.

Now try to solve each of the following problems. The answers to these problems, followed by full solutions are at the end of this lesson. **Do not** look at the answers until you have attempted these problems yourself. Please remember to mark off any problems you get wrong.

LEVEL 3: STATISTICS

2. If the average (arithmetic mean) of a, b, and 23 is 12, what is the average of a and b?

    F. 6.5
    G. 11
    H. 13
    J. 15
    K. It cannot be determined from the information given.

3. Set X contains only the integers 0 through 180 inclusive. If a number is selected at random from X, what is the probability that the number selected will be greater than the median of the numbers in X?

    A. $\frac{89}{180}$
    B. $\frac{90}{181}$
    C. $\frac{1}{2}$
    D. $\frac{91}{181}$
    E. $\frac{91}{180}$

253

4. Daniel and eight other students took two exams, and each exam yielded an integer grade for each student. The two grades for each student were added together. The sum of these two grades for each of the nine students was 150, 183, 100, 126, 151, 171, 106, 164, and Daniel's sum, which was the median of the nine sums. If Daniel's first test grade was 70, what is one possible grade Daniel could have received on the second test?

    F. 76
    G. 78
    H. 80
    J. 82
    K. 84

LEVEL 4: STATISTICS

5. The average (arithmetic mean) of 11 numbers is j. If one of the numbers is k, what is the average of the remaining 10 numbers in terms of j and k?

    A. $\dfrac{k}{11}$
    B. $11j + k$
    C. $\dfrac{10j-k}{11}$
    D. $\dfrac{11j-k}{10}$
    E. $\dfrac{11k-j}{10}$

6. The average (arithmetic mean) of a, $2a$, b, and $4b$ is $2a$. What is b in terms of a?

    F. $\dfrac{a}{4}$
    G. $\dfrac{a}{2}$
    H. a
    J. $\dfrac{3a}{2}$
    K. $2a$

7. On a certain exam, the median grade for a group of 25 students is 67. If the highest grade on the exam is 90, which of the following could be the number of students that scored 67 on the exam?

    I. 5
    II. 20
    III. 24

    A. I only
    B. III only
    C. I and II only
    D. I and III only
    E. I, II, and III

8. If the average (arithmetic mean) of k and $k + 7$ is b and if the average of k and $k - 11$ is c, what is the sum of b and c?

    F. $2k - 2$
    G. $2k - 1$
    H. $2k$
    J. $2k + \frac{1}{2}$
    K. $4k$

9. Twenty-six people were playing a game. 1 person scored 50 points, 3 people scored 60 points, 4 people scored 70 points, 5 people scored 80 points, 6 people scored 90 points, and 7 people scored 100 points. Which of the following correctly shows the order of the median, mode and average (arithmetic mean) of the 26 scores?

    A. average < median< mode
    B. average < mode < median
    C. median < mode < average
    D. median < average < mode
    E. mode < median < average

10. If the average (arithmetic mean) of the measures of two noncongruent angles of an isosceles triangle is 75°, which of the following is the measure of one of the angles of the triangle?

    F. 110°
    G. 120°
    H. 130°
    J. 140°
    K. 150°

LEVEL 5: STATISTICS

11. If $h = a + b + c + d + e + f + g$, what is the average (arithmetic mean) of a, b, c, d, e, f, g and h in terms of h?

    A. $\dfrac{h}{2}$

    B. $\dfrac{h}{3}$

    C. $\dfrac{h}{4}$

    D. $\dfrac{h}{5}$

    E. $\dfrac{h}{6}$

$$\frac{1}{x^3}, \frac{1}{x^2}, \frac{1}{x}, x^2, x^3$$

12. If $-1 < x < 0$, what is the median of the five numbers in the list above?

    F. $\dfrac{1}{x^3}$

    G. $\dfrac{1}{x^2}$

    H. $\dfrac{1}{x}$

    J. x^2

    K. x^3

Answers

1. E	5. D	9. A
2. F	6. H	10. G
3. B	7. E	11. C
4. H	8. F	12. K

Full Solutions

2.

* Solution by changing averages to sums: The Sum of the 3 numbers is $12 \cdot 3 = 36$. Thus, $a + b + 23 = 36$, and it follows that $a + b = 13$. So the Average of a and b is $\dfrac{13}{2} = 6.5$, choice **F**.

256

Solution by picking numbers: Let's let $a = 1$ and $b = 12$. We make this choice because 1 and 23 are both 11 units from 12. Then the Average of a and b is $\frac{a + b}{2} = \frac{1 + 12}{2} = \frac{13}{2} = 6.5$. So the answer is probably choice **F**.

Remark: We actually never quite ruled out choice K as the answer in the second solution. In this sense, the first solution is better.

    3.

* There are a total of 181 integers and 90 of them are greater than the median. So the desired probability is $\frac{90}{181}$, choice **B**.

Remark: By the fence-post formula there are $180 - 0 + 1 = 181$ integers in the list. Therefore, the median of the numbers in set X is $0 + \frac{180}{2} = 90$.

Again, by the fence-post formula, there are $180 - 91 + 1 = 90$ integers greater than the median.

    4.

* Let's begin by writing the sums in increasing order.

$$100, 106, 126, 150, 151, 164, 171, 183$$

Since Daniel's sum is the median, it is 150 or 151. Let's try one, say 150. Since Daniel's first test grade was 70, it follows that his second test grade was $150 - 70 = 80$, choice **H**.

Remark: The other choice for the median yields $151 - 70 = 81$, which is not an answer choice.

    5.

* **Solution by changing averages to sums:** The Sum of the 11 numbers is $11j$. The Sum of the remaining 10 numbers is $11j - k$ (after removing k). So the Average of the remaining 10 numbers is $\frac{11j - k}{10}$, choice **D**.

    6.

* **Solution by changing averages to sums:** Converting the Average to a Sum we have that $a + 2a + b + 4b = (2a)(4)$. That is, $3a + 5b = 8a$. Subtracting $3a$ from each side of this equation yields $5b = 5a$. Finally, we divide each side of this last equation by 5 to get $b = a$, choice **H**.

7.
* The highest exam grade must be 90. If the other 24 exam grades are 67, then the median will be 67. So III is possible.

If 5 of the exam grades are 90 and the remaining 20 are 67, then the median will be 67. So II is possible.

Finally, if 10 of the exam grades are 90, 10 are 60 and 5 are 67, then the median will be 67. So I is possible.

Therefore, the answer is choice **E**.

8.
* **Solution by changing averages to sums:** Note that the sum of k and $k + 7$ is $k + (k + 7) = 2k + 7$, so that $2k + 7 = 2b$. Similarly, the sum of k and $k - 11$ is $k + (k - 11) = 2k - 11$ so that $2k - 11 = 2c$. So,

$$2b + 2c = 4k - 4$$
$$2(b + c) = 4k - 4$$
$$b + c = \frac{4k - 4}{2} = \frac{4k}{2} - \frac{4}{2} = 2k - 2$$

Thus, the answer is choice **F**.

Solution by picking numbers: Let us choose a value for k, say $k = 5$. It follows that $k + 7 = 5 + 7 = 12$ and $k - 11 = 5 - 11 = -6$. So,

$$b = \frac{5+12}{2} = \frac{17}{2} = 8.5$$
$$c = \frac{5-6}{2} = -\frac{1}{2} = -0.5$$

and the sum of b and c is $b + c = 8.5 - 0.5 = 8$. **Put a nice big, dark circle around this number so that you can find it easily later.** We now substitute $k = 5$ into each answer choice.

F. 8
G. 9
H. 10
J. 10.5
K. 20

Compare each of these numbers to the number that we put a nice big, dark circle around. Since G, H, J, and K are incorrect we can eliminate them. Therefore, the answer is choice **F**.

Important note: F is **not** the correct answer simply because it is equal to 8. It is correct because all four of the other choices are **not** 8. **You absolutely must check all five choices!**

9.
* The median of 26 numbers is the average of the 13th and 14th numbers when the numbers are listed in increasing order (see remark below).

$$50, 60, 60, 60, 70, 70, 70, 70, 80, 80, 80, 80, \mathbf{80}, \mathbf{90}$$

So we see that the median is $\frac{80 + 90}{2} = 85$.

The mode is the number that appears most frequently. This is **100**.

Finally, we compute the average.

$$\frac{1 \cdot 50 + 3 \cdot 60 + 4 \cdot 70 + 5 \cdot 80 + 6 \cdot 90 + 7 \cdot 100}{26} = \frac{2150}{26} \approx 82.69.$$

Thus, we see that average < median < mode. This is choice **A**.

Remark: If n numbers are listed in increasing (or decreasing) order, with n even, then the median of these numbers is the average of the kth and $(k + 1)$st numbers where $k = \frac{n}{2}$. In this example, $n = 26$. So $k = 13$, and the 13th and 14th numbers are 80 and 90.

10.
* **Solution by changing averages to sums:** The Sum of the measures of the two noncongruent angles of the isosceles triangle is $(75)(2) = 150°$.

Thus, the third angle is $180 - 150 = 30°$. Since the triangle is isosceles, one of the original angles must also be $30°$. It follows that the other original angle was $180 - 30 - 30 = 120$, choice **G**.

11.

* The average of a, b, c, d, e, f, g and h is

$$\frac{a+b+c+d+e+f+g+h}{8}$$
$$=\frac{a+b+c+d+e+f+g+a+b+c+d+e+f+g}{8}$$
$$=\frac{2a+2b+2c+2d+2e+2f+2g}{8}$$
$$=\frac{2(a+b+c+d+e+f+g)}{8}$$
$$=\frac{2h}{8}$$
$$=\frac{h}{4}$$

This is choice **C**.

Alternate solution by picking numbers: Let's let $a = 1$, $b = 2, c = 3$, $d = 4$, $e = 5$, $f = 6$, and $g = 7$. Then $h = 28$, and the average of a, b, c, d, e, f, g and h is $\frac{1+2+3+4+5+6+7+28}{8} = \frac{56}{8} = 7$. Put a nice big, dark circle around this number. Now plug $h = 28$ in to each answer choice.

    A. 14
    B. 9.3333 ...
    C. 7
    D. 5.6
    E. 4.6666 ...

Since A, B, D, and E are incorrect we can eliminate them. Therefore, the answer is choice **C**.

12.

* **Solution by picking numbers:** Let's choose $x = -0.5$.

We use our calculator to compute the given expressions.

$$\frac{1}{x^3} = -8 \quad \frac{1}{x^2} = 4 \quad \frac{1}{x} = -2 \quad x^2 = 0.25 \quad x^3 = -0.125$$

Now let's place them in increasing order.

$$-8, -2, -0.125, 0.25, 4$$

The median is -0.125 which is x^3, choice **K**.

260

OPTIONAL MATERIAL

CHALLENGE QUESTIONS

1. Suppose that the average (arithmetic mean) of a, b, and c is h, the average of b, c, and d is j, and the average of d and e is k. What is the average of a and e?

   A. $h - j + k$

   B. $\dfrac{3h + 3j - 2k}{2}$

   C. $\dfrac{3h - 3j + 2k}{2}$

   D. $\dfrac{3h - 3j + 2k}{5}$

   E. $\dfrac{3h - 3j + 2k}{8}$

2. Show that if x is the least integer in a set of $n + 1$ consecutive integers, then the median of the set is $x + \dfrac{n}{2}$.

3. Show that in a set of consecutive integers, the average (arithmetic mean) and median are equal.

Solutions

1.

* Solution by changing averages to sums and using simple operations: We have that $a + b + c = 3h$, $b + c + d = 3j$, and $d + e = 2k$. If we subtract the second equation from the first, and then add the third equation we get $a + e = 3h - 3j + 2k$. So the average of a and e is $\dfrac{a + e}{2} = \dfrac{3h - 3j + 2k}{2}$, choice **C**.

Solution by picking numbers: Let's choose values for a, b, c, d, and e, say $a = 1$, $b = 2$, $c = 3$, $d = 4$, and $e = 6$. Then $h = 2$, $j = 3$, $k = 5$ and the average of a and e is 3.5. The answer choices become

A. 4
B. 2.5
C. 3.5
D. 1.4
E. 0.875

Since A, B, D, and E came out incorrect, the answer is choice **C**.

2.

Assume that the integers are written in increasing order. If n is even, then $n + 1$ is odd, and the median is in position $\frac{n+2}{2} = \frac{n}{2} + 1$. Note that $x = x + 0$ is in the 1st position, $x + 1$ is in the 2nd position, etc. Thus, $x + \frac{n}{2}$ is in position $\frac{n}{2} + 1$.

If n is odd, then $n + 1$ is even, and the median is the average of the integers in positions $\frac{n+1}{2}$ and $\frac{n+1}{2} + 1$. These integers are $x + \frac{n+1}{2} - 1$ and $x + \frac{n+1}{2}$. So their average is

$$\left(\tfrac{1}{2}\right)(2x + (n + 1) - 1) = \left(\tfrac{1}{2}\right)(2x + n) = x + \frac{n}{2}.$$

3.

Let $\{x, x + 1, x + 2, ..., x + n\}$ be a set of $n + 1$ consecutive integers. The average is equal to

$$\frac{(n + 1)x + (1 + 2 + \cdots + n)}{n + 1} = \frac{(n + 1)x}{n + 1} + \frac{n(n + 1)}{2(n + 1)} = x + \frac{n}{2}.$$

Remark: $1 + 2 + \cdots + n = \frac{n(n + 1)}{2}$.

To see that this we can formally write out the sum of the numbers from 1 through n forwards and backwards, and then add term by term.

$$
\begin{array}{ccccccc}
1 & + & 2 & + & 3 & + \cdots + (n - 1) + & n \\
n & + (n - 1) & + (n - 2) & + \cdots + & 2 & + & 1 \\
\end{array}
$$
$$(n + 1) + (n + 1) + (n + 1) + \cdots + (n + 1) + (n + 1)$$

We are adding $n + 1$ to itself n times, so that $2(1 + \cdots + n) = n(n + 1)$. So $1 + \cdots + n = \frac{n(n+1)}{2}$.

LESSON 21
NUMBER THEORY

Reminder: Before beginning this lesson remember to redo the problems from Lessons 1, 5, 9, 13 and 17 that you have marked off. Do not "unmark" a question unless you get it correct.

Search for a Pattern

If a question is asking about large numbers, it may be helpful to start with smaller numbers and search for a pattern.

Try to answer the following question by searching for a pattern. **Do not** check the solution until you have attempted this question yourself.

LEVEL 5: NUMBER THEORY

1. In an empty square field, m rows of m trees are planted so that the whole field is filled with trees. If k of these trees lie along the boundary of the field, which of the following is a possible value for k?

    A. 14
    B. 49
    C. 86
    D. 125
    E. 276

Solution

* We will systematically try values for m, and draw a picture of the situation to determine the corresponding value for k.

Here is the picture for $m = 3$.

Note that $k = 9 - 1 = 8$.

263

Here is the picture for $m = 4$.

Note that $k = 16 - 4 = 12$.

So the pattern appears to be $8, 12, 16, 20, 24, 28, \ldots$ Make sure that you keep drawing pictures until this is clear to you. So we see that the answer must be divisible by 4.

Beginning with choice C we have $\frac{86}{4} = 21.5$. So choice C is not the answer. We can eliminate choices B and D because they end in an odd digit. Trying choice E, we have $\frac{276}{4} = 69$. Thus, 276 is divisible by 4, and the answer is choice **E**.

Some rigorous mathematics: Let's prove that for each m, the corresponding k is divisible by 4. For fixed m, the total number of trees is m^2, and the total number of trees that are **not** on the boundary is $(m - 2)^2 = m^2 - 4m + 4$. Thus, the number of trees on the boundary is

$$k = m^2 - (m^2 - 4m + 4) = m^2 - m^2 + 4m - 4$$
$$= 4m - 4 = 4(m - 1)$$

which is divisible by 4.

Sums and Products of Odd and Even Integers

The following describes what happens when you add and multiply various combinations of even and odd integers.

$$\begin{array}{ll} e + e = e & ee = e \\ e + o = o & eo = e \\ o + e = o & oe = e \\ o + o = e & oo = o \end{array}$$

For example, the sum of an even and an odd integer is odd ($e + o = o$).

Try to answer the following question. **Do not** check the solution until you have attempted this question yourself.

LEVEL 5: NUMBER THEORY

2. If x and y are integers and $x^2y + xy^2 + x^2y^2$ is odd, which of the following statements must be true?

> I. x is odd
> II. xy is odd
> III. $x + y$ is odd

    F. I only
    G. II only
    H. III only
    J. I and II only
    K. I, II, and III

Solution

* Note that $x^2y + xy^2 + x^2y^2 = xy(x + y + xy)$. The only way a product can be odd is if each factor is odd. Therefore, x, y and $x + y + xy$ all must be odd. Since the product of two odd integers is odd, xy must also be odd. If $x + y$ were odd, then $x + y + xy$ would be the sum of two odds, thus even. Thus, $x + y$ cannot be odd. Therefore, the answer is choice **J**.

Sequences and Products of Consecutive Integers

In a sequence of two consecutive integers, one of the integers is always divisible by 2 (even). In a sequence of three consecutive integers, one of the integers is always divisible by 3. In general, in a sequence of n consecutive integers, one of the integers is always divisible by n.

It follows that the product of n consecutive integers is divisible by $n!$. For example, the product of two consecutive integers is divisible by $2! = 2$, the product of three consecutive integers is divisible by $3! = 6$, and the product of four consecutive integers is divisible by $4! = 24$, etc.

Try to answer the following question. **Do not** check the solution until you have attempted this question yourself.

LEVEL 5: NUMBER THEORY

3. If n is a positive integer and $k = n^3 - n$, which of the following statements about k must be true for all values of n?

> I. k is a multiple of 3
> II. k is a multiple of 4
> III. k is a multiple of 6

>   **A.** I only
>   **B.** II only
>   **C.** III only
>   **D.** I and III only
>   **E.** I, II, and III

Solution

$$n^3 - n = n(n^2 - 1) = n(n - 1)(n + 1) = (n - 1)n(n + 1).$$

Thus, $n^3 - n$ is a product of 3 consecutive integers. The product of 3 consecutive integers is divisible by $3! = 6$, and therefore also by 3. If we let $n = 2$, then $k = 6$. So k does **not** have to be a multiple of 4. Thus, the answer is choice **D**.

Before we go on, try to also answer this question by picking numbers.

Solution

Let's try some values for n.

$n = 2$. Then $k = 6$. This shows that II can be false. So we can eliminate choices B and E.

$n = 3$. Then $k = 24$. This is divisible by both 3 and 6.

$n = 4$. Then $k = 60$. This is again divisible by both 3 and 6.

The evidence seems to suggest that the answer is choice **D**.

Remark: This method is a bit risky. Since this is a Level 5 problem, there is a chance that some large value of n might provide a counterexample. In this problem, it turns out not to be the case, and the answer is in fact choice D.

Now try to solve each of the following problems. The answers to these problems, followed by full solutions are at the end of this lesson. **Do not** look at the answers until you have attempted these problems yourself. Please remember to mark off any problems you get wrong.

LEVEL 5: NUMBER THEORY

4. The first two numbers of a sequence are 5 and 7, respectively. The third number is 12, and, in general, every number after the second is the sum of the two numbers immediately preceding it. How many of the first 400 numbers in the sequence are odd?

   F. 268
   G. 267
   H. 266
   J. 134
   K. 133

5. If $\frac{jk}{v}$ is an integer which of the following must also be an integer?

   A. jkv

   B. $\frac{3j^2k^2}{v^2}$

   C. $\frac{jv}{k}$

   D. $\frac{kv}{j}$

   E. $\frac{j}{kv}$

6. In how many of the integers from 1 to 150 does the digit 7 appear at least once?

   F. 14
   G. 15
   H. 23
   J. 24
   K. 25

267

7. If n is a positive integer such that the units (ones) digit of $n^2 + 4n$ is 7 and the units digit of n is <u>not</u> 7, what is the units digit of $n + 3$?

    A. 1
    B. 2
    C. 3
    D. 4
    E. 5

8. A list consists of 20 consecutive positive integers. Which of the following could be the number of integers in the list that are divisible by 19?

      I. None
      II. One
      III. Two

    F. I only
    G. II only
    H. III only
    J. II and III only
    K. I, II, and III

9. If k, m, and n are distinct positive integers such that n is divisible by m, and m is divisible by k, which of the following statements must be true?

      I. n is divisible by k.
      II. $n = mk$.
      III. n has more than 2 positive factors.

    A. I only
    B. III only
    C. I and II only
    D. I and III only
    E. I, II, and III

10. If $a_k = 5 + 5^2 + 5^3 + 5^4 + \cdots 5^k$, for which of the following values of k will a_k be divisible by 10?

    F. 5
    G. 17
    H. 66
    J. 81
    K. 99

268

11. The sum of c and $2d$ is equal to k, and the product of c and $2d$ is equal to j. If j and k are positive numbers, what is $\frac{10}{c} + \frac{5}{d}$ in terms of j and k?

   A. $\dfrac{j}{10k}$

   B. $\dfrac{10k}{j}$

   C. $10jk$

   D. $\dfrac{10}{j} + \dfrac{5}{k}$

   E. $\dfrac{10}{2j+k}$

12. The integer k is equal to m^2 for some integer m. If k is divisible by 20 and 24, what is the smallest possible positive value of k?

   F. 44
   G. 240
   H. 480
   J. 2500
   K. 3600

Answers

1. E	5. B	9. D
2. J	6. J	10. H
3. D	7. B	11. B
4. G	8. J	12. K

Full Solutions

4.

* Start writing out the terms of the sequence.

$$5, 7, 12, 19, 31, 50, 81, 131, 212, \ldots$$

Notice that the pattern is odd, odd, even, odd, odd, even, ...

The greatest number less than 400 that is divisible by 3 is 399. So of the first 399 numbers in the sequence $\frac{2}{3} \cdot 399 = 266$ are odd. The 400th term is odd, and therefore the answer is $266 + 1 = 267$, choice **G**.

269

Remark: Notice that this is also a "remainders in disguise" problem. We checked divisibility by 3 because the pattern repeats every third term. Any term which is divisible by 3 behaves like the third term of the sequence. Any term which has a remainder of 1 when divided by 3 behaves like the first term of the sequence. And any term which has a remainder of 2 when divided by 3 behaves like the second term of the sequence. Here is the sequence listed while keeping track of which remainder it goes with.

remainder 1 (odd)	remainder 2 (odd)	No remainder (even)
5	7	12
19	31	50
81	131	212
343	...	...

5.

Solution by picking numbers: Let's choose values for j, k, and v, say $j = 3$, $k = 4$, and $v = 2$. Then $\frac{jk}{v} = \frac{3 \cdot 4}{2} = 6$, an integer. So the given condition is satisfied. Now let's check the answer choices.

A. $jkv = 3 * 4 * 2 = 24$

B. $\frac{3j^2k^2}{v^2} = (3)(9)(16)/4 = 108$

C. $\frac{jv}{k} = (3)(2)/4 = 1.5$

D. $\frac{kv}{j} = (4)(2)/3 \approx 2.67$

E. $\frac{j}{kv} = 3/(4*2) = 0.375$

So we can eliminate choices C, D, and E. Let's try another set of numbers, say $j = 0.5$, $k = 1$, and $v = 0.5$. Then $\frac{jk}{v} = \frac{0.5 \cdot 1}{0.5} = 1$. Let's check the remaining answer choices.

A. $jkv = 0.5 * 1 * 0.5 = 0.25$

B. $\frac{3j^2k^2}{v^2} = (3)(0.25)(1)/0.25 = 3$

So we can eliminate choice A, and the answer is choice **B**.

* Advanced method: Let $\frac{jk}{v}$ be an integer. Then $\frac{3j^2k^2}{v^2} = 3\left(\frac{jk}{v}\right)^2$ is an integer because the product of integers is an integer.

270

Remark: If you are having trouble seeing that the expression in the advanced method is an integer, the following might help. Since $\frac{jk}{v}$ is an integer, we can write $\frac{jk}{v} = n$ for some integer n. It then follows that $\frac{3j^2k^2}{v^2} = 3\left(\frac{jk}{v}\right)^2 = 3n^2$ is an integer because when we multiply integers together we get an integer.

6.
* Let's list these integers **carefully**.

$$7, 17, 27, 37, 47, 57, 67, \mathbf{70, 71, 72, 73, 74, 75, 76, 77, 78, 79},$$

$$87, 97, 107, 117, 127, 137, 147$$

We see that there are 24 such integers, choice **J**.

7.
* By plugging in values of n, we find that for $n = 9$,

$$n^2 + 4n = 9^2 + 4 \cdot 9 = 81 + 36 = 117.$$

So $n = 9$ works, and $n + 3 = 9 + 3 = 12$. So the units digit of $n + 3$ is 2, choice **B**.

Advanced solution showing the independence of n:

$n^2 + 4n = n(n + 4)$. So we are looking at positive integers 4 units apart whose product ends in 7. Since 7 is odd, n must be odd. So n must end in 1, 3, 5, or 9. Note that we skip $n = 7$ since the problem forbids us from using it.

If n ends in 1, then $n + 4$ ends in 5, and $n(n + 4)$ ends in 5.
If n ends in 3, then $n + 4$ ends in 7, and $n(n + 4)$ ends in 1.
If n ends in 5, then $n + 4$ ends in 9, and $n(n + 4)$ ends in 5.
If n ends in 9, then $n + 4$ ends in 13, and $n(n + 4)$ ends in **7**.

So n ends in a 9, and $n + 3$ ends in a 2, choice **B**.

8.
* **Solution by picking numbers:** Consider the following two lists.

$$1, 2, 3, \dots, 19, 20$$
$$19, 20, 21, \dots, 37, 38$$

The first list consists of twenty consecutive integers with one integer divisible by 19, and the second list consists of twenty consecutive integers with two integers divisible by 19. Thus, the answer is either choice J or K.

Now recall that remainders are cyclical. If we start with a positive integer not divisible by 19, then within 19 integers we will arrive at one that is divisible by 19. Therefore, the answer is choice **J**.

As an example, if we begin with a positive integer that has a remainder of 1 when divided by 19, then the sequence of remainders is as follows.

$$1, 2, 3, 4, \dots, 17, 18, 0, 1$$

Recall: In a sequence of n consecutive integers, one of the integers is always divisible by n. In this example we have 20 consecutive integers. So if we take the first 19, then one of these is divisible by 19.

9.
* Let's pick some numbers. Let $k = 3$, $m = 15$, and $n = 30$. Then n is divisible by m, and m is divisible by k. Let's look at each roman numeral now.

      I. 30 is divisible by 3. True.
      II. $30 = 15 \cdot 3$. False.
      III. The factors of 30 are $1, 2, 3, 5, 6, 10, 15$, and 30. True.

Since II is false we can eliminate choices C and E. Answer choice D would be a good guess at this point. There are now 2 ways to complete this problem:

Method 1: Pick another set of numbers and verify that I and III are still true. This will give more evidence that choice D is correct, thus making choice **D** the best guess.

Method 2 (advanced): Let's show that I and III always hold under the given conditions.

Let's start with I. Since n is divisible by m, there is an integer b such that $n = mb$. Since m is divisible by k, there is an integer c such that $m = kc$. Thus, $n = mb = (kc)b = k(cb)$. Since cb is an integer it follows that n is divisible by k.

And now III. Since n is divisible by m, m is a factor of n. We also just showed that n is divisible by k. So k is a factor of n. Also, every integer is a factor of itself. Thus, n is a factor of n. So k, m, and n are 3 factors of n. The problem tells us they are distinct.

Therefore, the answer is choice **D**.

10.
* Solution by searching for a pattern:
$a_1 = 5$ which is **not** divisible by 10.
$a_2 = 5 + 5^2 = 30$ which is divisible by 10.
$a_3 = 5 + 5^2 + 5^3 = 155$ which is **not** divisible by 10.
$a_4 = 5 + 5^2 + 5^3 + 5^4 = 780$ which is divisible by 10.

Note that a_k is divisible by 10 precisely when k is even. Thus, the answer is choice **H**.

Remarks: (1) Make sure to write out as many values of a_k as you need to convince yourself that a_k is divisible by 10 precisely when k is even.

(2) Note that $5 + 5^2 + 5^3 + \cdots + 5^k = 5(1 + 5 + 5^2 + \cdots + 5^{k-1})$. This expression is 5 times an integer so that it is divisible by 5. It will therefore be divisible by 10 if and only if $1 + 5 + 5^2 + \cdots + 5^{k-1}$ is even (divisible by 2). Since each term here is odd, this sum will be even if and only if there is an even number of terms, i.e. k is even.

11.
Solution by picking numbers: Let's choose values for c and d, say $c = 10$ and $d = 5$. Then $k = c + 2d = 10 + 2(5) = 20$, and $j = c(2d) = 10(2 \cdot 5) = 100$. Now, $\frac{10}{c} + \frac{5}{d} = \frac{10}{10} + \frac{5}{5} = 2$. **Put a nice big, dark circle around this number so that you can find it easily later.** We now substitute $k = 20$ and $j = 100$ into each answer choice and use our calculator.

A. $\frac{j}{10k} = \frac{100}{10*20} = 0.5$

B. $\frac{10k}{j} = 10 * \frac{20}{100} = 2$

C. $10jk = 10 * 100 * 20 = 20,000$

D. $\frac{10}{j} + \frac{5}{k} = 10/100 + 5/20 = 0.35$

E. $\frac{10}{2j+k} = 10/(2*100 + 20) \approx 0.045$

Compare each of these numbers to the number that we put a nice big, dark circle around. Since A, C, D and E are incorrect we can eliminate them. Therefore, the answer is choice **B**.

* **Algebraic solution:** We get a common denominator of $2cd$ by multiplying the numerator and denominator of the left term by $2d$, and the right term by $2c$.

$$\frac{10}{c} + \frac{5}{d} = \frac{10(2d)}{c(2d)} + \frac{5(2c)}{d(2c)} = \frac{20d}{2cd} + \frac{10c}{2cd} = \frac{10(2d+c)}{2cd} = \frac{10k}{j}.$$

This is answer choice **B**.

    12.
* We are looking for the smallest perfect square that is divisible by the least common multiple of 20 and 24. Now $20 = 2^2 \cdot 5$, and $24 = 2^3 \cdot 3$. So $\text{lcm}(20,24) = 2^3 \cdot 3 \cdot 5$. The least perfect square divisible by this number is $2^4 \cdot 3^2 \cdot 5^2 = 3600$, choice **K**.

Download additional solutions for free here:

www.satprepget800.com/28LesAdv

LESSON 22
ALGEBRA AND FUNCTIONS

Reminder: Before beginning this lesson remember to redo the problems from Lessons 2, 6, 10, 14 and 18 that you have marked off. Do not "unmark" a question unless you get it correct.

Standard Form for a Quadratic Function

The standard form for a quadratic function is

$$y - k = a(x - h)^2 \quad \text{or} \quad y = a(x - h)^2 + k$$

The graph is a parabola with **vertex** at (h, k). The parabola opens upwards if $a > 0$ and downwards if $a < 0$.

Example 1: Let the function f be defined by $f(x) = 7(x - 3)^2 + 5$. For what value of x will the function f have its minimum value?

The graph of this function is an upward facing parabola with vertex $(3,5)$. Therefore, the answer is $x = \mathbf{3}$.

Remark: Note that in this example $k = 2$ and k is on the right hand side of the equation.

General Form for a Quadratic Function

The general form for a quadratic function is

$$y = ax^2 + bx + c.$$

The graph of this function is a parabola whose vertex has x-coordinate

$$-\frac{b}{2a}$$

The parabola opens upwards if $a > 0$ and downwards if $a < 0$.

Example 2: Let the function f be defined by $f(x) = -3x^2 - 8x + 1$. For what value of x will the function f have its maximum value?

The graph of this function is a downward facing parabola, and we see that $a = -3$, and $b = -8$. Therefore, the x-coordinate of the vertex is $x = \frac{8}{-6} = \mathbf{-4/3}$.

Sum and Product of Roots of a Quadratic Function

Let r and s be the roots (or solutions, or zeros) of the quadratic equation $x^2 + bx + c = 0$. Then

$$b = -(r+s) \quad \text{and} \quad c = rs.$$

Try to answer the following question using these formulas. **Do not** check the solution until you have attempted this question yourself.

LEVEL 3: ALGEBRA AND FUNCTIONS

1. What is the sum and product of the two solutions of the equation $x^2 - x + 15 = 0$?

    A. sum = $-$ 1,   product =   15
    B. sum =   1,   product =   15
    C. sum =   1,   product = -15
    D. sum = -15,   product = $-$ 1
    E. sum =   15,   product =   1

Solution

* We have $b = -1$ and $c = 15$. So the sum is $-b = -(-1) = 1$ and the product is $c = 15$, choice **B**.

Remark: In plain English, the product of the solutions is equal to the constant term (in this case 15), and the sum of the solutions is the negative of the coefficient of x (in this case, the coefficient of x is -1, and therefore the sum of the solutions is $-(-1) = 1$).

Special Factoring

Students that are trying for a 36 may want to memorize the following three special factoring formulas.

$$(x+y)^2 = x^2 + y^2 + 2xy$$
$$(x-y)^2 = x^2 + y^2 - 2xy$$
$$(x+y)(x-y) = x^2 - y^2$$

Try to answer the following question using the appropriate formula. **Do not** check the solution until you have attempted this question yourself.

LEVEL 4: ALGEBRA AND FUNCTIONS

2. If $c > 0$, $s^2 + t^2 = c$, and $st = c + 5$, what is $(s + t)^2$ in terms of c ?

    F. $c + 5$
    G. $c + 10$
    H. $2c + 5$
    J. $2c + 10$
    K. $3c + 10$

Solution

* $(s + t)^2 = s^2 + t^2 + 2st = c + 2(c + 5) = c + 2c + 10 = 3c + 10$, choice **K**.

Polynomial Functions

A **polynomial function** has the form

$$y = a_n x^n + a_{n-1} x^{n-1} + \cdots + a_1 x + a_0$$

where $a_0, a_1, \ldots, a_n$ are real numbers. If $a_n \neq 0$, then n is the degree of the polynomial.

The definition of a polynomial looks a lot messier than it actually is.

Examples: (1) $y = 5x^4 - 2x^3 + x^2 - 2x + 1$ is a polynomial function of degree 4.

(2) $y = x - 1$ is a polynomial function of degree 1. Note that $y = x - 1$ can be written as $y = x^1 - 1$. Polynomials of degree 1 are also called **linear functions**.

(3) $y = 2x^2 - 5x + 1$ is a polynomial function of degree 2. Polynomials of degree 2 are also called **quadratic functions**.

(4) $y = 5$ is a polynomial function of degree 0. Polynomials of degree 0 are also called **constant functions**.

(5) $y = 4 - x$ is a polynomial of degree 1 (or a linear function). Note that we can rewrite this polynomial as $y = -x^1 + 4$.

(6) $y = x^2 + x - x^{\frac{1}{2}} + 1$ is **not** a polynomial function. To be a polynomial, all powers of x must be positive integers (exponents cannot be negative, fractions, or decimals).

Rational Functions

A **rational function** is a quotient of polynomials (one polynomial divided by another polynomial).

Examples: (1) $y = x - 1$ is a rational function since it can be written as $y = \frac{x-1}{1}$. In fact, every polynomial is a rational function.

(2) $y = \frac{x^2-3x+2}{2x-3}$ is a rational function.

(3) $y = x^{-1}$ is a rational function since it can be written as $y = \frac{1}{x}$. Unlike polynomials, negative exponents are allowed in rational functions.

(4) $y = x^{\frac{1}{2}}$ is **not** a rational function. Exponents cannot be fractions or decimals.

The **domain** of a function is the set of all values that can be plugged into the function for x that result in a numerical output.

Examples: (1) The domain of $y = 5x^4 - 2x^3 + x^2 = 2x + 1$ is the set of "all real numbers." In fact, the domain of every polynomial is "all real numbers."

(2) The domain of $y = \frac{x^2-3x+2}{2x-3}$ is the set of all real numbers except $x = \frac{3}{2}$. In general, the domain of a rational function is the set of all x-values that do not make the denominator zero.

Note: If we set $2x - 3 = 0$, we can add 3 to each side of this equation to get $2x = 3$. We then divide each side of this last equation by 2 to get $x = \frac{3}{2}$. So x CANNOT be $\frac{3}{2}$.

Vertical Asymptotes

The vertical line $x = a$ is a **vertical asymptote** for the graph of the function $y = f(x)$ if y approaches ∞ or $-\infty$ as x approaches a from either the left or right (or both).

For rational functions it is sufficient to know the following:

If the rational function $y = \frac{p(x)}{q(x)}$ has the property that $q(a) = 0$ and $p(a) \neq 0$, then $x = a$ is a vertical asymptote for the graph.

Example: If $x = a$ is a vertical asymptote of $y = \frac{x^2-5}{x-3}$, then $a =$

Solution: Since 3 makes the denominator zero, and 3 does not make the numerator zero, the vertical line $x = 3$ is a vertical asymptote of the given function. So $a = $ **3**.

Note: On the ACT, you really do not even have to worry about the numerator. In other words, to find vertical asymptotes of a rational function on the ACT simply find all numbers that will make the denominator of the function 0.

If plugging in the number a makes the denominator 0, then the vertical line $x = a$ is a vertical asymptote for the function. You can usually find these numbers by simple observation, but if necessary you can set the denominator equal to zero and formally solve the resulting equation.

So in the previous example it was actually sufficient to notice that setting x equal to 3 in the denominator gives zero.

Horizontal Asymptotes

The horizontal line with equation $y = b$ is a **horizontal asymptote** for the graph of $y = f(x)$ if y approaches b as x gets larger and larger, or smaller and smaller (as in very large in the negative direction).

For the rational function $y = \frac{p(x)}{q(x)}$ it is sufficient to know the following 3 rules:

Rule 1: If p has a higher degree than q, then the rational function has no horizontal asymptote.

Rule 2: If p has a lower degree than q, then the rational function has the horizontal asymptote $y = 0$.

Rule 3: If p and q have equal degree, then the rational function has the horizontal asymptote $y = \frac{m}{n}$ where m is the leading coefficient of p and n is the leading coefficient of q.

Examples: (1) Find all horizontal asymptotes of $y = \frac{x^2-5}{x-3}$.

Solution: Since the numerator has degree 2 and the denominator has degree 1, there are no horizontal asymptotes.

(2) Find all horizontal asymptotes of $y = \frac{x-3}{x^2-5}$.

Solution: Since the numerator has degree 1 and the denominator has degree 2, there is a horizontal asymptote of $y = 0$

(3) Find all horizontal asymptotes of $y = \frac{5x^2+2x-3}{3x^2-7}$.

Solution: Since the numerator and denominator both have degree 2, there is a horizontal asymptote of $y = \frac{5}{3}$.

Try to answer the following question about asymptotes. **Do not** check the solution until you have attempted this question yourself.

LEVEL 4: ALGEBRA AND FUNCTIONS

3. Consider the rational function $r(x) = \frac{x^2-5}{x-3}$. Let $m = r(5)$, let n be the number of horizontal and/or vertical asymptotes there are for the graph of r. What is the value of $m \cdot n$?

    A. 10
    B. 9
    C. 8
    D. 7
    E. 6

Solution: $m = r(5) = \frac{5^2-5}{5-3} = \frac{25-5}{2} = \frac{20}{2} = 10$.

The graph also has a vertical asymptote of $x = 3$. There are no horizontal asymptotes. So $n = 1$.

So $m \cdot n = 10(1) = 10$, choice **A**.

Now try to solve each of the following problems. The answers to these problems, followed by full solutions are at the end of this lesson. **Do not** look at the answers until you have attempted these problems yourself. Please remember to mark off any problems you get wrong.

LEVEL 4: ALGEBRA AND FUNCTIONS

$$y = -5(x - 3)^2 + 2$$

4. In the xy-plane, line ℓ passes through the point $(-1,5)$ and the vertex of the parabola with the equation above. What is the slope of line ℓ ?

    F. $-\dfrac{4}{3}$

    G. $-\dfrac{3}{4}$

    H. 0

    J. $\dfrac{3}{4}$

    K. $\dfrac{4}{3}$

5. In the standard (x, y) coordinate plane, for what value(s) of x, if any, is there NO value of y such that (x, y) is on the graph of $y = \dfrac{7-x}{(x-5)(x+4)(x-4)}$?

    A. $-5, -4$, and 4 only
    B. $-4, 4$, and 5 only
    C. -5 only
    D. 5 only
    E. There are no such values of x.

6. The graph of $y = \dfrac{1-x}{2+x}$ in the standard (x, y) coordinate plane has an asymptote with which of the following equations?

    F. $x = -1$
    G. $x = 1$
    H. $x = 2$
    J. $y = -1$
    K. $y = \dfrac{1}{2}$

7. The function g is defined by $g(x) = 4x^2 - 7$. What are all possible values of $g(x)$ where $-3 < x < 3$?

    A. $4 < g(x) < 36$
    B. $0 < g(x) < 36$
    C. $0 < g(x) < 29$
    D. $-7 \leq g(x) < 29$
    E. $-7 \leq g(x) < 0$

281

$$-2x^2 + bx + 5$$

8. In the xy-plane, the graph of the equation above assumes its maximum value at $x = 2$. What is the value of b?

    F. -8
    G. -4
    H. 4
    J. 8
    K. 10

LEVEL 5: ALGEBRA AND FUNCTIONS

9. If $x + y = 2k - 1$, and $x^2 + y^2 = 9 - 4k + 2k^2$, what is xy in terms of k?

    A. $k - 2$
    B. $(k - 2)^2$
    C. $k + 2$
    D. $(k + 2)^2$
    E. $k^2 - 4$

10. Let the function g be defined by $g(x) = a(x - h)^2$, where h is a positive constant, and a is a negative constant. For what value of x will the function g have its maximum value?

    F. $-h$
    G. $-a$
    H. 0
    J. a
    K. h

11. Which of the following quadratic equations has solutions $x = -3u$ and $x = 7v$

    A. $x^2 - 21uv = 0$
    B. $x^2 - x(7v - 3u) - 21uv = 0$
    C. $x^2 - x(7v - 3u) + 21uv = 0$
    D. $x^2 + x(7v - 3u) - 21uv = 0$
    E. $x^2 + x(7v - 3u) + 21uv = 0$

12. Which of the following linear equations gives the vertical asymptote for the graph of $y = \frac{329x+147}{331x+149}$?

    F. $x = -\frac{329}{331}$

    G. $x = -\frac{147}{329}$

    H. $x = -\frac{147}{149}$

    J. $x = -\frac{149}{331}$

    K. $x = -\frac{476}{480}$

Answers

1. B	5. B	9. E
2. K	6. J	10. K
3. A	7. D	11. B
4. G	8. J	12. J

Full Solutions

4.

* Solution using the standard form of a quadratic equation: The vertex of the parabola is (3,2). Therefore, the slope of the line is

$$\frac{5-2}{-1-3} = \frac{3}{-4} = -\frac{3}{4}$$

This is answer choice **G**.

5.

* We are looking to find all values for x that make the denominator zero. So we solve the following equation

$$(x-5)(x+4)(x-4) = 0$$
$$x - 5 = 0 \qquad x + 4 = 0 \qquad x - 4 = 0$$
$$x = 5 \qquad x = -4 \qquad x = 4$$

So the answer is choice **B**.

6.

Solution: Since the numerator and denominator both have degree 1, there is a horizontal asymptote of $y = \frac{-1}{1} = -1$, choice **J**.

283

Notes: (1) Choosing choice **K** is a common mistake. Remember to always look at the highest power of x for each polynomial. If there is any confusion it may help to rewrite the given rational function as $y = \frac{-x+1}{x+2}$.

(2) Another way to see that $y = -1$ is a horizontal asymptote is to note that for large x,

$$y = \frac{1-x}{2+x} \approx \frac{-x}{x} = -1.$$

(3) We can also find the horizontal asymptote by plugging in a really large value for x such as 999,999,999. We get

$$(1 - 999{,}999{,}999) / (2 + 999{,}999{,}999) = -0.999999997$$

which is practically -1.

(4) In this problem plugging in -2 makes the denominator of the function 0 and the numerator nonzero. So $x = -2$ is a vertical asymptote for the graph of the given function. Note however that this is not an answer choice.

7.

Solution by picking a number: Let's try a value for x in the given range, say $x = 0$. Then $g(x) = -7$. So we can eliminate choices A, B, and C. Let's try $x = 2$ next. Then $g(x) = 4(2)^2 - 7 = 4 \cdot 4 - 7 = 16 - 7 = 9$. So we can eliminate choice E. Thus, the answer is choice **D**.

* **Quick solution:** g is an **even** function. So we need only check the possible values of $g(x)$ for which $0 \le x < 3$. We have $g(0) = -7$ and $g(3) = 4(3)^2 - 7 = 4(9) - 7 = 36 - 7 = 29$. So the answer is **D**.

Solution using the general form for a quadratic function: Using the formula $x = -\frac{b}{2a}$ we see that the x-coordinate of the vertex of the parabola is $x = 0$ (since $b = 0$). The parabola opens upwards because $a = 4 > 0$. So the minimum value of $g(x)$ is $g(0) = -7$. We substitute $x = 3$ (or $x = -3$) to find the upper bound:

$$g(3) = 4(3)^2 - 7 = 4 \cdot 9 - 7 = 36 - 7 = 29.$$

So we must have $-7 \le g(x) < 29$, choice **D**.

Graphical solution: In your graphing calculator press Y=, and under Y1=, type 4X^2 − 7. Press WINDOW and set Xmin = −3, Xmax = 3, Ymin = −7, and Ymax = 29. Then press GRAPH. The graph is a perfect fit, so the answer is choice **D**.

Remark: We chose the window in the last solution by using the smallest and largest values that appear in the answer choices.

8.

Solution using the general form for a quadratic function: Using the formula $x = -\dfrac{b}{2a}$ we have $-\dfrac{b}{2(-2)} = 2$. So $b = 8$, choice **J**.

Solution using differential calculus: The derivative of the function $y = -2x^2 + bx + 5$ is $y' = -4x + b$. We set the derivative equal to 0 and plug in $x = 2$ to get $-4(2) + b = 0$, or $b = 8$, choice **J**.

9.

Solution by picking numbers: Let $k = 0$. Then $x + y = -1$, and $x^2 + y^2 = 9$.

$$(x + y)^2 = (x + y)(x + y) = x^2 + 2xy + y^2 = x^2 + y^2 + 2xy$$
$$(-1)^2 = 9 + 2xy$$
$$1 = 9 + 2xy$$
$$-8 = 2xy$$
$$-4 = xy$$

Put a nice big dark circle around the number -4. Now substitute $k = 0$ into each answer choice.

    A. -2
    B.   4
    C.   2
    D.   4
    E. -4

Since A, B, C, and D came out incorrect we can eliminate them, and the answer is choice **E**.

* Algebraic solution: We use the first special factoring formula.

$$(x + y)^2 = x^2 + y^2 + 2xy.$$
$$(2k - 1)^2 = 9 - 4k + 2k^2 + 2xy$$
$$4k^2 - 4k + 1 = 9 - 4k + 2k^2 + 2xy$$
$$2k^2 - 8 = 2xy$$
$$2(k^2 - 4) = 2xy$$
$$k^2 - 4 = xy$$

So $xy = k^2 - 4$, choice **E**.

10.

* Solution using the standard form of a quadratic equation: The function $g(x) = a(x - h)^2$ is in standard form and thus has a graph that is a parabola with $(h, 0)$ for its vertex. Since $a < 0$ the parabola opens downwards. Thus, the maximum occurs at $x = h$, choice **K**.

Graphical solution: Let's choose values for h and a, say $h = 2$ and $a = -1$. So $g(x) = -(x - 2)^2$. If we put this in our graphing calculator we see that the maximum occurs when $x = 2$. Substituting our chosen values for h and a into each answer choice yields

    F. -2
    G. 1
    H. 0
    J. -1
    K. 2

We can therefore eliminate choices F, G, H, and J. Thus, the answer is choice **K**.

11.

* The sum of the solutions is $-3u + 7v = 7v - 3u$ and the product of the solutions is $(-3u)(7v) = -21uv$. An equation with these roots is therefore

$$x^2 - (7v - 3u)x - 21uv = 0.$$

This is equivalent to choice **B**.

12.

* We set the denominator equal to zero to get

$$331x + 149 = 0$$
$$331x = -149$$
$$x = -\frac{149}{331}$$

This is choice **J**.

OPTIONAL MATERIAL

CHALLENGE QUESTIONS

1. Let f and g be functions such that $f(x) = ax^2 + bx + c$ and $g(x) = ax + b$. If $g(1) = 2b - a + 25$ and $g(2) = 2a - 24$, then for what value of x does $f(x) = f(8)$, where $x \neq 8$?

2. Show that $x^2 + y^2 + z^2 \geq xy + yz + zx$ for positive numbers $x, y,$ and z.

Solutions

1.

* $g(1) = a(1) + b = a + b$. So $a + b = 2b - a + 25$, and therefore $2a = b + 25$. $g(2) = a(2) + b = 2a + b$, and so $2a + b = 2a - 24$. Thus, $b = -24$. We also have $2a = b + 25 = -24 + 25 = 1$. Thus, $a = \frac{1}{2}$.

So $f(x) = \frac{x^2}{2} - 24x + c$, and $f(8) = \frac{8^2}{2} - 24(8) + c = -160 + c$. If $f(x) = f(8)$, then $\frac{x^2}{2} - 24x + c = -160 + c$, so $\frac{x^2}{2} - 24x + 160 = 0$. Let's multiply each side of this equation by 2 to eliminate the denominator. We get $x^2 - 48x + 320 = 0$. There are several ways to solve this equation.

Factoring: $(x - 8)(x - 40) = 0$. So $x = \mathbf{40}$.

Completing the square: We take half of -48, which is -24, and square this number to get 576. We then add 576 to each side of the equation to get $x^2 - 48x + 576 + 320 = 576$. This is equivalent to $(x - 24)^2 = 256$. We now apply the square root property to get $x - 24 = \pm 16$. So $x = 24 \pm 16$. This yields the solutions $24 - 16 = 8$, and $24 + 16 = \mathbf{40}$.

The quadratic formula:

$$x = \frac{-b \pm \sqrt{b^2 - 4ac}}{2a} = \frac{48 \pm \sqrt{2304 - 1280}}{2} = \frac{48 \pm \sqrt{1024}}{2} = \frac{48 \pm 32}{2} = \mathbf{24 \pm 16.}$$

As in the previous solution we get $x = 8$ or $x = \mathbf{40}$.

Graphically: In your graphing calculator press the Y= button, and enter the following.

$$Y1 = X^2 - 48X + 320$$

Now press ZOOM 6 to graph the parabola in a standard window. It needs to be zoomed out, so we will need to extend the viewing window. Press the WINDOW button, and change Xmax to 100, Ymin to -50, and Ymax to 50. Then press 2nd TRACE (which is CALC) 2 (or select ZERO). Then move the cursor just to the left of the second x-intercept and press ENTER. Now move the cursor just to the right of the second x-intercept and press ENTER again. Press ENTER once more, and you will see that the x-coordinate of the second x-intercept is **40**.

Remark: The choices made for Xmax, Ymin and Ymax were just to try to ensure that the second x-intercept would appear in the viewing window. Many other windows would work just as well.

2.
The following inequalities are equivalent.

$$x^2 + y^2 + z^2 \geq xy + yz + zx$$
$$2x^2 + 2y^2 + 2z^2 \geq 2xy + 2yz + 2zx$$
$$(x^2 - 2xy + y^2) + (y^2 - 2yz + z^2) + (z^2 - 2zx + x^2) \geq 0$$
$$(x - y)^2 + (y - z)^2 + (z - x)^2 \geq 0$$

Since the last inequality is obviously true, so is the original inequality.

Download additional solutions for free here:

www.satprepget800.com/28LesAdv

LESSON 23
GEOMETRY

Reminder: Before beginning this lesson remember to redo the problems from Lessons 3, 7, 11, 15 and 19 that you have marked off. Do not "unmark" a question unless you get it correct.

Cylinders and Cones

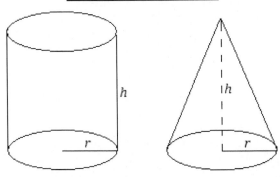

If a cylinder has base radius r, and height h, then we have the following:

Volume of cylinder: $V = \pi r^2 h$

Lateral Surface Area of Cylinder: $L = 2\pi r h$

Total Surface Area of Cylinder: $S = 2\pi r^2 + 2\pi r h$

If a cone has base radius r, and height h, then we have the following:

Volume of cone: $V = \frac{1}{3}\pi r^2 h$

Note that the volume of a cone is $\frac{1}{3}$ the volume of a cylinder with the same base radius and height.

See the solution to problem 6 for a visual method of computing the lateral surface area of a cylinder.

LEVEL 3: GEOMETRY

1. A small capsule is created from two congruent right circular cones and a right circular cylinder with measurements shown in the figure below. Of the following, which is closest to the volume of the capsule, in cubic inches?

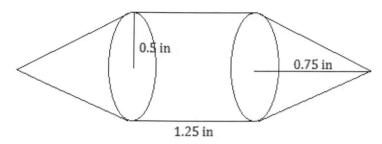

0.5 in

0.75 in

1.25 in

    A. 0.39
    B. 0.98
    C. 1.18
    D. 2.16
    E. 1.37

Solution

* The volume is

$$V = \pi(0.5)^2 \cdot 1.25 + 2\left(\frac{1}{3}\right)\pi(0.5)^2 \cdot 0.75 \approx 1.37$$

This is choice **D**.

Notes: (1) The capsule consists of a cylinder and two cones. We get the volume of the capsule by adding up the volumes of the three individual solids.

(2) The radius of a base of the cylinder is $r = 0.5$ and the height of the cylinder is $h = 1.25$. Therefore, the volume of the cylinder is

$$V = \pi(0.5)^2 \cdot 1.25 \approx 0.98.$$

(4) The radius of the base of the cone is $r = 0.5$ and the height of the cone is $h = 0.75$. Therefore, the volume of the cone is

$$V = \frac{1}{3}\pi(0.5)^2 \cdot 0.75 \approx 0.196.$$

(5) To get the total volume of the capsule, we add the volume of the cylinder and the volume of the two cones to get approximately

$$0.98 + 2 \cdot 0.196 \approx 1.372$$

Equations of Lines in General Form

The **general form of an equation of a line** is $ax + by = c$ where a, b and c are real numbers. If $b \neq 0$, then the slope of this line is $m = -\frac{a}{b}$. If $b = 0$, then the line is vertical and has no slope.

Let us consider 2 such equations.

$$ax + by = c$$
$$dx + ey = f$$

(1) If there is a number r such that $ra = d$, $rb = e$, and $rc = f$, then the two equations represent the **same line**. Equivalently, the two equations represent the same line if $\frac{a}{d} = \frac{b}{e} = \frac{c}{f}$. In this case the system of equations has **infinitely many solutions**.

(2) If there is a number r such that $ra = d$, $rb = e$, but $rc \neq f$, then the two equations represent **parallel** but distinct lines. Equivalently, the two equations represent parallel but distinct lines if $\frac{a}{d} = \frac{b}{e} \neq \frac{c}{f}$. In this case the system of equations has **no solution**.

(3) Otherwise the two lines intersect in a single point. In this case $\frac{a}{d} \neq \frac{b}{e}$, and the system of equations has a **unique solution**.

These three cases are illustrated in the figure below.

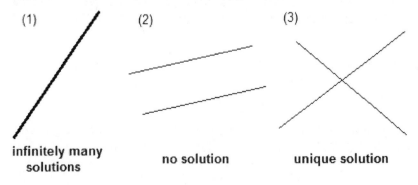

(1)	(2)	(3)
infinitely many solutions	no solution	unique solution

291

Example: The following two equations represent the same line.

$$2x + 8y = 6$$
$$3x + 12y = 9$$

To see this, note that $\frac{2}{3} = \frac{8}{12} = \frac{6}{9}$.(or equivalently, let $r = \frac{3}{2}$ and note that $\left(\frac{3}{2}\right)(2) = 3$, $\left(\frac{3}{2}\right)(8) = 12$, and $\left(\frac{3}{2}\right)(6) = 9$).

The following two equations represent parallel but distinct lines.

$$2x + 8y = 6$$
$$3x + 12y = 10$$

This time $\frac{2}{3} = \frac{8}{12} \neq \frac{6}{10}$.

The following two equations represent a pair of intersecting lines.

$$2x + 8y = 6$$
$$3x + 10y = 9$$

This time $\frac{2}{3} \neq \frac{8}{10}$.

Try to answer the following question. **Do not** check the solution until you have attempted this question yourself.

LEVEL 4: GEOMETRY

$$3x - 7y = 12$$
$$kx + 21y = -35$$

2. For which of the following values of k will the system of equations above have no solution?

> **F.**   9
> **G.**   3
> **H.**   0
> **J.** -3
> **K.** -9

Solution

As mentioned above, the system of equations

$$ax + by = c$$
$$dx + ey = f$$

292

has no solution if $\frac{a}{d} = \frac{b}{e} \neq \frac{c}{f}$. So we solve the equation $\frac{3}{k} = \frac{-7}{21}$. Cross multiplying yields $63 = -7k$ so that $k = 63/(-7) = -9$, choice **K**.

Note: In this problem $\frac{b}{e} \neq \frac{c}{f}$. Indeed, $\frac{-7}{21} \neq \frac{12}{-35}$. This guarantees that the system of equations has no solution instead of infinitely many solutions.

* **Quick solution:** We multiply -7 by -3 to get 21. Therefore, $k = (3)(-3) = -9$, choice **K**.

Now try to solve each of the following problems. The answers to these problems, followed by full solutions are at the end of this lesson. **Do not** look at the answers until you have attempted these problems yourself. Please remember to mark off any problems you get wrong.

LEVEL 3: GEOMETRY

3. A tank in the shape of a right circular cylinder is completely filled with water as shown below. If the volume of the tank is 160π cubic yards, what is the <u>diameter</u> of the base of the cylinder, in yards?

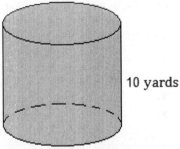

10 yards

    A. 8
    B. 10
    C. 12
    D. 14
    E. 15

LEVEL 4: GEOMETRY

4. The volume of a right circular cylinder is 375π cubic centimeters. If the height is three times the base radius of the cylinder, what is the base <u>diameter</u> of the cylinder?

    F. 5
    G. 10
    H. 12
    J. 15
    K. 18

293

5. Mike has identical containers each in the shape of a cone with internal diameter of 5 inches. He pours liquid from a half-gallon bottle into each container until it is full. If the height of liquid in each container is 8 inches, what is the largest number of full containers that he can pour a half-gallon of liquid? (Note: There are 231 cubic inches in 1 gallon.)

    A. 5
    B. 4
    C. 3
    D. 2
    E. 1

6. The figure below is a right circular cylinder with a height of 10 inches and a base radius of 7 inches. What is the surface area, in square inches, of the cylinder to the nearest integer?

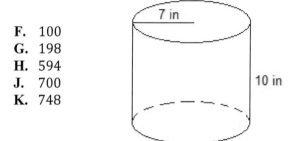

    F. 100
    G. 198
    H. 594
    J. 700
    K. 748

7. A container in the shape of a right circular cylinder has an inside base diameter of 10 centimeters and an inside height of 6 centimeters. This cylinder is completely filled with fluid. All of the fluid is then poured into a second right circular cylinder with a larger inside base diameter of 14 centimeters. What must be the minimum inside height, in centimeters, of the second container?

    A. $\dfrac{5}{\sqrt{7}}$

    B. $\dfrac{7}{5}$

    C. 5

    D. $\dfrac{150}{49}$

    E. $2\sqrt{78}$

8. In the xy-plane, line ℓ is the graph of $5x + ky = 8$, where k is a constant. The graph of $10x + 22y = 17$ is parallel to line ℓ. What is the value of k?

F. $\dfrac{1}{11}$

G. $\dfrac{11}{25}$

H. $\dfrac{25}{11}$

J. 11

K. 25

9. The height of a solid cone is 22 centimeters and the radius of the base is 15 centimeters. A cut parallel to the circular base is made completely through the cone so that one of the two resulting solids is a smaller cone. If the radius of the base of the small cone is 5 centimeters, what is the height of the small cone, in centimeters?

A. $\dfrac{3}{22}$

B. 3

C. 7

D. 11

E. $\dfrac{22}{3}$

LEVEL 5: GEOMETRY

10. The figure shown below is a right circular cylinder. The circumference of each circular base is 20, the length of AD is 14, and AB and CD are diameters of each base respectively. If the cylinder is cut along AD, opened, and flattened, what is the length of AC?

F. $3\sqrt{3}$
G. $\sqrt{74}$
H. $2\sqrt{74}$
J. $\sqrt{149}$
K. $2\sqrt{149}$

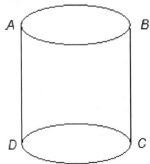

11. The circumference of the base of a right circular cone is 10π and the circumference of a parallel cross section is 8π. If the distance between the base and the cross section is 6, what is the height of the cone?

    A. 30
    B. 20
    C. 15
    D. 7.5
    E. 4.8

12. A right circular cylinder has a base diameter of 4 and height 7. If point O is the center of the top of the cylinder and B lies on the circumference of the bottom of the cylinder, what is the straight-line distance between O and B ?

    F. 3
    G. 7
    H. 11
    J. $\sqrt{11}$
    K. $\sqrt{53}$

Answers

1. D	5. D	9. E
2. K	6. K	10. H
3. A	7. D	11. A
4. G	8. J	12. K

Full Solutions

3.

* Algebraic solution:

$$V = \pi r^2 h$$
$$160\pi = \pi r^2 (10)$$
$$16 = r^2$$
$$4 = r.$$

So $d = 2r = 2 \cdot 4 = 8$, choice **A**.

Notes: (1) To get from the second to the third equation, we divided each side of the equation by 10π.

296

(2) The equation $16 = r^2$ would normally have the two solutions $\pm 4 = r$. But the radius of a circle must be positive, and so we reject the negative solution.

(3) The diameter of a circle is twice the radius. Symbolically, $d = 2r$.

4.

Solution by taking a guess: Let's start with a guess of $d = 6$. Then we have $r = 3$, so that $h = 9$ and $V = \pi r^2 h = \pi(3)^2(9) = 81\pi$, too small.

Let's try $d = 10$ next. Then $r = 5$, and so $h = 15$ and $V = \pi r^2 h = \pi(5)^2(15) = 375\pi$. This is correct, and so the base diameter is 10, choice **G**.

* Algebraic solution:

$$V = \pi r^2 h$$
$$375\pi = \pi r^2 (3r)$$
$$125 = r^3$$
$$5 = r.$$

Since $r = 5$, we have $d = 2r = 2 \cdot 5 = 10$, choice **G**.

5.

* The volume of 1 container is $V = \frac{1}{3}\pi r^2 h = \frac{1}{3}\pi \left(\frac{5}{2}\right)^2 \cdot 8 \approx 52.35988$ cubic inches.

The volume of a half-gallon of liquid in cubic inches is $\frac{231}{2} = 115.5$.

We divide the two volumes to get the number of containers:

$$\frac{115.5}{52.35988} \approx 2.2$$

So the largest number of *full* containers is 2, choice **D**.

6.

* When we cut and unfold the cylinder we get the following rectangle.

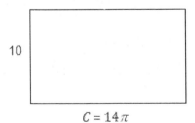

10

$C = 14\pi$

297

Notice that the width of the rectangle is the circumference of the base of the cylinder. Thus, the width is $C = 2\pi r = 2\pi(7) = 14\pi$ inches.

The **lateral** surface area of the cylinder is the area of this rectangle.

$$L = 10(14\pi) = 140\pi \text{ inches.}$$

We also need the area of the two bases. Each of these is a circle with area $A = \pi r^2 = \pi(7)^2 = 49\pi$ inches. Therefore, the total surface area is $S = L + 2A = 140\pi + 2(49\pi) = 238\pi \approx 747.699$ inches.

To the nearest integer this is 748 inches, choice **K**.

Note: We can also just use the formula for the surface area of a cylinder as given in the beginning of this lesson.

7.

* First note that the base radius of the first cylinder is 5 and the base radius of the second cylinder is 7. Therefore, the volume of the first cylinder is $V = \pi r^2 h = \pi(5)^2(6) = 150\pi$ and the volume of the second cylinder is $V = \pi r^2 h = \pi(7)^2 h = 49\pi h$. We set the two volumes equal to each other and solve for h.

$$49h\pi = 150\pi$$

$$h = \frac{150}{49}$$

This is choice **D**.

8.

* Since we multiply 5 by 2 to get 10, we multiply k by 2 to get 22. Therefore, $k = 11$, choice **J**.

9.

Complete solution. A picture of the problem looks like this:

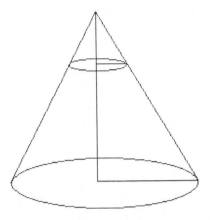

In the above picture we have the original cone together with a cut forming a smaller cone. We have also drawn two triangles that represent the 2 dimensional cross sections of the 2 cones. Let's isolate the triangles:

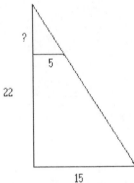

The two triangles formed are **similar**, and so the ratios of their sides are equal. We identify the 2 key words "height" and "radius."

height	22	h
radius	15	5

We now find h by cross multiplying and dividing.

$$\frac{22}{15} = \frac{h}{5}$$
$$110 = 15h$$
$$h = \frac{110}{15} = \frac{22}{3}$$

299

This is choice **E**.

Notes: For a review of similar triangles, see Lesson 11.

* Quick calculator computation: $\left(\frac{22}{15}\right) * 5 = \frac{22}{3}$, choice **E**.

10.

* When we cut and unfold the cylinder as described we get the following rectangle.

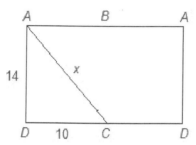

Notice that C is right in the middle of the rectangle. A common error would be to put C as one of the vertices. Note also that the length of the rectangle is 20 so that DC is 10. We can now use the Pythagorean Theorem to find AC.

$$x^2 = 10^2 + 14^2 = 100 + 196 = 296$$
$$x = \sqrt{296} = 2\sqrt{74}$$

This is choice **H**.

11.

* Let's start by drawing a picture (to the right).

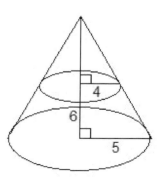

Since the circumference of the base of the cone is 10π, the radius is 5. Similarly, since the circumference of a parallel cross section is 8π, its radius is 4. We now have a pair of similar right triangles. If we let h be the height of the larger triangle, then the height of the smaller triangle is $h - 6$, and we get the ratio $\frac{h-6}{h} = \frac{4}{5}$.

Cross multiplying, we get $5h - 30 = 4h$, and so $h = 30$, choice **A**.

300

12.

* Solution: We draw a right circular cylinder with a right triangle inside as seen below.

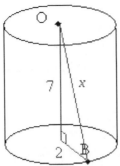

Note that the bottom leg of the triangle is equal to the radius of the circle (not the diameter) which is why it is 2 and not 4. We can now use the Pythagorean Theorem to find x.

$$x^2 = 2^2 + 7^2 = 4 + 49 = 53$$

So $x = \sqrt{53}$, choice **K**.

OPTIONAL MATERIAL

CHALLENGE QUESTIONS

1. Draw a rectangular solid with sides of length a, b and c, and let the long diagonal have length d. Show geometrically that $d^2 = a^2 + b^2 + c^2$.

2. A cube is inscribed in a cone of radius 1 and height 2 so that one face of the cube is contained in the base of the cone. What is the length of a side of the cube?

Solutions

1.

Let's begin by drawing a picture.

301

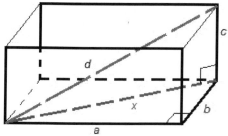

We first use the Pythagorean Theorem on the right triangle with sides of length a, b, and x to get $x^2 = a^2 + b^2$. Then we use the Pythagorean Theorem on the triangle with sides of length x, c, and d to get

$$d^2 = x^2 + c^2 = a^2 + b^2 + c^2.$$

2.

Let x be the length of a side of the cube. Slice the cone from the vertex to the base so that it cuts through the diagonal of the square base of the cube. We get the following picture.

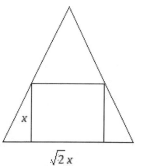 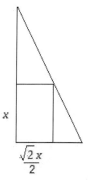

We can now set up the following ratio: $\frac{1}{2} = \frac{1 - \frac{x\sqrt{2}}{2}}{x}$. Cross multiplying gives $x = 2 - x\sqrt{2}$ or $x + x\sqrt{2} = 2$. So we have $x(1 + \sqrt{2}) = 2$, and therefore $x = \frac{2}{1+\sqrt{2}}$. By rationalizing the denominator, this can be simplified to $x = 2\sqrt{2} - 2$.

LESSON 24
TRIGONOMETRY

Reminder: Before beginning this lesson remember to redo the problems from Lessons 4, 8, 12, 16 and 20 that you have marked off. Do not "unmark" a question unless you get it correct.

Trigonometry in the Four Quadrants

The following diagram contains the information you need to evaluate trigonometric functions of angles that are NOT between 0° and 90° (or 0 and $\frac{\pi}{2}$ radians). The only difference between the two images is that the image on the left is in degrees and the image on the right is in radians.

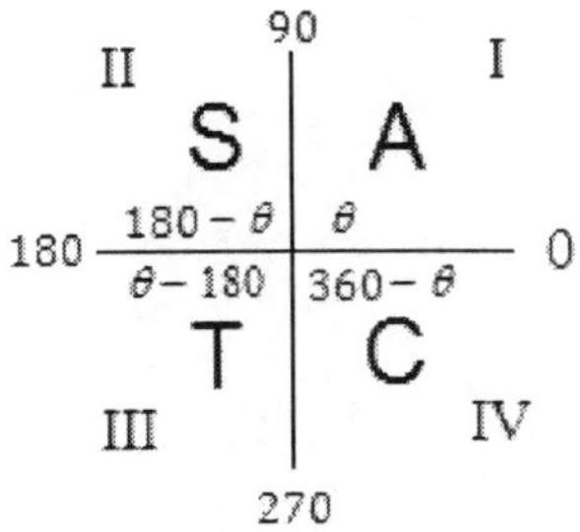

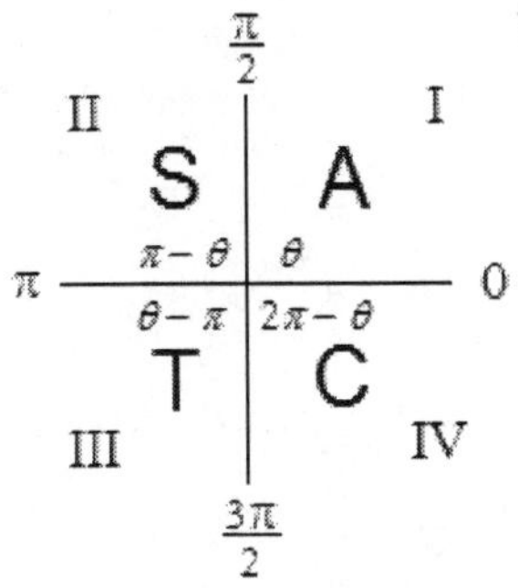

The roman numerals I, II, III, and IV are the quadrant numbers.

The letters A, S, T, and C stand for "all, sine, tangent," and "cosine." These letters tell us the sign we get when we evaluate a trig function of any angle. For example, if an angle is in the second quadrant, then its sine is positive, whereas its tangent and cosine are negative. Since taking a reciprocal does not change the sign, cosecant is also positive in the second quadrant, whereas cotangent and secant are negative there.

Examples:

$\cos 200° < 0$ $\sin 200° < 0$ $\tan 200° > 0$ ($200°$ is in quadrant III)

$\cos \frac{7\pi}{4} > 0$ $\sin \frac{7\pi}{4} < 0$ $\tan \frac{7\pi}{4} < 0$ ($\frac{7\pi}{4}$ is in quadrant IV)

Finally, the expressions toward the center of the images tells us how to find the **reference angle**. This is essentially the first quadrant angle that "mirrors" the given angle.

303

Trig functions give the same value on an angle and its reference angle, except for possibly the sign. To evaluate a trig function on an angle that is not between $0°$ and $90°$ (or 0 and $\frac{\pi}{2}$ radians), there are three simple steps:

<u>Step 1</u>: Make sure the angle is between $0°$ and $360°$ (or 0 and 2π radians). If not, add or subtract an appropriate multiple of $360°$ (or 2π).

<u>Step 2</u>: Evaluate the trig function on the reference angle.

<u>Step 3</u>: Use the letters A, S, T, C to choose whether the answer is positive or negative.

LEVEL 4: TRIGONOMETRY

1. If $0 \le x \le 2\pi$, $\tan x < 0$ and $\cos x \tan x > 0$, then which of the following is a possible value for x ?

    A. $\frac{\pi}{6}$

    B. $\frac{\pi}{2}$

    C. $\frac{5\pi}{6}$

    D. $\frac{7\pi}{6}$

    E. $\frac{11\pi}{6}$

<u>Solution</u>

$\tan x < 0$ in Quadrants II and IV. Since $\cos x \tan x > 0$ we must have $\cos x < 0$. This is true in Quadrants II and III. So x must be in Quadrant II, and therefore $\frac{\pi}{2} < x < \pi$. So the answer is choice **C**.

Note: The quickest way to see that $\frac{5\pi}{6}$ is between $\frac{\pi}{2}$ and π is to simply enter each number into your calculator and compare the decimal approximations.

Graphs of Sine and Cosine

Below are pictures of the basic sine and cosine graphs. Note that the graphs keep repeating infinitely in both directions, but rectangles have been drawn around one **period** of each graph. The period for the functions $y = \sin x$ and $y = \cos x$ is 360° or 2π radians. The **amplitude** of each of these functions is 1.

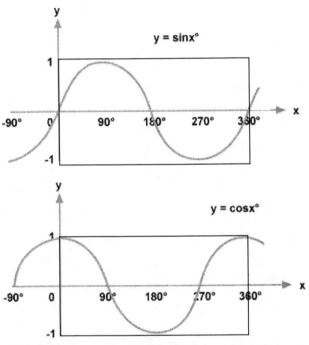

From these graphs we can evaluate the sine and cosine of the **quadrantal angles** quite easily. For example, we have $\sin 90° = 1$ and $\cos \frac{3\pi}{2} = \cos 270° = 0$.

Let's look at more general sine and cosine functions.

$$y = a\sin(bx + c) \qquad\qquad y = a\cos(bx + c)$$

The amplitude and period for each of these functions is as follows:

$$\text{Amplitude} = |a| \qquad \text{Period} = \frac{2\pi}{b}$$

Examples: $y = \frac{3}{2}\sin 4x$ has Amplitude $= \frac{3}{2}$ and Period $= \frac{2\pi}{4} = \frac{\pi}{2}$

$y = -2\cos\left(\frac{x}{4} - 3\right)$ has Amplitude = 2, and Period $= \frac{2\pi}{\frac{1}{4}} = 2\pi \cdot 4 = 8\pi$

305

Laws of Sines and Cosines

Basic trigonometry together with the Pythagorean Theorem can be used to find the side lengths and angle measures in a right triangle. But what if we would like to find the side lengths and/or angle measures in an arbitrary angle? This is where the Laws of Sines and Cosines can be extremely useful.

Consider the arbitrary triangle on the right:

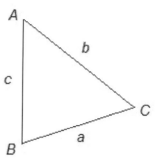

The **Law of Sines** says

$$\frac{a}{\sin A} = \frac{b}{\sin B} = \frac{c}{\sin C}$$

where A, B and C are the angles of the triangle, and a, b and c are the lengths of the sides opposite these angles (in that order).

The **Law of Cosines** is a generalization of the Pythagorean Theorem to arbitrary triangles. It says

$$c^2 = a^2 + b^2 - 2ab \cos C$$

where a, b, and c are the lengths of the sides of the triangle, and the side of length c is opposite angle C.

Note: On the ACT, problems requiring the law of sines of the law of cosines have always given the appropriate formula in the question. Since there is no absolute guarantee that this will continue to happen in the future, we will <u>not</u> include the formulas in each question here.

LEVEL 4: TRIGONOMETRY

2. In $\triangle ABC$ below, $AB = 12$ inches. To the nearest tenth of an inch, $BC = ?$

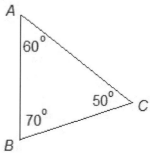

    F. 9.8
    G. 10.6
    H. 13.5
    J. 13.6
    K. 13.9

Solution

By the law of sines, we have $\frac{AB}{\sin C} = \frac{BC}{\sin A}$, so that $\frac{12}{\sin 50°} = \frac{BC}{\sin 60°}$. So we have $BC = \frac{12}{\sin 50°} \cdot \sin 60°$. We type this last expression into our calculator to get approximately 13.5661905. which we round to 13.6, choice **J.**

Notes: (1) In this problem we used angles A and C, and their opposite sides.

(2) Make sure that your calculator is in degree mode. Otherwise you will get the incorrect answer 13.9 (choice K).

If you are using a TI-84 (or equivalent) calculator press MODE, and on the third line make sure that DEGREE is highlighted. If it is not, scroll down and select it.

LEVEL 5: TRIGONOMETRY

3. Triangle PQR is shown in the figure below. The measure of $\angle P$ is 32°, $PQ = 9$ in, and $PR = 15$ in. Which of the following is the length, in inches, of $\overline{QR}$?

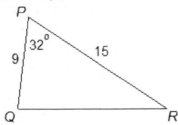

A. $9 \sin 32°$
B. $15 \sin 32°$
C. $\sqrt{15^2 - 9^2}$
D. $\sqrt{15^2 + 9^2}$
E. $\sqrt{15^2 + 9^2 - 2(15)(9)\cos 32°}$

Solution

We use the law of cosines to get
$$QR^2 = 15^2 + 9^2 - 2(15)(9)\cos 32°$$
So $QR = \sqrt{15^2 + 9^2 - 2(15)(9)\cos 32°}$, choice **E.**

Notes: (1) This problem gives the most direct use of the law of cosines. In this example two side lengths of a triangle and the angle between these two sides are known. We are trying to find the length of the side opposite the known angle.

(2) Observe that QR is by itself on one side of the equation because it is opposite angle C.

Try to solve each of the following problems. The answers to these problems, followed by full solutions are at the end of this lesson. **Do not** look at the answers until you have attempted these problems yourself. Please remember to mark off any problems you get wrong.

LEVEL 3: TRIGONOMETRY

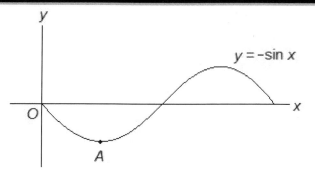

4.   The figure above shows one cycle of the graph of the function $y = -\sin x$ for $0 \le x \le 2\pi$. If the minimum value of the function occurs at point A, then the coordinates of A are

   F. $(\frac{\pi}{3}, -\pi)$

   G. $(\frac{\pi}{3}, -1)$

   H. $(\frac{\pi}{3}, 0)$

   J. $(\frac{\pi}{2}, -\pi)$

   K. $(\frac{\pi}{2}, -1)$

LEVEL 4: TRIGONOMETRY

5. If $\cos x = 0.36$, then $\cos(180° - x) =$

    A. -0.64
    B. -0.36
    C. 0
    D. 0.36
    E. 0.64

6. The vertex of $\angle P$ is the origin of the standard (x, y) coordinate plane. One ray of $\angle P$ is the positive x-axis. The other ray, $\overrightarrow{PQ}$, is positioned so that $\tan P < 0$ and $\sin P > 0$. In which quadrant, if it can be determined, is point Q ?

    F. Quadrant I
    G. Quadrant II
    H. Quadrant III
    J. Quadrant IV
    K. Cannot be determined from the given information

7. In the triangle shown below, $\sin x =$

    A. $\dfrac{7}{8 \sin 40°}$

    B. $\dfrac{8}{7 \sin 40°}$

    C. $\dfrac{7 \sin 40°}{8}$

    D. $\dfrac{8 \sin 40°}{7}$

    E. $(8)(7) \sin 40°$

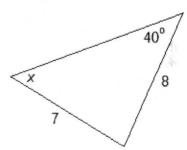

LEVEL 5: TRIGONOMETRY

8. If $0 \leq x \leq 2\pi$, $\cot x > 0$ and $\sec x \cot x < 0$, then which of the following is a possible value for x ?

    F. $\dfrac{\pi}{6}$

    G. $\dfrac{\pi}{2}$

    H. $\dfrac{5\pi}{6}$

    J. $\dfrac{7\pi}{6}$

    K. $\dfrac{11\pi}{6}$

9. What is the period of the graph of $y = \dfrac{2}{3}\sin(\dfrac{5}{2}\pi\theta - 2)$?

    A. $\dfrac{4}{15}$

    B. $\dfrac{2}{5}$

    C. $\dfrac{4}{5}$

    D. $\dfrac{4\pi}{15}$

    E. $\dfrac{2\pi}{5}$

10. Points P and Q lie on a circle of radius 8 with center O. If the measure of $\angle OPQ$ is $50°$, what is the length of chord $\overline{PQ}$ to the nearest tenth?

    F.   10.0
    G.   10.1
    H.   10.2
    J.   10.3
    K.   10.4

11. What is the degree measure of the largest angle of a triangle that has sides of length 7, 8, and 9 to the nearest degree?

    A. $75°$
    B. $73°$
    C. $17°$
    D. $16°$
    E. $1°$

12. If $\tan \theta = -\frac{3}{4}$ and $\frac{3\pi}{2} < \theta < 2\pi$, then $\cos \theta = ?$

  F. $-\frac{5}{4}$

  G. $-\frac{4}{5}$

  H. $-\frac{3}{5}$

  J. $\frac{3}{5}$

  K. $\frac{4}{5}$

Answers

1. C	5. B	9. C
2. J	6. G	10. J
3. E	7. D	11. B
4. K	8. J	12. K

Full Solutions

4.

* Let's add the key points into the figure.

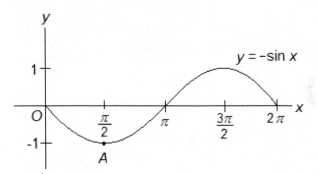

From this picture we can see that A has coordinates $(\frac{\pi}{2}, -1)$, choice **K**.

5.

* **Quick solution:** We use the chart on the right.

Since $\cos x$ is positive, we can assume that x is in the first quadrant. It follows that $180° - x$ is in the second quadrant, and so we have

311

$$\cos(180° - x) = -\cos x = -0.36.$$

This is choice **B**.

Calculator solution: $x = \cos^{-1} 0.36,$ so we can simply type

$$\cos(180 - \cos^{-1} 0.36) \approx -0.36$$

This is choice **B**.

Notes: (1) The computation above will give the correct answer only if your calculator is in degree mode.

(2) If your calculator is in radian mode you can get the correct answer by using π instead of 180.

Solution using an identity: We use the following difference identity:

$$\cos(x - y) = \cos x \cos y + \sin x \sin y$$

$$\cos(180° - x) = \cos 180° \cos x + \sin 180° \sin x$$

$\cos 180° = -1,$ $\sin 180° = 0.$ So $\cos(180° - x) = -\cos x = -0.36,$ choice **B**.

6.
* $\sin P > 0$ in Quadrants I and II and $\tan P < 0$ in Quadrants II and IV. So point Q must be in Quadrant II, choice **G**.

Note: We used the diagram to the right.

So, for example, if an angle A in **standard position** (this just means that its initial side is the positive x-axis) has its terminal side in the second quadrant, then $\sin A > 0,$ $\tan A < 0$ and $\cos A < 0.$

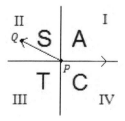

7.
* **Solution using the Law of Sines:** By the Law of Sines we have

$$\frac{\sin x}{8} = \frac{\sin 40°}{7}$$

So $\sin x = \frac{8 \sin 40°}{7},$ choice **D**.

8.

* $\cot x > 0$ in Quadrants I and III. Since $\cot x > 0$, we must have $\sec x < 0$ (otherwise $\sec x \cot x$ would be positive). Now, $\sec x < 0$ in Quadrants II and III. So point Q must be in Quadrant III. So we probably have $\pi < x < \frac{3\pi}{2}$. The only number in the choices that satisfies this requirement is $\frac{7\pi}{6}$, choice **J**.

Note: In order to see that $\frac{7\pi}{6}$ is the only answer choice between π and $\frac{3\pi}{2}$, it might be helpful to rewrite the latter two numbers with a denominator of 6. We have

$$\pi = \pi \cdot \frac{6}{6} = \frac{6\pi}{6} \qquad \text{and} \qquad \frac{3\pi}{2} = \frac{3\pi}{2} \cdot \frac{3}{3} = \frac{9\pi}{6}$$

Now it is obvious that $\frac{6\pi}{6} < \frac{7\pi}{6} < \frac{9\pi}{6}$, and also that none of the other answer choices lie between $\frac{6\pi}{6}$ and $\frac{9\pi}{6}$.

9.

* The period of the graph of $y = a\sin(bx + c)$ is $\frac{2\pi}{b}$. So the period of the graph of the given function is $\frac{2\pi}{\frac{5\pi}{2}} = 2\pi \div \frac{5\pi}{2} = 2\pi \cdot \frac{2}{5\pi} = \frac{4}{5}$, choice **C**.

10.

Solution: Let's draw a picture (on the right)

By drawing in segment $\overline{OQ}$ we get an isosceles triangle. Since $\angle OPQ$ has measure $50°$, so does $\angle OQP$, and it follows that $\angle POQ$ has measure $180 - 50 - 50 = 80°$. We can now use the Law of Sines to find PQ.

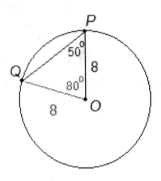

$$\frac{\sin 80°}{PQ} = \frac{\sin 50°}{8}$$

So $PQ \sin 50° = 8 \sin 80°$, and $PQ = \frac{8\sin 80°}{\sin 50°} \approx 10.3$, choice **J**.

11.

* Let's draw a picture (on the right).

Note that the largest angle in a triangle is always opposite the longest side. So we are looking for θ in the figure. We use the law of cosines.

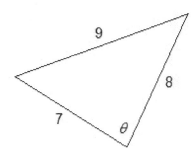

$$9^2 = 7^2 + 8^2 - 2(7)(8)\cos\theta$$
$$81 = 113 - 112\cos\theta$$
$$-32 = -112\cos\theta$$
$$\cos\theta \approx 0.286$$
$$\theta \approx \cos^{-1} 0.286 \approx 73°$$

This is choice **B**.

12.

We can actually ignore the minus sign in this problem and pretend that we are given $\tan\theta = \frac{3}{4}$. Let's draw a right triangle.

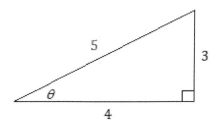

Since $\tan\theta = \frac{\text{OPP}}{\text{ADJ}}$, we label the leg opposite to θ with a 3 and the leg adjacent to theta with 4. We can use the Pythagorean triple 3, 4, 5 to see that the hypotenuse is 5.

Next, $\cos\theta = \frac{\text{ADJ}}{\text{HYP}} = \frac{4}{5}$.

Finally, we need to decide if the answer should be positive or negative. $\frac{3\pi}{2} < \theta < 2\pi$, θ is actually in the fourth quadrant. Since cosine is positive in the fourth quadrant, the answer is choice **K**.

Notes: (1) For this problem to be technically correct, we must have $\tan\theta$ negative. This is because we are given that θ is in the fourth quadrant. Although we must have the minus sign before the $\frac{3}{4}$ for the problem to be written correctly, when we solve the problem we can ignore the minus sign.

(2) An alternative way to solve this problem is to draw the triangle in the correct quadrant as follows.

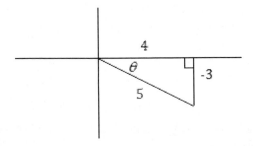

Notice how we drew the triangle in the fourth quadrant. The opposite leg is negative because we went down to draw it (up is positive, down is negative). We used the Pythagorean Theorem (or the Pythagorean triple 3, 4, 5) to get the hypotenuse. Finally, $\cos \theta = \dfrac{\text{ADJ}}{\text{HYP}} = \dfrac{4}{5}$, choice K.

Download additional solutions for free here:

www.satprepget800.com/28LesAdv

LESSON 25
NUMBER THEORY

Try to solve each of the following problems. The answers to these problems are at the end of this lesson.

Full solutions to these problems are available for free download here:
www.satprepget800.com/28LesAdv

LEVEL 3: NUMBER THEORY

1. Which of the following number properties is illustrated in the statement below?

$$3(5 + 2) = 3 \cdot 5 + 3 \cdot 2$$

   A. Identity: $1 \cdot x = x$
   B. Inverse: $x \cdot \frac{1}{x} = 1$
   C. Associative: $x(yz) = (xy)z$
   D. Commutative: $xy = yx$
   E. Distributive: $x(y + z) = xy + xz$

LEVEL 4: NUMBER THEORY

2. If $n \leq -5$. which of the following has the least value?

   F. $\frac{1}{(n+3)^2}$
   G. $-\frac{1}{(n+3)^2}$
   H. $\frac{1}{n+3}$
   J. $\frac{1}{n+4}$
   K. $\frac{1}{n-4}$

3. A mixture is made by combining a red liquid and a blue liquid so that the ratio of the red liquid to the blue liquid is 17 to 3 by weight. How many liters of the blue liquid are needed to make a 420 liter mixture?

    A. 21
    B. 42
    C. 63
    D. 147
    E. 357

4. What is the value of $\log_4 64$?

    F. 3
    G. 4
    H. 6
    J. 10
    K. 16

5. 10 fence posts are evenly spaced along a fence 900 feet long, with one of the posts at each end of the fence. About how many feet apart any two consecutive fence posts?

    A. 75
    B. 82
    C. 90
    D. 100
    E. 113

$$2, 50, 4, 50, 6, 50, 8, \ldots$$

6. In the sequence above, all odd-numbered terms beginning with the first term are the consecutive positive even integers. The even-numbered terms are all 50. What is the difference between the 51st term and the 50th term?

    F. 1
    G. 2
    H. 49
    J. 50
    K. 51

317

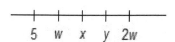

5   w   x   y   2w

7. If the tick marks are equally spaced on the number line above, what is the value of x?

    A. 14
    B. 13
    C. 12
    D. 11
    E. 10

8. When the positive integer k is divided by 14 the remainder is 4. When the positive integer m is divided by 14 the remainder is 9. What is the remainder when the product km is divided by 7?

    F. 0
    G. 1
    H. 2
    J. 3
    K. 4

9. Each term of a certain sequence is greater than the term before it. The difference between any two consecutive terms in the sequence is always the same number. If the third and tenth terms of the sequence are 46 and 81, respectively, what is the ninth term?

    A. 72
    B. 74
    C. 75
    D. 76
    E. 78

LEVEL 5: NUMBER THEORY

10. The positive number k is the product of four different positive prime numbers. If the sum of these four prime numbers is a prime number greater than 20, what is the least possible value for k?

    F. 354
    G. 390
    H. 462
    J. 490
    K. 770

11. A cheetah ran 12 miles at an average rate of 50 miles per hour and then traveled the next 12 miles at an average rate of 43 mile per hour. What was the average speed, in miles per hour, of the cheetah for the 24 miles? (Round your answer to the nearest tenth)

    A. 47.2
    B. 46.5
    C. 46.4
    D. 46.2
    E. 45.8

12. What is $\frac{1}{7}\%$ of $\frac{14}{3}$?

    F. $\frac{1}{150}$
    G. $\frac{1}{15}$
    H. $\frac{1127}{3500}$
    J. $\frac{49}{150}$
    K. $\frac{2}{3}$

Answers

1. E	5. D	9. D
2. J	6. G	10. G
3. C	7. E	11. D
4. F	8. G	12. F

LESSON 26
ALGEBRA AND FUNCTIONS

Try to solve each of the following problems. The answers to these problems are at the end of this lesson.

Full solutions to these problems are available for free download here:
www.satprepget800.com/28LesAdv

LEVEL 3: ALGEBRA AND FUNCTIONS

1. Which of the expressions below is a factor of the polynomial $2x^3 - x^2 - 15x$?

  I. x
  II. $2x - 5$
  III. $x + 3$

  A. I only
  B. I and II only
  C. I and III only
  D. II and III only
  E. I, II, and III

2. Tickets for a concert cost $4.50 for children and $12.00 for adults. 4460 concert tickets were sold for a total cost of $29,220. Solving which of the following systems of equations yields the number of children, c, and number of adults, a, that purchased concert tickets?

  F. $c + a = 4460$
     $4.50c + 12a = 58,440$

  G. $c + a = 4460$
     $4.50c + 12a = 29,220$

  H. $c + a = 4460$
     $4.50c + 12a = 14,610$

  J. $c + a = 29,220$
     $4.50c + 12a = 4460$

  K. $c + a = 14,610$
     $4.50c + 12a = 4460$

320

LEVEL 4: ALGEBRA AND FUNCTIONS

$$P = \frac{G}{G + N}$$

3. The formula above is used to compute the percentage P of people in any population that play the guitar, where G is the number of people from the population that play the guitar, and N is the number of people from the population that do not play the guitar. Which of the following expresses the number of people that play the guitar in terms of the other variables?

    A. $G = \frac{N}{P-1}$

    B. $G = \frac{N}{1-P}$

    C. $G = \frac{PN}{1-P}$

    D. $G = \frac{PN}{P-1}$

    E. $G = \frac{P}{N-1}$

4. If $x \neq 0$ and x is directly proportional to y, which of the following is inversely proportional to $\frac{1}{y^2}$?

    F. x^2

    G. x

    H. $\frac{1}{x}$

    J. $\frac{1}{x^2}$

    K. $-\frac{1}{x^2}$

5. Seven years ago, Melissa invested $4500 at 5% interest compounded quarterly. Which of the following expressions represents today's value of the investment?

    A. $\$4500e^{0.5t}$

    B. $\$4500(1 + 0.05)^7$

    C. $\$4500\left(1 + \frac{0.05}{4}\right)^{28}$

    D. $\$4500\left(1 + \frac{0.05}{12}\right)^{84}$

    E. $\$4500 + \$4500(4)(7)$

321

6. For all $x \neq -5$, which of the following expressions is equal to $\dfrac{x^2+3x-10}{x+5} + 2x - 3$?

    F. $x - 5$

    G. $3x - 5$

    H. $2x^2 - 7x - 6$

    J. $\dfrac{3x-5}{x+5}$

    K. $\dfrac{x^2+5x-13}{x+5}$

7. What is the matrix product $\begin{bmatrix} -1 \\ 0 \\ 1 \end{bmatrix} \begin{bmatrix} s & t & u \end{bmatrix}$?

    A. $\begin{bmatrix} -s + u \end{bmatrix}$

    B. $\begin{bmatrix} -s & 0 & u \end{bmatrix}$

    C. $\begin{bmatrix} -s \\ 0 \\ u \end{bmatrix}$

    D. $\begin{bmatrix} -s & -t & -u \\ 0 & 0 & 0 \\ s & t & u \end{bmatrix}$

    E. $\begin{bmatrix} -s & 0 & s \\ -t & 0 & t \\ -u & 0 & u \end{bmatrix}$

LEVEL 5: ALGEBRA AND FUNCTIONS

8. In the equation $\log_4 2 + \log_4 8 = \log_6 x^2$, what is the positive real value of x ?

    F. 6

    G. 7

    H. 8

    J. 9

    K. 10

9. Two numbers have a product of -75 and a sum of 0. What is the lesser of the two numbers?

    A. $-5\sqrt{3}$

    B. $-3\sqrt{5}$

    C. $-3\sqrt{2}$

    D. 0

    E. 5

10. For all values of k where the expression is defined, $\dfrac{1}{\frac{1}{k+1}+\frac{1}{k-1}} = ?$

    F. $2k$

    G. $k^2 - 1$

    H. $\dfrac{1}{k^2-1}$

    J. $\dfrac{k^2-1}{2k}$

    K. $\dfrac{2k}{k^2-1}$

11. The equation $y = \dfrac{3x^2-27}{x^2-2x}$ has 2 vertical asymptotes and 1 horizontal asymptote. What are the equations of these 3 asymptotes?

    A. $x = 0, x = 2, y = 3$

    B. $x = 0, x = 2, y = \dfrac{27}{2}$

    C. $x = 2, y = -3, y = 3$

    D. $x = 3, y = 0, y = 2$

    E. $x = \dfrac{27}{2}, y = 0, y = 2$

12. If $x^2 + y^2 = k^2$, and $xy = 8 - 4k$, what is $(x + y)^2$ in terms of k?

    F. $k - 4$

    G. $(k - 4)^2$

    H. $k^2 - 4k + 8$

    J. $(k - 2)^2 + 4$

    K. $(k + 4)^2$

Answers

1. A	5. C	9. A
2. G	6. G	10. J
3. C	7. D	11. A
4. F	8. F	12. G

Full solutions to these problems are available for free download here:

www.satprepget800.com/28LesAdv

LESSON 27
GEOMETRY

Try to solve each of the following problems. The answers to these problems are at the end of this lesson.

LEVEL 3: GEOMETRY

1. Which of the following is an equation of the line in the xy-plane that passes through the point $(0, -7)$ and is perpendicular to the line $6x - y = 2$?

   A. $6x + y = 7$
   B. $6x + y = 14$
   C. $x + 6y = 36$
   D. $x + 6y = -42$
   E. $x + 6y = 42$

2. Line k contains the point $(4,0)$ and has slope 5. Which of the following points is on line k?

   F. $(1,5)$
   G. $(3,5)$
   H. $(5,5)$
   J. $(7,5)$
   K. $(9,5)$

LEVEL 4: GEOMETRY

3. Points P and Q are on the surface of a sphere that has a volume of 972π cubic meters. What is the greatest possible length, in meters, of line segment $\overline{PQ}$? (The volume of a sphere with radius r is $V = \frac{4}{3}\pi r^3$.)

   A. 9
   B. 12
   C. 18
   D. 27
   E. 36

325

4. If a square has a side of length $x + 5$ and a diagonal of length $x + 10$, what is the value of x ?

    F. 5
    G. 10
    H. 20
    J. $5\sqrt{2}$
    K. $10\sqrt{2}$

5. The height of a right circular cylinder is 3 times the diameter of its base. If the volume of the cylinder is 5, what is the radius of the cylinder to the nearest hundredth?

    A. 0.32
    B. 0.64
    C. 0.76
    D. 0.85
    E. 1.26

6. In the xy-plane, line k passes through the point $(0, -3)$ and is parallel to the line with equation $5x + 3y = 4$. If the equation of line k is $y = sx + t$, what is the value of st?

    F. -3
    G. $-\frac{5}{3}$
    H. $\frac{5}{3}$
    J. 3
    K. 5

7. The points $(0,4)$ and $(5,4)$ are the endpoints of one of the diagonals of a square. What is a possible y-coordinate of one of the other vertices of this square?

    A. -3.0
    B. -1.5
    C. 1.0
    D. 3.0
    E. 6.5

LEVEL 5: GEOMETRY

8. In $\triangle ABC$, the length of side $\overline{BC}$ is 16 and the length of side $\overline{AC}$ is 17. What is the least possible integer length of side $\overline{AB}$?

    F. 5
    G. 4
    H. 3
    J. 2
    K. 1

9. A sphere with volume 36π cubic inches is inscribed in a cube so that the sphere touches the cube at 6 points. What is the surface area, in square inches, of the cube?

    A. 216
    B. 184
    C. 108
    D.   96
    E.   36

10. A square is inscribed in a circle of diameter d. What is the perpendicular distance from the center of the circle to a side of the square, in terms of d ?

    F. $\dfrac{d}{2}$

    G. $\dfrac{d\sqrt{2}}{4}$

    H. $\dfrac{d\sqrt{2}}{2}$

    J. d

    K. $d\sqrt{2}$

11. The figure below is a pyramid with four isosceles triangular faces and a base that is a regular pentagon. Points A, B, C, D and E (not shown) are the midpoints of the edges that are not in the plane of the base. Line segments are to be drawn on the triangular faces such that each segment connects two of these points. Which of the following is a representation of how these line segments could appear if viewed through the pentagonal base?

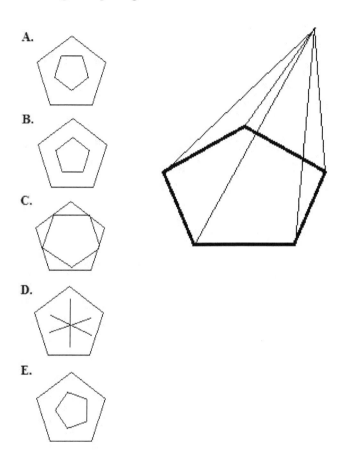

A.

B.

C.

D.

E.

12. The intersection of a plane with a cone could be which of the following?

    I. A circle
    II. A parabola
    III. A trapezoid

    F. I only
    G. II only
    H. I and II only
    J. I and III only
    K. I, II, and III

Answers

1. D	5. B	9. A
2. H	6. K	10. G
3. C	7. E	11. B
4. J	8. J	12. H

Full solutions to these problems are available for free download here:

www.satprepget800.com/28LesAdv

LESSON 28
PROBABILITY, STATISTICS, COMPLEX NUMBERS, AND TRIGONOMETRY

Try to solve each of the following problems. The answers to these problems are at the end of this lesson.

Full solutions to these problems are available for free download here:

www.satprepget800.com/28LesAdv

LEVEL 3: PROBABILITY

1. There are y bricks in a row. If one brick is to be selected at random, the probability that it will be cracked is $\frac{3}{11}$. In terms of y, how many of the bricks are <u>not</u> cracked?

    A. $\frac{y}{11}$

    B. $\frac{8y}{11}$

    C. $\frac{11y}{8}$

    D. $\frac{3y}{11}$

    E. 11y

LEVEL 4: COMPLEX NUMBERS

2. If $i^2 = -1$, then $\frac{(3+5i)(3-5i)}{17} + i^{86} =$

    F. -3

    G. -2

    H. -1

    J. 0

    K. 1

330

LEVEL 4: TRIGONOMETRY

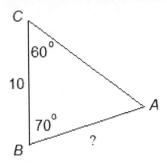

3. In $\triangle ABC$ shown above, the measure of $\angle B$ is 70°, the measure of $\angle C$ is 60°, and $\overline{BC}$ is 10 inches long. Which of the following is an expression for the length, in inches of $\overline{AB}$?

   A. $\dfrac{10\sin 50°}{\sin 70°}$

   B. $\dfrac{10\sin 60°}{\sin 50°}$

   C. $\dfrac{10\sin 130°}{\sin 70°}$

   D. $\dfrac{10\sin 70°}{\sin 50°}$

   E. $\dfrac{10\sin 60°}{\sin 70°}$

LEVEL 4: PROBABILITY

4. The integers 1 through 5 are written on each of five cards. The cards are shuffled and one card is drawn at random. That card is then replaced, the cards are shuffled again and another card is drawn at random. This procedure is repeated one more time (for a total of three times). What is the probability that the sum of the numbers on the three cards drawn was between 13 and 15, inclusive?

   F. 0.04
   G. 0.05
   H. 0.06
   J. 0.07
   K. 0.08

LEVEL 4: STATISTICS

5. The average (arithmetic mean) of 17 numbers is j. If two of the numbers are k and m, what is the average of the remaining 15 numbers in terms of j, k and m?

    A. $\frac{k+m}{17}$

    B. $17j + k + m$

    C. $\frac{16j-k-m}{17}$

    D. $\frac{17j-k-m}{15}$

    E. $\frac{17(k-m)-j}{15}$

6. A farmer purchased several animals from a neighboring farmer: 6 animals costing $50 each, 10 animals costing $100 each, and k animals costing $200 each, where k is a positive odd integer. If the median price for all the animals was $100, what is the greatest possible value of k?

    F. 14
    G. 15
    H. 16
    J. 17
    K. 18

7. The average (arithmetic mean) age of the people in a certain group was 32 years before one of the members left the group and was replaced by someone who is 10 years younger than the person who left. If the average age of the group is now 30 years, how many people are in the group?

    A. 1
    B. 2
    C. 3
    D. 4
    E. 5

LEVEL 5: TRIGONOMETRY

8. In the right triangle below, $b > a > 0$. One of the angle measures in the triangle is $\cos^{-1} \frac{b}{\sqrt{a^2+b^2}}$. What is $\csc[\cos^{-1}\left(\frac{b}{\sqrt{a^2+b^2}}\right)]$?

    F. $\dfrac{b}{a}$

    G. $\dfrac{a}{b}$

    H. $\dfrac{b}{\sqrt{a^2+b^2}}$

    J. $\dfrac{a}{\sqrt{a^2+b^2}}$

    K. $\dfrac{\sqrt{a^2+b^2}}{a}$

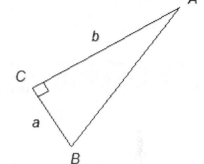

9. The polar equation $r \cos \theta = 2$ defines a

    A. point.
    B. circle.
    C. noncircular ellipse.
    D. line.
    E. parabola.

10. If $\cos x = k$, then for all x in the interval $0 < x < \frac{\pi}{2}$, $\cot x = $?

    F. $\dfrac{1}{1+k}$

    G. $\dfrac{k}{\sqrt{1+k^2}}$

    H. $\dfrac{1}{\sqrt{1+k^2}}$

    J. $\dfrac{k}{\sqrt{1-k^2}}$

    K. $\dfrac{1}{\sqrt{1-k^2}}$

11. In the figure below, if $PR = 5$ and $PQ = 6$, then find RQ to the nearest hundredth.

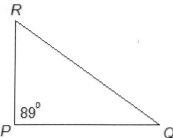

    A. 3.12
    B. 3.33
    C. 5.01
    D. 6.23
    E. 7.74

LEVEL 5: COUNTING

12. Seven cards, each of a different color are shuffled and placed in a row. In how many ways can the cards be placed so that the blue card is placed at an end?

    F. 1440
    G. 720
    H. 28
    J. 21
    K. 14

Answers

1. B	5. D	9. D
2. K	6. G	10. J
3. B	7. E	11. E
4. K	8. K	12. F

Full solutions to these problems are available for free download here:

www.satprepget800.com/28LesAdv

Congratulations! By completing the lessons in this book you have given yourself a significant advantage in ACT math. Go ahead and take a practice ACT. The math score you get should be much higher than the score you received before completing these lessons.

If you found that you were still getting many problems wrong in the last four lessons, this means that you can still show improvement by going through this book again. You can also use these last four lessons to determine exactly what you need more practice in. For example, if you got all the questions correct in Lesson 25 (Number Theory), then there is no need to review the number theory lessons in this book. But if you found, for example, that you got some questions wrong in Lesson 27 (Geometry), you may want to spend the next week or so redoing all the geometry lessons from this book.

For additional practice you may want to read *320 ACT Math Problems Arranged by Topic and Difficulty Level.*

If you decide to use different materials for practice problems, please remember to try to solve each problem that you attempt in more than one way. Remember – the actual answer is not very important. What is important is to learn as many techniques as possible. This is the best way to simultaneously increase your current score, and increase your level of mathematical maturity.

I really want to thank you for putting your trust in me and my materials, and I want to assure you that you have made excellent use of your time by studying with this book. I wish you the best of luck on the ACT, on getting into your choice college, and in life.

Dr. Steve Warner
steve@SATPrepGet800.com

ACTIONS TO COMPLETE AFTER YOU HAVE READ THIS BOOK

1. Take another practice ACT

You should see a substantial improvement in your score.

2. Continue to practice ACT math problems for 10 to 20 minutes each day

You may want to purchase *320 ACT Math Problems arranged by Topic and Difficulty Level* for additional practice problems.

3. 'Like' my Facebook page

This page is updated regularly with ACT prep advice, tips, tricks, strategies, and practice problems. Visit the following webpage and click the 'like' button.

www.facebook.com/ACTPrepGet800

4. Review this book

If this book helped you, please post your positive feedback on the site you purchased it from; e.g. Amazon, Barnes and Noble, etc.

5. Claim your FREE bonuses

If you have not done so yet, visit the following webpage and enter your email address to receive solutions to all the supplemental problems in this book and other materials.

www.satprepget800.com/28LesAdv

About the Author

Dr. Steve Warner, a New York native, earned his Ph.D. at Rutgers University in Pure Mathematics in May, 2001. While a graduate student, Dr. Warner won the TA Teaching Excellence Award.

After Rutgers, Dr. Warner joined the Penn State Mathematics Department as an Assistant Professor. In September, 2002, Dr. Warner returned to New York to accept an Assistant Professor position at Hofstra University. By September 2007, Dr. Warner had received tenure and was promoted to Associate Professor. He has taught undergraduate and graduate courses in Precalculus, Calculus, Linear Algebra, Differential Equations, Mathematical Logic, Set Theory and Abstract Algebra.

Over that time, Dr. Warner participated in a five year NSF grant, "The MSTP Project," to study and improve mathematics and science curriculum in poorly performing junior high schools. He also published several articles in scholarly journals, specifically on Mathematical Logic.

Dr. Warner has more than 15 years of experience in general math tutoring and tutoring for standardized tests such as the SAT, ACT and AP Calculus exams. He has tutored students both individually and in group settings.

In February, 2010 Dr. Warner released his first SAT prep book "The 32 Most Effective SAT Math Strategies," and in 2012 founded Get 800 Test Prep. Since then Dr. Warner has written books for the SAT, ACT, SAT Math Subject Tests and AP Calculus exams.

Dr. Steve Warner can be reached at

steve@SATPrepGet800.com

BOOKS BY DR. STEVE WARNER

 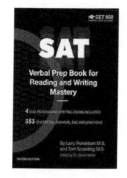 

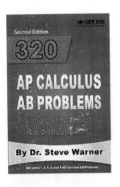

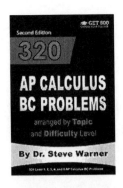

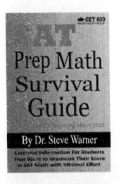

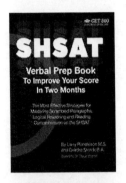

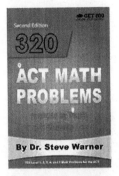

Made in the USA
Lexington, KY
04 March 2017